8.00

The Paternoster Church History, Vol. VI

General Editor: PROFESSOR F. F. BRUCE, M.A., D.D.

LIGHT IN THE NORTH

LIGHT IN THE NORTH

The Story of the Scottish Covenanters

by

J. D. DOUGLAS

M.A., B.D., S.T.M., Ph.D.
Organizing Editor, *New Bible Dictionary*
British Editorial Director, Christianity Today

THE PATERNOSTER PRESS

Made and Printed in Great Britain for
the Paternoster Press
Paternoster House, 3 Mount Radford Crescent
Exeter, Devon, England, by
Latimer, Trend & Co Ltd, Plymouth

CONTENTS

FOREWORD

AT FIRST BLUSH THE INCLUSION OF A WHOLE VOLUME ON THE Scottish Covenanters in a series covering two thousand years of Christian history may be put down to an excess of provincialism on someone's part. But the inclusion of this volume is due to something more than an exaggerated estimate of the importance of seventeenth-century Scotland in the on-going story of the Church in the world. Thucydides wrote the history of the Peloponnesian War not simply because of the part which it played in his own career, but also because in the record of this conflict, waged over a period of twenty-seven years between the leading city-states of the Greek world, he discerned principles and patterns of action which tended to recur in the fortunes of men and nations. So, too, the story of the Scottish Covenanters, limited as it is in space and time, brings out in sharp outline a crucial issue which the Christian Church has had to face from its earliest days, and which is as acute today as ever it was.

This issue is not the question whether episcopacy or presbytery is the more apostolic church order. To this question there are more than two possible answers. The issue is that of the relation between Church and State. The highest authority that Christians recognize bids them "render to Caesar the things that are Caesar's, and to God the things that are God's." But it is not easy to fix the limits of those things that are Caesar's, and less easy than ever when Caesar himself turns Christian. Extreme positions were taken up on either side in seventeenth-century Scotland, when the divine right of kings was opposed by the divine right of presbytery—the divine right of presbytery, moreover, not only in the Scottish Kirk but in England and Ireland as well. The kindly, tolerant, hospitable English people have often been bewildered, and at times even exasperated, by the stiff-necked behaviour of the other nations that share with them the islands of Great Britain and Ireland, with their inordinate sense of history and their contempt for the suggestion of reasonable compromise when principles are at stake. Even where a national symbol like the Stone of Destiny is concerned, Scots know where they stand on the point of legal principle and call from time to time upon the sister nation to honour the Treaty of Northampton. But it was not national honour that was at stake in the seventeenth century, but

7

the Crown Rights of the Redeemer—the claim of Christ to be Master in His own house. On this principle an Aberdeen doctor will insist as strenuously as the most zealous Protester from the west lands.

For, whatever may be thought about the interpretation which Andrew Melville and his followers put upon the doctrine of the Two Kingdoms, it is a fundamental Christian doctrine. On the one hand, there are still times when it must be emphasized that the civil ruler as such, even when he is a Christian, has no authority in church councils beyond that of the humblest church member. On the other hand, the obedience which a Christian man, or the Christian community, owes to the civil ruler, even when the ruler is a Christian, is never absolute. There are times when it may be not merely a Christian right, but a Christian duty, to disobey the civil ruler: when his claims clash with the law of God, the Christian will say with the apostles: "We must obey God rather than men." Where men so conscious of their Christian right and duty as the Covenanters were confronted by men so blindly insistent on imposing their own will as the Stuarts, the resultant conflict revealed the issues involved with exceptional clarity.

On 25th November, 1666, Samuel Pepys records that the recent rising in Galloway (see p. 111) was all the talk of court circles in London. "My Lord Lauderdale," he goes on, "do make nothing of it, it seems, and people do censure him for it, he from the beginning saying that there was nothing in it, whereas it do appear to be a pure rebellion; but no persons of quality being in it, all do hope that it cannot amount to much." This hope seemed to be realized when news of Rullion Green arrived. He concludes his entry for December 3rd: "So to bed, and with more cheerfulness than I have done a good while, to hear that for certain the Scot rebels are routed; they having been so bold as to come within three miles of Edinburgh, and there given two or three repulses to the King's forces, but at last were mastered. Three or four hundred killed or taken, among which their leader, one Wallis, and seven ministers, they all having taken the Covenant a few days before, and sworn to live and die in it, as they did; so all is likely to be there quiet again." As appears from p. 113, Samuel's information was at fault if it reported that Wallis (Wallace) was captured. Apart from that, his estimate of the matter was no doubt that of most people of his station in London at the time. Yet what the Covenanters—an obscure body of conscientious men and women, with "no persons of quality" among them—thought of the Stuarts in 1666 was what the majority of responsible citizens of

Scotland and England thought of them little more than twenty years later. This aspect of the matter is rarely given the weight that it deserves, and Dr. Douglas has done well to emphasize it in the following pages.

It may be pointed out that the monarchs who appear in this volume as James VI and James VII were known south of the border as James I and James II. With that, let the editor make way for the author.

F. F. B.

PREFACE

"IT'S DYNAMITE!" EXCLAIMED A HISTORIAN FRIEND WHEN HE heard I was preparing a volume on the Scottish Covenanters. Long before the task was done I saw what he meant, and saw too the truth of Dr. W. S. Provand's words when some decades ago he said: "The path of investigation is perilous; it is thorny; it is strewn with the ashes of long past controversies, which yet when stirred develop heat as well as smoke; the air of it is potent, like Circe's wine, so that the traveller who breathes it is strangely changed." Here, then, is a field which in modern times has been largely surrendered to the extremists on both sides. Their numbers are happily dwindling as we learn both Christian charity and a decent reticence.

The problem of religious freedom is at least as pertinent to our own day as it was to seventeenth-century Scotland, yet Covenanting literature is now remarkably little known. This book seeks to show how the Covenanters reacted, especially in their writings, to the attack by the Stuart kings upon their ways of worship and living.

So far as possible I have let Covenanting authors illustrate their own position, but in matters of historical fact I have sought verification from more disinterested sources. Wherever feasible I have tried to standardize the vagaries of sixteenth- and seventeenth-century Scots spelling. This applies to most long quotations and to the Appendices; in short quotations I have retained the original spelling where it is more vivid and where the meaning is clear. For volumes listed in the Bibliography the date given is usually that of the first publication of the work; wherever footnotes to the text refer to a different edition, that fact is made clear.

Much of the material for this volume was collected and written at St. Andrews University and at the Hartford Seminary Foundation, Connecticut, and I am most grateful for the encouragement and help given by my supervisory committee: Professors J. H. Baxter, Matthew Spinka and Ford Lewis Battles. Much appreciated facilities were readily made available also by the Trustees of Taradale House, Muir of Ord, and by Dr. Guy S. Klett of the Presbyterian Historical Association Library, Philadelphia. Professor F. F. Bruce has made many valuable suggestions which have been incorporated in the manuscript, and has graciously written the Foreword, and Mr. B. Howard Mudditt of The Paternoster Press has been a model of patience and courtesy in coping with a dilatory author.

J. D. Douglas

CHAPTER I

INTRODUCTION

THE SCOTTISH REFORMATION OF 1560, CONCERNED CHIEFLY with the errors and corruptions of the Church of Rome, necessarily left many practical questions unanswered. The Reformers abolished the papal religion and established a Protestant faith, but they did not prescribe a definite form of church government. Knox and his colleagues asserted the claim of Christ's prophetic and priestly offices; those who came after them contended mainly for his kingly prerogatives. Where the sixteenth century Reformers in Scotland, following Luther, took as their watchword "None but Christ saves," those of the seventeenth century were forced by political developments to add a further word, "None but Christ reigns."

The Covenants emerged as the direct result of the Stuart theory of the Divine Right of Kings, which held that the "legislative and architectonick" power of making laws resides solely in the king. The conception of Divine Right was a Byzantine product; in it we can see, suggests A. J. Carlyle, "some of the bad effects of Semitic and Oriental traditions which the Christian Church inherited with the Old Testament."[1] It did not make the same impression in the West, chiefly because of the influence and opposition of the popes. Nevertheless, echoes of it are found in Western history, and the Stuart kings adopted the principle. Continually stressing that parliaments were expedient, they just as steadfastly maintained that members sat there only through a special privilege accorded by the ruler. This ill-fated theory was to lead Mary Queen of Scots and Charles I to execution, cost James VII his throne, and spell the doom of the Stuart dynasty.

The English lawyer Sir John Fortescue, writing in the fifteenth century, remarked that the King of Scots "may not rule his people by other laws than such as they assent unto." This idea of a monarchy limited by the will of the subject survived in Scotland (and to some extent in Holland) into the Reformation era, long after it had been forgotten or ignored in other countries, but strong tides were now running against it. The Absolutist movement was

[1] *The Christian Church and Liberty*, 1924, p. 65.

greatly stimulated by nationalism coming into its own. Kings began to appropriate powers previously associated with Pope and Emperor; petty Germany princelings blossomed overnight into absolute monarchs. As early as the Peace of Augsburg (1555) it was laid down that these rulers were to be supreme over the consciences of their subjects, as well as being free to determine their own convictions. Thus was enunciated the notorious principle, *cujus regio ejus religio*, which made the religion of the subject dependent on the will of the monarch.

Turning back to Scotland itself, we find that when in the early fourteenth century the pope, not without justification, declared against Robert Bruce, the Scots replied that Providence, the laws, the customs of the country, and the choice of the people, had made him their king, and that if he betrayed his country they would elect another. They cared not for glory or riches, but for that liberty which no man renounces till death. This Declaration, made at Arbroath in 1320, is a landmark in Scottish history.[1]

Two centuries later, the discussion of this claim was taken up by John Major, professor of philosophy and theology at Glasgow University and later professor at St. Andrews. Affirming that the people first made kings and could dethrone them, Major went on to state that "as is it for the benefit of the whole body that an unhealthy member be removed, so is it for the welfare of the State that a tyrant be cut off."[2] But the king, Major continues, is to be deposed only where it is indisputably best for the State. Major had studied and taught at Paris University, and there had adopted the views of Conciliarists such as John Gerson and Pierre d'Ailly, which sought to limit papal power in ecclesiastical affairs.

In Reformation Germany, the killing of tyrants was held to be a worthy task. Thus Melanchthon expressed the wish that some good man would kill the "English Nero," Henry VIII, who had put to death in England some who had accepted and spread Lutheran teachings. By the middle of the sixteenth century, liberal doctrines were more frequently affirmed. They received much support in Scotland a little later because the triumph of the Reformation in that country involved a political revolution. From the start the

[1] See W. Bower, *Scotichronicon*, ed. Goodall, 1759, xii, 1–3. This work was compiled originally toward the end of the fourteenth century by John Fordun, and about the middle of the fifteenth century was revised and completed by Walter Bower, Abbot of Inchholm. For background consult J. A. Duke, *The Church of Scotland to the Reformation*, 1937, pp. 92–102. For the Declaration itself, a good translation is given by Lord Cooper of Culross in his *The Declaration of Arbroath Revisited*, 1950.
[2] *A History of Greater Britain*, Scottish History Society, 1892, pp. 213ff. Though George Buchanan had a poor opinion of his scholarship, and referred disparagingly to *solo cognomine Major*, Major was regarded by John Eck, Luther's opponent, as among the first of theologians.

new Church of Scotland showed no respect for the heads of the
State as such.

In England, Christopher Goodman attacked the government of
Mary Tudor in 1558 with his *How Superior Powers Should Be
Obeyed*. A fellow-refugee of Knox on the Continent, Goodman
in his writings held that whenever kings became blasphemers of
God and oppressors and murderers of their subjects, they should
no longer be regarded as kings or lawful magistrates, but rather
as private men—and as such should be examined, accused, and
punished by the law of God. This view, greeted with approval by
John Milton, was probably used as the basis of Samuel Rutherford's position in *Lex Rex*, a work which we shall discuss later in
this volume.

In France, the writer Jean Boucher criticized the rule of Henry
III (1551–89) on the grounds that it was outrageous to suggest
that kings are subject to no laws. He asserted that the people have
the supreme power, and that kings are established merely for the
public convenience. Therefore, maintained Boucher, the people
possess the right of life and death over the king, as violators of
public faith are unworthy to rule.

John Knox, in 1563, expressed similar theories in a single pun-
gent sentence flung in the face of the young Mary Queen of Scots.
"The blind zeal of princes," he said, "is nothing but a mad frenzy,
and therefore to take the sword from them, to bind their hands,
and to cast them into prison, till they be brought to a more sober
mind . . . agreeth with the Word of God." Knox further declared
that right religion took neither its origin nor its authority from
worldly princes, but from the Eternal God alone.[1] This controversy between Knox and Mary goes deeper than the mutual dislike, the clashing of personalities, to which it is often attributed.
It is linked up with the two completely different views of independence which had been growing since the days of Bruce. Mary's
ideas were nurtured in the autocratic court of France where much
of her early life had been spent. She could not be expected to take
kindly to the alarming democracy evinced by the Scottish Reformers which was so completely at variance with her view of the
royal prerogative. Her strong Catholicism also ensured an
irreparable breach with her Protestant subjects.

The school whose theories were crystallized by Knox, on the
other hand, was to prove a great stimulus to the cause of democracy. It is noteworthy that at this point Knox did not follow his
master, John Calvin, perhaps because, as in our own day, the real
extent of Calvin's liberalism in such matters is open to discussion.
Calvin's Protestantism was a law-abiding religion, but in certain

[1] *Knox's History of the Reformation*, ed. W. C. Dickinson, 1949, Vol. II, p. 17.

circumstances it decreed that recognized and responsible constitutional authorities in the State could defend their rights against a tyrannical prince. In some cases, moreover, the latter could lawfully be resisted by all.

There are echoes all through history of theories which would thus limit the royal power—one may find them scattered throughout the writings of classical antiquity[1]—but it is significant that just prior to the Reformation there seems to have been a kind of unofficial rivalry among rulers as to which would govern most autocratically. Machiavelli's *Prince* is a true product of its age. Even James IV of Scotland was infected: he tried to do away with Parliament and to govern through the Privy Council. It may be that the partial success he achieved encouraged James VI and Charles I in similar projects.

In 1579 George Buchanan published his famous treatise, *De Jure Regni apud Scotos*, and this marks the real beginning of that conflict in Scotland which was to rend the country asunder and to end more than a century later with the overthrow of the House of Stuart, and the subsequent fulfilment at every point of the political doctrines advocated by Buchanan in this work—with one exception which we shall see in a moment. Buchanan dedicated *De Jure* to James VI, ". . . that it may guide you beyond the rocks of flattery and not only give you advice, but also keep you in the road you are so happily entered, and in case of any deviation, replace you in the line of duty." Buchanan taught, briefly, that kings are chosen and continued in office by the people, that they are subject to both human and divine laws (he did not elaborate on how the true "human" law was to be determined), and that the Scots had always claimed and exercised the right to call wicked rulers to account.

From this it would appear that the only one of the more essential doctrines in which Buchanan stands isolated from his French companions and his English and Scottish predecessors, is in his advocacy of tyrannicide. He held that a manifest tyrant is a public enemy and may be lawfully slain by *any* subject whose conscience would justify the act. On the other hand, Buchanan tells of his ideal view of the kingship: "I wish," he says, "to see him beloved by his subjects; and guarded not by terror but by affection; the only armour that can render kings perfectly secure." This greatest of Scottish humanists, who was to exert such an influence on later writers, had an enormous reputation even outside his own country. "The three great sources of a free spirit in politics," says Hallam, "admiration of antiquity, zeal for religion, and persuasion

---

[1] Alexander Shields gives some examples at the end of his Preface to *A Hind Let Loose*, 1687.

of positive right, which separately had animated La Boetie, Languet, and Hottoman, united their streams to produce in another country the treatise of George Buchanan, a scholar, a Protestant, and the subject of a very limited monarchy."[1] In the following century, as we shall see, Buchanan's theories of government were adopted and made popular by Samuel Rutherford, Richard Cameron and others, and became a potent force in the stand taken by the persecuted Covenanters against the Stuart kings. Further publicized by John Locke in 1690, the doctrine came probably by way of Rousseau to immortality at the hands of Thomas Jefferson in 1776.

But James VI, who as an infant had succeeded Mary in 1567, was now expressing very different ideas. Pointedly he opposed the teaching of Buchanan, his former tutor, in the instruction which he (James) gave to his son some years later: the young prince was to know and love God, who had made him "a little God to sit on his throne, and to rule over other men." According to the king, "as to dispute what God may do is blasphemy, so is it to dispute what a King may do in the height of his power."[2] James may have been strengthened in his reasoning by what he saw south of the border, where in her latter years Elizabeth gave the impression of being virtually an absolute monarch.

It was not surprising, then, that James had Buchanan's book condemned by Act of Parliament in 1584. Indeed, the book was still considered dangerous enough to be singled out for public burning in 1683 by the University of Oxford, and important enough (we may add) to run through three new editions in the eighteenth century. When it was recalled that the Jesuit Juan Mariana had written a book (*De Rege et Regis Institutione*) in 1599 which also justified tyrannicide, someone made this unlikely alliance the ground of the doggerel lines:

> A Scot and Jesuit, hand in hand,
>   First taught the world to say
> That subjects ought to have command
>   And monarchs to obey.

It was James, again, who was responsible for the passing of the Black Acts which declared, contrary to the teaching of Knox, that the king was head of the Church as of the State, that there should be Crown-appointed bishops in the Church of Scotland, and that ministers should not discuss public affairs under penalty of treason.

Andrew Melville, who had succeeded John Knox as eccle-

---

[1] H. Hallam, *History of the Literature of Europe*, 1873, Vol. II, p. 38.
[2] James VI, *Works*, 1616, p. 532.

siastical leader in Scotland, inveighed against the "bloodie gullie" (i.e. knife) of absolute authority, and the Scots pawkily made it clear to the king that they had no objection to bishops as long as he maintained parity by making all of them bishops. Melville, like Knox, was no respecter of persons. "There will never be quietness in this country," blustered the Earl of Morton on one occasion, "till half a dozen of you be hanged or banished the country." "Tush, Sir," replied Melville, "threaten your courtiers after that manner. It is the same to me whether I rot in the air or in the ground. The earth is the Lord's. . . . Let God be glorified; it will not be in your power to hang or exile His truth."[1] We might point out that Morton's was no idle threat, for he had already been responsible for the hanging of two poets and a minister, all of whom had dared to criticize him.[2]

In spite of this clerical opposition James not only had his way, but in 1587 was able to persuade Parliament to declare that all church property belonged to the Crown, except for teinds, glebes and manses. Thereafter he seemed satisfied for a time, and even showed a tendency to favour Presbyterianism on a modified scale. At the General Assembly in 1590 James "praised God that he was born in such a place as to be king in such a kirk, the purest kirk in the world." He went on to condemn the service of the Church of England as "an ill mumbled mass in English."[3] In June 1592 the Presbyterian polity was formally restored by Parliament, and the Black Acts abrogated in so far as they interfered with the church's authority in matters of religion.

But this phase was short-lived. The king was determined to have no competing authority in the land, and wrote: "Some of our fiery ministers got such a guiding of the people at that time of confusion as finding the gust [taste] of government sweet, they began to fantasy to themselves a democratic form of government . . . and after usurping the liberty of the time in my long minority, settled themselves so fast upon that imagined democracy, as they felt themselves to become *tribuni plebis*. . . ."[4] It is not hard to understand James's exasperation and his resolve that he would be no ministers' king. Despite all his fine words on previous occasions, Presbyterianism in his eyes was to monarchy what the devil was to God.

In vain did Melville in 1596 call him "God's sillie vassal." In vain did he grip the royal sleeve, and "through much hot reason-

---

[1] T. McCrie, *Life of Andrew Melville*, 1899, p. 69.
[2] Cf. J. Cunningham, *The Church History of Scotland*, 1882, Vol. I, p. 449.
[3] D. Calderwood, *The History of the Kirk of Scotland*, Vol. V, p. 106.
[4] Quoted from James's work *Basilikon Doron* by W. C. Dickinson and G. Donaldson, *A Source Book of Scottish History*, Vol. III, pp. 50f.

ing and many interruptions" remind James in a speech for which he is chiefly remembered:

> There are two Kings and two kingdoms in Scotland. There is Christ Jesus the King, and His kingdom the Kirk, whose subject King James the Sixth is, and of whose Kingdom he is not a king, nor a lord, nor a head, but a member. And those whom Christ has called and commanded to watch over His Kirk, and govern His spiritual Kingdom, have sufficient power of Him, and authority so to do, both together and severally, the which no Christian King nor Prince should control or discharge, but fortify and assist, otherwise they are not faithful subjects nor members of Christ. And, Sir, when you were in your swaddling clothes Christ Jesus reigned freely in this land in spite of all His enemies, and His officers and ministers convened and assembled for the ruling and weal of His Kirk, which was ever for your welfare, defence, and preservation also, when these same enemies were seeking your destruction and cutting off.[1]

These views, which closely paralleled those of the contemporary Thomas Cartwright in England, were in Scotland to lead later to the theory of the Divine Right of Presbytery, as we shall see in a later chapter. Melville had drawn an arbitrary distinction between civil and ecclesiastical, and in this he was followed by many of the Covenanters in the next century. Academic hairsplitting apart, however, is it a real distinction, or even a reasonable one? Can human life and interests be simply and conveniently divided up into neat little spiritual and secular packages? The complexities of life are continually throwing up questions which resist all attempt to fit them into either category inasmuch as they are both spiritual and secular.

Although he undoubtedly resented it (a king could do no other), James VI received Melville's outburst fairly calmly. Nevertheless his standard maxim seems to have been *qui nescit dissimulare, nescit regnare*, sufficient testimony to the necessary connection he assumed there was between guile and government. Step by step, by exercising what he was pleased to call "kingcraft," he contrived to advance his own and the episcopal cause by persuading Parliament to agree that such ministers as James made bishops should have the right to vote in the legislature. The object of this was given out as the necessity to uphold the dignity of the ministerial office, not to emulate Romans or Anglicans. The more discerning of his subjects were not deceived by all this. Said John Davidson: "Busk [dress] him, busk him as bonnilie as ye can, we see him weill eneuch. We see the horns of his mitre."[2] A riot

---

[1] James Melville, *Autobiography and Diary*, 1556–1610, ed. R. Pitcairn, 1842, p. 370.
[2] Ibid., Melville, p. 437.

which flared up in Edinburgh soon afterwards only strengthened James's hand and gave him excuse for reprisals. Finally, casting aside tradition, he called a General Assembly on his own authority, and forced it and succeeding Assemblies to carry out the royal dictates.

James's accession to the English throne after the death of Elizabeth in 1603 marked a distinct stage in the controversy. It was no stroke of good fortune for the southern nation—he will be sorely misled who extends the theory of scriptural inerrancy to the Dedication prefaced to the King James Version. It is not the James we know! However, from his appearance on the English scene, "as of the sun in his strength," it became apparent that James's ruling passion was the complete union of his two kingdoms. As a necessary step toward this end, he set about de-Presbyterianizing Scotland and making its kirk a northern counterpart of the Church of England. This programme involved two features primarily: the setting up of a bench of bishops with diocesan powers, and the introduction of Episcopalian practices into public worship. In 1610, therefore, a completely Episcopal system was introduced into Scotland; in 1612 the Estates obediently ratified the new order of church government.

The battle was short and sharp. The king proved to be a good tactician. He marked out individual opponents of his ecclesiastical policy, and by devious means rendered them *hors de combat*, or made others yield by witnessing the sufferings of such men—a policy which was conspicuously successful. After this may still be heard what David Masson describes as dropping shots in the dying battle between king and kirk. It was, however, a dying battle, because when the smoke lifted we find Andrew Melville a prisoner in the Tower of London as a result of his audacious speeches, never again allowed to set foot in his native land; James Melville, his nephew and staunch supporter, likewise banished; and twenty other leading ministers either deposed or in exile. A determined despot could have taken no milder action. James had won his fight. He was not slow to tell the English Parliament so: "This I may say for Scotland, and may truly vaunt it," he said loftily. "Here I sit and govern it with my pen. I write and it is done, and by a Clerk of the Council I govern Scotland now—which others could not do by the sword." Individual presbyteries were still functioning, but only the form remained. The bishops had the real power.

Andrew Melville died at Sedan at the age of seventy-seven. He has with some justification been referred to as the Hildebrand of Presbyterianism. To the Kirk of Scotland he bequeathed High Church principles which, though acquired in Geneva under Calvin, stemmed ultimately from the Church of Rome, especially in so far as they dealt with the autonomy of the Church.[1] There was no hint here of the Erastian traits found in Anglicanism and Lutheranism. This point also we shall meet later. Melville's contact with Geneva was not an unmixed blessing from the point of view of Church-State relations in Scotland. The example of the Genevan model caused the Scottish Reformers to make demands on the State for support and protection—demands impracticable in the political circumstances of sixteenth-century Scotland, and feasible in Geneva only because Calvin himself had drawn up most of the civil code there. As State and Church in Geneva were both of the republican type, they got on fairly well together after an initial period of minor dissension. It was very different in Scotland. Presbyterianism was suspect at court because it had had its beginnings in a republic, and was thus held to be a potential danger to the Crown.

Now that he had changed the government of the Church, King James turned to the customs and forms of worship. The General Assembly of 1616 was obliged to plan a new Confession of Faith, a Catechism, a Liturgy, and a Book of Canons; that of 1618 at Perth, again under direct royal coercion, passed the notorious Five Articles which constituted a startling innovation in the Scottish ritual and ways of worship. These Articles decreed kneeling at communion, private communion in cases of necessity, private baptism in like cases, observance of the great annual festivals of the Church, and confirmation by the bishops. In this the Scots saw the hand of a despot tearing the crown from the head of Christ, the only King of His Church. Such was the eventual reaction to the article on private communion, for example, that it was not until 1954 that the General Assembly of the Church of Scotland formally revoked the Act of 1690 which, after the deposition of the Stuarts, prohibited the private celebration of communion.

When the government of the Church had thus been changed and its ritual modified, the king again for a space lay low, content with this exercise and recognition of his supremacy. While he still showed his adherence to the Divine Right idea, he ruled the Church through General Assemblies, thus showing lip-service to the generally recognized machinery of legislation. James knew his own strength, and never quite overstepped the mark in all his dealings with Scotland.

[1] On this point see H. Macpherson, *The Covenanters under Persecution*, 1923, pp. 127ff. A good recent treatment is the first two chapters of R. Stuart Louden, *The True Face of the Kirk*, 1963.

CHAPTER II

THE CHURCH UNDER CHARLES I

CHARLES I SUCCEEDED BOTH TO HIS FATHER'S THRONE AND TO his belief in the royal supremacy in all things. He promptly cleared up the disorder at court that James had tolerated, and declared that whoever had business with him "must never approach him by backstairs or private doors." During the opening years of his reign he was preoccupied with domestic troubles in England and by abortive military attempts on the Continent; Scotland was thus for a time left alone. Ultimately, however, Charles went further than James had gone, building upon the foundation which the latter had laid. In Scotland he continued, without the tact and discretion which his father had exhibited, the assertion of royal absolutism. It had been James's boast that he "knew the stomach" of his Scottish subjects. Charles never did, or he would never have assumed the role of a sovereign "ruling in accordance with his own inscrutable counsels."

In England, people who knew the court soon expressed alarm at the resurgence of Popery—due, they alleged, to the baneful influence of Queen Henrietta. This was seen in the cordial welcome extended to papal nuncios, and, according to Burnet, in the "many proselytes who were daily falling off to the Church of Rome." In Scotland, the ceremonies in connection with Charles's coronation in Edinburgh in 1633 made the Scots suspicious of the king, and even more of William Laud who later that year was to become Archbishop of Canterbury. Charles had requested that the crown of Scotland be forwarded to him in London, but the Scots had no mind to save him the 400-mile journey or to bestow on him the honour *in absentia*.

Without the sanction of either Assembly or Parliament, the king tried in January 1636 to impose a Book of Canons on the Scottish Church. About a year later, once more on his sole authority, with the connivance of Laud, a liturgy afterwards known as Laud's Liturgy was decreed for use throughout Scotland. Evidently the details of this service form were drawn up, not by Laud himself (he protested that he never meddled with the Scots except by the king's command), but, Burnet says, "all was

22

managed by three or four aspiring bishops, Maxwell, Sidserfe, Whitford, and Banautine, the Bishops of Ross, Galloway, Dunblane, and Aberdeen."[1] Even if this is so, it is certain that, whether with the king's command or not, Laud at least approved the finished article. James Kirkton claims to "have seen the principal book, corrected with Bishop Laud's own hand, where, in every place he corrected, he brings the word as near the missall as English can be to Latine."[2]

The Canons made little impact, although the more discerning Scots detected here a drastic exercise of the royal power; but the Liturgy roused a popular clamour. It prompted George Gillespie in 1638 to write his *Reasons for which the Service Book urged upon Scotland should be refused*. This pamphlet said of the Liturgy: "It quenches the Holy Spirit because he gets no employment." (It also asserted the Presbyterian right to spread that form of church polity in the southern kingdom.)

A riot occurred in the High Church of St. Giles, which is usually associated with the doughty conduct of one Jenny Geddes. It has been for long an object of wonder to us how this resourceful lady appears to be the sheet anchor of many a foreigner's knowledge of Scottish Church history. A little investigation might suggest that the only historically authenticated Jenny figured in the High Street of Edinburgh at the Restoration of Charles II more than twenty years later, *as a staunch Royalist*. (It may, of course, have been the same lady, older and wiser.) On that festive occasion, it is recorded, at a bonfire near the Tron Church she burned her "chair of State and all her creels, baskets, creepies, and furms." Could anything be more lucid?

John Brown of Wamphray says simply of the St. Giles's uproar that it was "begun by some women"—and in somewhat misogynistic fashion evidently regarded that as sufficient comment. "First," says Kirkton, "ane unknown obscure woman threw her stool at his [the officiating minister's] head." According to Henry Guthry, at that time minister of Stirling and afterwards Bishop of Dunkeld, the whole thing was a premeditated Covenanting plot devised by two leading laymen, Lord Balmerino and Sir Thomas Hope. The ministers "did afterwards meet at the house of Nicholas Balfour in the Cowgate, with Nicholas, Eupham Henderson, Bethia and Elspa Craig, and several other matrons, and recommended to them, that they and their adherents might give the first affront to the book, assuring them that men should afterwards

---

[1] Something is wrong here. The implication is that Whitford was Bishop of Dunblane (for the others are in their correct respective order), but he had been consecrated in September 1634, when he became Bishop of Brechin (cf. Keith's *Scottish Bishops*, 1824, pp. 167, 182).

[2] *The Secret and True History*, ed. C. K. Sharpe, 1817, p. 30.

take the business out of their hands."[1] It seems almost sacrilegious
to suggest that despite the memorial in St. Giles's the monu-
mental Jenny is a myth. Whoever was responsible for the riot
inaugurated a revolution which soon spread through the greater
part of the country. "Are we so modest spirits," asked Robert
Baillie, "that we shall embrace in a clap such a mass of novelties?"

The political implications of the new measures bear examination. The Book of Canons required explicit acknowledgment of
the royal supremacy; it swept away the remaining framework of
the Presbyterian Church, at which James VI had been chipping
sporadically for years; transferred full power to the bishops;
threatened excommunication on those who for biblical reasons
condemned the Liturgy, and on those who rejected Episcopacy.
All was done in striking defiance of the known wishes of most of
the people, and under the aegis of the king, the English, and an
ecclesiastical system which the entire country was increasingly
learning to dislike.

The Scottish Privy Council advised the king that it would be
dangerous to the peace of the nation to go on with the attempt to
impose a more rigid Episcopacy on the land, in fact as well as in
form. Not only did Charles reject the proffered advice and censure
the Council for its temerity in questioning his actions, but he
further commanded that no one should hold office of any sort in
Scotland unless he became an Episcopalian. This showed Charles
at his most obstinate, bent on self-destruction, inviting trouble.
Trouble came. At first the Scots limited themselves to formal protests against the bishops. Charles, with incredible stupidity, retorted
by charging the people who opposed the bishops with rebellion
against himself—and that was a capital offence. The Scots, ever
fond of legal bonds of association, prepared a document known
as the National Covenant.[2] Drawn up by Alexander Henderson
and Archibald Johnston of Wariston, the Covenant was signed by
multitudes, by some (it is said) even with their blood.

This Covenant began by repeating the Negative or King's Confession[3] of 1581 which had condemned Roman Catholic errors and
"the usurped authority of that Roman antichrist upon the Scriptures of God, upon the Kirk, the civil magistrate, and consciences
of men; all his tyrannous laws made upon indifferent things against
our Christian liberty." It went on to detail numerous Acts of
Parliament which had established the Reformed faith and church

---

[1] H. Guthry, *Memoirs*, 1748, pp. 23f. Those interested in pursuing this intriguing
subject should consult John Brown, *An Apologetical Relation*, 1665, p. 45; J. Kirkton,
op. cit., p. 31; R. Chambers, *Domestic Annals*, 1868, Vol. I, p. 103; W. Stephen,
History of the Scottish Church, 1896, Vol. II, pp. 254f.
[2] See Appendix II for text of this document.
[3] See Appendix I.

government. Thereafter, more specifically, the subscribers bound themselves to maintain the freedom of the Church, to defend the Presbyterian religion, "and the King's majesty . . . in the preservation of the foresaid true religion, liberties, and laws of the kingdom." The date was 28th February, 1638. On the previous day Robert Baillie, writing to the minister of the Scots congregation at Campvere in Holland, mentions that the leaves and sheets of the odious Liturgy were already being used by Edinburgh shopkeepers to cover spice and tobacco.[1]

Such was the impression produced that Archbishop Spottiswoode of St. Andrews exclaimed: "We have been making a tub these forty years, and now the bottom thereof is fallen out." Yet it should be noted that the Covenant had omitted any explicit condemnation of Episcopacy. Even Charles was alarmed nevertheless, but he insisted that the Covenant should be renounced, otherwise he would have no more power than the Doge of Venice. To Samuel Rutherford this appeared a pertinent analogy, for in his *Lex Rex*, published six years later, he observed: "The Duke of Venice to me cometh nearest to the King moulded by God. . . ."

However, Charles at first pretended to yield, but wrote to Hamilton, from June 1638 his appointed Commissioner in Scotland: "I give you leave to flatter them with what hopes you please; your chief end being now to win time, until I be ready to suppress them . . . I will rather die than yield to those impertinent and damnable demands."[2] The Covenanters were not to be denounced as traitors until the king's fleet had set sail for Scotland. It is not surprising that no reconciliation was ever effected with a monarch who could resort to such blatant subterfuge, and to whom moderation signified a "meanness of spirit."

A word might be added here about the recipient of these royal instructions, whom John Buchan calls "a diligent tramper of backstairs." (Perhaps Charles had discovered the value of such after all.) While the Covenanters tended to look upon Laud as the instigator of their troubles, they declared that Hamilton's head "was the shop where those cursed counsells were first forged for the taking off of his Majestie's."[3] The implication against the thirty-two-year-old Oxford-educated bankrupt is carried further in the scurrilous verses entitled "*Digitus Dei*" in *Thomason Tracts*, thus:

'Twas he that first alarmed the Kirk
To this preposterous bloody work
Upon the king's to place Christ's throne
A step and footstool to his own.

[1] R. Baillie, *Letters and Journals*, 1775, Vol. I, p. 14.
[2] A. Peterkin, *Records*, 1838, p. 70.
[3] *Digitus Dei*, p. 21.

Yet Robert Baillie speaks well of Hamilton, and suggests that if Charles had many like him he was indeed "a well-served prince."[1]

What can we say of "those impertinent and damnable demands"? The Covenant was no rebellious document. It was a legal appeal from the Crown to the people, a fact which is not always fully comprehended. Charles consulted his law officers in Scotland, and was advised by them that the Covenanting action was not a contravention of statute law. In a country remarkable for legal acumen, no lawyer could be persuaded to support the king on this issue. Wariston, indeed, cited more than sixty Acts of Parliament in defence of the Covenanters' action. That the act of signing the Covenant lay within the law is corroborated by a more modern advocate, Lord President Inglis.[2] Moreover, the Covenant expressly provided for the order and maintenance of the king. Andrew Cant said he knew of "no other means under heaven to make many loyal subjects, but by renewing our Covenant," in a sermon preached at Glasgow in 1638. More than three centuries later, it is still true that nothing undermines the foundations of totalitarian power more surely than a free Christian Church which gets right its priorities in dealing with God and man.

But freedom had not yet been won. Apart from the king's attitude, Laud was unflinching. "He would break ere he bow one inch," recorded Baillie, "he is born it seems for his own and our destruction; yet there is a God."[3] A General Assembly met at Glasgow in November 1638, its main purpose to settle the burning question of the day: who is Head of the Scottish Church? This had obvious dangers for the Royalist position, a fact which did not go unnoticed. The king's Commisioner, Hamilton, finding this was not "ane tractable convocation," declared the proceedings illegal; but ignoring him, the Assembly continued without the royal warrant.

This was only one episode in the battle which raged all over Europe during the seventeenth century, between the traditional royal absolutism and those popular rights which the common people were increasingly claiming as their due. Alexander Henderson's reply to the king's claim to control the Church by dissolving her Assemblies at will is a noble defence of Christian liberty. "Whatsoever is ours," he said, "we shall render it to his Majesty, even our lives, lands, liberties, and all; but for that which is God's, and the liberties of his House we do think, neither will his majesty's

---

[1] *Letters and Journals*, Vol. I, p. 98.
[2] "Montrose and the Covenant of 1638," *Blackwood's Magazine*, CXLII, November 1887, p. 624.
[3] *Letters and Journals*, Vol. I, p. 51.

piety suffer him to crave, neither may we grant them, although he
should crave it."[1]

The proceedings of this Glasgow Assembly lasted one month.
Robert Baillie recounts that Alexander Henderson, "incomparably
the ablest man of us all," was elected Moderator, while in Archibald Johnston they found "a nonsuch for a clerk." The bishops
were deposed, and eight of them excommunicated. Spottiswoode
was condemned for, *inter alia*, "drinking over late in taverns";
Sydserff ("that Roman snaikie viper") for "conversing with excommunicated Papists"; Maxwell for being "a bower at the
altar"; Graham for being "a curler on the ice on the Sabbath-
day."[2] The Book of Canons, the offending Liturgy, and the Five
Articles of Perth, were all condemned, the Court of High Commission abolished. (The latter had had its foundation in the royal
prerogative of James VI, and had by him been invested with
plenary powers.)

Arguments were adduced for the deposition also of such
ministers as persisted in opposing the Covenanters' policy. The
case of Thomas Foster, minister at Melrose, was a *cause célèbre*.
Baillie narrates it thus:

> He was accused of avowing, that said service was better than
> preaching, that preaching was no part of God's essential worship,
> that all prayers should be read out of books. He made his altar and
> rails himself, stood within, and reached the elements to those who
> kneeled without. He avowed Christ's presence there; but whether
> sacramentally, or by way of consubstantiation or transubstantiation,
> he wist not; but thought it a curiosity to dispute it. He maintained
> Christ's universal redemption, and all that was in our service-book
> was good. Yet he used to sit at preaching and prayer, baptize in his
> own house, made a way through the church for his kine and sheep,
> made a waggon of the old communion-table to lead his peats in; that
> to make the Sabbath a moral precept was to Judaize; that it was lawful
> to work on it; he caused lead his corns on it; that our Confession of
> Faith was faithless, only an abjuration of better things than those we
> swore to; he kept no thanksgiving after communion; affirmed our
> reformers to have brought more damage to the church in one age,
> than the Pope and his factions had done in 1000 years.

"This monster," concluded the outraged Baillie, "was justly
deposed."[3]

At the close of the Glasgow Assembly, Alexander Henderson
made a characteristically Covenanting application of Scripture.

---

[1] T. McCrie, *Sketches of Scottish Church History*, 1846, Vol. I, p. 228.
[2] J. Brown, *An Apologetical Relation*, p. 52; cf. Robert Baillie, Vol. I, pp. 127ff.
The Bishops of Dunkeld and Caithness requested to be allowed to continue in the
ministry; the Assembly agreed on condition of their good behaviour.
[3] *Letters and Journals*, Vol. I, p. 139.

"We have now cast down the walls of Jericho," he declaimed. "Let him that rebuildeth them beware of the curse of Hiel the Bethelite." (An interesting amalgam of 1 Kings 16: 34 and Joshua 6: 26.) It was now becoming more and more clear that if Scotland were to preserve her liberties in Church and State the only way open, peaceful protests having failed, was the way of revolution.

On the day after the Glasgow Assembly had dispersed, the Earl of Argyle, impressed out of his neutrality by its proceedings, threw in his lot with the Covenanters and gave his whole-hearted support thereafter to what has been called the Magna Charta of Scottish liberty. Anticipating the trouble that would result, Samuel Rutherford wrote to Henderson: "The wind is now on Christ's face in this land, and seeing ye are with Him ye cannot expect the leeside, or the sunny side of the brae." The results of the Covenant and of the Glasgow Assembly cannot better be expressed than in Dr. King Hewison's summary, thus:

> The Word of God, as the sole rule of faith and morals, was restored to its authoritative position; the Lord Jesus Christ was again enthroned as the Head of the Church; the principle of autocracy was condemned; the seat of power was asserted to be in the People, as taught by Buchanan, Goodman, and other Reformers; the national will regarding religion expressed in the Covenant was unmistakably announced; Episcopacy, as a barren and unwelcome imposition, was extinguished; Scottish Presbytery, as a polity warranted by Scripture, was revived; the right of the laity to representation in Church Courts was ratified. . . .[1]

In addition, John Buchan characteristically points out, this same Assembly prohibited salmon fishing on Sundays.

These developments opened up in Scotland the whole question of the validity of the king's assumption of an absolute authority in ecclesiastical affairs. Scottish thinkers began to concern themselves increasingly with the grounds and limits of obedience. It was no light matter for a people to take such a stand, for this was an age when resistance to the Stuarts in England had resulted in dire reprisals against Nonconformists. They had ears cut off, noses slit, tongues torn out, cheeks branded with hot irons—not the least result of all which was the sailing of the *Mayflower* to the New World in 1620.

But there is another side to all this. In the north-east there was a minority opposed to the Covenant, led by the so-called Aberdeen Doctors. According to their *Generall Demands Concerning the Late Covenant*, a manifesto which they issued that same year in reply to the subscribers, the Covenant was a very different thing from the

---

[1] *The Covenanters*, 1908, Vol. I, p. 316.

Negative Confession of 1581 on which it purported to be based. In the first place, they objected, the National Covenant was not published by the king or by any recognized authority. A modern Doctor of Aberdeen lists their other objections thus:

> The Covenant was unnecessary, as the King had now withdrawn the proposed innovations in religion. The assumption was false that the Perth Articles and Episcopacy were contrary to the terms of the Negative Confession. The Covenant makes binding for ever certain external rites (which the Scots Confession did not do). In condemning the Articles of Perth, the Covenant separates from the practice of the ancient Church and much Reformed opinion. Conscience would not permit them to condemn as Popish certain practices to which they had long been accustomed. The Covenant states *conditions* on which the defence of the King will be accepted. The Covenant seems to require defence of the royal authority and at the same time disobedience to certain royal commands. To accept the Covenant is to prejudge what should be brought before a free Assembly or Parliament. The acceptance of the Scots Confession should be sufficient to prove adherence to Protestantism without this interpretation of the Negative Confession and without the "military part" of the Covenant with which the Churchmen have no concern . . . The Covenant involves dissent from Reformers and the early Church and perjury for those who at ordination swore obedience to the Perth Articles and to their Bishop. How could persons with such scruples be expected to sign the Covenant?[1]

It would be beside our purpose to discuss this point further, except to suggest that not everyone would agree with this interpretation of the Negative Confession.

Both the Doctors and the Town Council of Aberdeen received from the king a letter of thanks for their efforts in the anti-Covenanting cause. Montrose, Henderson, David Dickson and Andrew Cant, with others, had earlier been sent to enlist support for the Covenant in Aberdeen, an area in which the antagonistic Marquis of Huntly had great influence. The city had received the emissaries hospitably (Montrose was a freeman of Aberdeen), and prepared some refreshment for them. They refused to accept this until the city fathers had subscribed the Covenant. The provost and bailies thereupon spiritedly distributed the wine among the poor.

Dr. John Forbes, Professor of Divinity in the University of Aberdeen, and chief spokesman of the dissentients, was one of Scotland's greatest theologians. For disagreeing with Covenanting policy he was deposed from his Chair, and evicted from the resi-

[1] G. D. Henderson, *Religious Life in Seventeenth-Century Scotland*, 1937, pp. 168f.; for an account of the remarkable authors of this protest, see D. Macmillan, *The Aberdeen Doctors*, 1909, especially pp. 227ff.

dence which, formerly his own, he had made over to the university. Worse was to follow. Being reluctant later to sign the
Solemn League and Covenant, he felt himself compelled in 1644
to leave the country for Holland, where he spent two years. Even
then the Presbyterians were not finished with him: it was Forbes's
wish to be buried beside his wife and father in St. Machar's
Cathedral, Aberdeen, but this last request was refused, and he
rests in the kirkyard at Leochel.

These Doctors were men of learning and moderation ("the
learnedest, without question, of our opposites," acknowledges
Baillie[1]), but this was an age of extremes; however courageous and
reasonable an objection, it was unfashionable, even dangerous, to
go against the tide in that time of turmoil and intense patriotism,
and temperate men suffered accordingly.

War was inevitable, and the Scottish army made ready for the
battle. In command was General Alexander Leslie, the "old, little,
crooked soldier," formerly in the service of Gustavus Adolphus,
and, it was said, a match for the redoubtable Wallenstein himself.
The Covenanters had such a high regard for Leslie's wisdom and
authority that all "with ane incredible submission . . . gave over
themselves to be guided by him, as if he had been Great Soly-
man." Leslie received his commission on 17th April, 1640.

Charles had no money for a war. The English Parliament could
have made him a grant, but no English Parliament had met for ten
years—the result of the king's determination to be sole ruler. He
did now call the Short Parliament, but it refused the necessary
supplies and he dissolved it after three weeks. Moreover, a growing proportion of the English people was looking askance at
Charles's brand of Episcopacy, and many about this time turned
to Independency.

After Charles had been defeated by the Scottish army at New-
burn, 28th August, 1640, Henderson was one of the Scottish
Commissioners appointed to draw up a treaty with the king.
Baillie, Gillespie and Blair accompanied him, first to Ripon in
Yorkshire, then to London where negotiations were resumed.
Baillie, in a letter to his wife, thus describes the situation in the
metropolis:

> Many ministers used greater freedom than ever here was heard of.
> Episcopacy itself beginning to be cried down, and a covenant cried
> up, and the liturgy to be scorned. The town of London, and a world
> of men, minds to present a petition, which I have seen, for the aboli-
> tion of bishops, deans, and all their appurtenances. It is thought
> good to delay it till the parliament have pulled down Canterbury,

---

[1] *Letters and Journals*, Vol. I, p. 73.

and some prime bishops, which they mind to do so soon as the King has a little digested the bitterness of his Lieutenant's censure. Huge things are here in working. The mighty hand of God be about this great work. We hope this shall be the joyful harvest of the tears that thir many years has been sown in thir kingdoms. All here are weary of bishops ... Yet how soon, if God but wink, might the devil, and his manifold instruments here watching, turn our hopes in fear![1]

The king tried to enlist English sympathy against Scotland by a clumsy trick: he reported that the Scots were preparing an invasion—which was something less than the truth. However, troubles in England[2] soon forced Charles to yield to the Scottish demands. The Glasgow Assembly was given legal validity, and the Church requested the Privy Council to require every one in the nation to sign the Covenant.

Thus did the Covenanters take upon themselves the power which they had denied to the Crown. The alternative form of government which they would have established was, on one view, as impossible as the absolutism of the Stuart kings. On the other hand, Charles's aim was the imposition of a system which ran clean contrary to Scottish constitutional procedure and to the country's wishes; the Covenanters' aim, whatever its disadvantages, was legal, was in the true Reformation tradition, and was acceptable to a majority of the nation. Nevertheless, this violation of the religious toleration principle was to become almost synonymous with the name of Covenanter in the years that lay ahead, and was one, moreover, which was to cost many of them their lives during the reigns of Charles's sons. But when we have said all that, the onus of blame lies squarely on the head of Charles Stuart for his obtuseness in converting what began as a protest against Episcopacy into a rebellion against himself.

Meanwhile in Scotland most of the clergy, including the two bishops mentioned earlier, renounced former ways and allegiances and threw in their lot with the Covenanters who for a time accepted all who came. Purging was not yet the order of the day.

On the outbreak of the English Civil War in 1642, both sides sought the aid of the Scots. The latter, though themselves divided on the issue, were very largely favourable to the Parliamentary cause. In August 1643, the General Assembly, with the approval of the Scottish Estates, put forward the Solemn League and Covenant, drafted mainly by Alexander Henderson, as the condition of an alliance. Just before this, on 12th June, 1643, the Scots had

---

[1] *Letters and Journals*, Vol. I, pp. 218f.
[2] For an account of the contemporary English scene, see J. K. Hewison, *op. cit.*, Vol. I, pp. 352f.; for the background of the Anglo-Scottish negotiations of 1640–1, see comments by Charles L. Hamilton in the *Scottish Historical Review*, XLI, No. 131, April, 1962, pp. 34ff.

accepted an invitation from the English Parliament to send representatives to an Assembly of Divines at Westminster. It was convened for "the settling of the Government and Liturgy of the Church of England, and for vindicating and clearing of the said Doctrine of said Church from false aspersions and interpretations." The divines took their task seriously. According to Baillie, writing in 1644, they were in session for nearly nine and a half hours a day, Monday to Friday, and had only Saturday off, for seldom were any of the Scots participants free of Sunday preaching engagements. Even when the Assembly's sessions were over for the day there were committee meetings to be attended, correspondence to be dealt with, and pamphlets to be written.

In view of the charge later made against them of interference in English affairs, it is important to note that the Scots acted only by invitation of the English Parliament and the Puritan ministers, and without any malicious design on the Church of England. Indeed, the Scottish representatives (five ministers and three laymen) were officially not members of the Assembly, but only "observers." It had at one time been hoped that an invitation to participate would have been sent also to the Reformed Churches on the Continent, but the English Parliament insisted on an English Assembly commisioned to reform the English Church.

The subscribers to the Solemn League and Covenant[1] (the English Parliament had accepted it) were to bind themselves to preserve the Reformed religion in Scotland, and to secure in England and Ireland a reform in doctrine, worship, discipline and government, according to the "Word of God and the example of the best Reformed Churches." It is incredible that the lynx-eyed Presbyterians did not spot the surreptitious monkey-wrench which had been cunningly slipped into the works. To the Scots, the words quoted had but one connotation: Reformation according to the Word of God would necessarily result in the adoption of Presbyterianism. They did not imagine that to many of the English Puritans the clause would convey a very different meaning—that it might signify Independency.[2] It might by the same token have denoted for others some different form of church polity.

This Covenant further bound the subscribers to seek the extirpation of Popery, Prelacy, superstition, heresy and schism; and to defend the privileges of Parliament, and also the person and authority of the king. The last point particularly should be noted, in the light of future English action. The Solemn League was

---

[1] See Appendix III for the text of the Solemn League, and for a good discussion of it consult W. L. Mathieson, *Politics and Religion*, 1902, Vol. II, pp. 60ff.

[2] On this point see J. L. Ainslie, "Scotland and English Puritanism," *Scottish Church History Society Records*, Vol. VIII, p. 89ff.

distributed over the whole of the two kingdoms, and those who declined to subscribe were threatened with ecclesiastical censures and civil penalties.

In an address at St. Margaret's, Westminster, on 25th September, 1643, when the Covenant was to be publicly subscribed, Henderson declaimed: "Had the Pope at Rome the knowledge of what is doing this day in England, and were this Covenant written on the plaster of the wall over against him, where he sitteth, Belshazzar-like, in his sacrilegious pomp, it would make his heart to tremble, his countenance to change, his head and mitre to shake, his joints to loose, and all his cardinals and prelates to be astonished. . . ."[1] There is no indication of papal reaction, but hell's foundations certainly did not tremble as a result of that day's work. The consequences of the Solemn League and Covenant were far-reaching—and, so far as concerned the immediate future, almost all bad.

At least one of Henderson's colleagues may have had reservations. "The play is begun," wrote Robert Baillie, "the good Lord give it a happie end." His prayer was not granted. The alliance was an unhappy one from the beginning, for the respective national causes differed radically. The ground of the Scottish quarrel, after all superficialities had been cleared away, was religion; that of the English was essentially the more mundane constitutional point of legal taxation. "The English Commissioners did not in the first place see why God had to be a party to the alliance."[2] It would have been better, as Alexander Shields was later to point out, if in 1643 two covenants had been drawn up, one dealing with civil, the other with religious affairs.

The abolition of monarchy and the setting up of Cromwell's Commonwealth and Protectorate was the inevitable outcome of the English success. The Scots, on the other hand, despite all their assertions of the rights of the people, were deeply attached to the kingship. Charles I, the man, alienated them, both by his despotic rule and by his refusal to take the Covenant; but that monarchy was still their first love (the principle, not the person) was seen when, after the king's death on the scaffold at Whitehall, they turned to his son and offered him the kingdom on the same terms as the father had refused.

Another great gulf fixed between English and Scottish outlooks is seen in the different interpretations of the Solemn League made by two great poets. To the English John Milton, as we shall see more fully in the following chapter, it brought in the civil sword

---

[1] T. McCrie, *Sketches*, Vol. I, p. 280.
[2] C. V. Wedgwood, "The Covenanters in the First Civil War," *Scottish Historical Review*, XXXIX, No. 127, April, 1960.

B

"to force our consciences that Christ set free." To the Scottish Robert Burns, "it sealed Freedom's noble cause." Though Lord (Charles J.) Guthrie suggests that Burns had made a slip, and that it was rather the National Covenant which the poet had here in mind, it is worth observing that the Covenanters who later suffered almost all explicitly professed their adherence to both Covenants. Yet each Covenant in its own way, shrewdly forged by canny and scholarly hands, was a necessary contribution toward a true democracy. The twentieth-century Presbyterian who seriously studies his heritage is not likely to deny this fact.

The English Parliament had accepted the Solemn League in September 1643, and in the following January, in accordance with its terms, General Leslie led an army into England and helped to secure the victory of Marston Moor over the king's forces. In February Charles, in difficulties, granted a commission in Scotland and a marquisate to the Earl of Montrose, and sent a motley horde of Irish Roman Catholics to augment the Scottish Highlanders of his command. Montrose had been won over to the king's side, partly because of disagreements with the Covenanters, though not with the Covenant (an important point). In June 1641 he had been imprisoned in Edinburgh Castle because he had corresponded with the king and allegedly conspired against Argyle. It would seem also that he had no inkling of Charles's secret negotiations earlier with Hamilton. Montrose, a learned and well-travelled young man, is possibly now best remembered for his famous lines:

> He either fears his fate too much
> Or his deserts are small,
> That does not put it to the touch,
> To gain or lose it all.

Montrose had been told by an astrologer that he would prosper exceedingly for a time, but that "all was to be overthrown in conclusion."

So it happened. Victory after victory was won by him on the king's behalf in the course of a meteoric campaign, but horrible cruelties were perpetrated by the savages of his army who were Royalists for no idealistic motives. Their commander's success, paradoxically, was the king's undoing, for it gave Charles a quite erroneous idea of the strength at his disposal, luring him into wrong decisions.

Montrose went undefeated until his first meeting with trained troops, at Philiphaugh in September 1645—a triumph which brought relief and jubilation to the Covenanters, and death later by execution to Sir Robert Spottiswoode and other leading Malig-

nants, as the Scottish Royalists were called. John Buchan seems
determined to make a case for Covenanting atrocities, where he
is selective in his choice and use of sources. Thus Leslie's account,
according to him, is not to be believed because he "does not
appear to be a man of scrupulous honour," and even Sir James
Turner's narrative is deprecated because he "was naturally anxious
to defend his general."[1] These seem to be very shaky bases from
which to draw historical conclusions.

In England the Parliamentary party, after their victory at
Naseby, had no further need of Scottish help, but they had now
to reckon with the opposition of the Independents under Oliver
Cromwell, who were becoming a force in the land. Charles,
gauging the situation and shrewdly weighing his chances, threw
himself in May 1646 into the hands of the Scots. Nevertheless, to
his eternal credit, he still did not budge from what he considered
to be his kingly prerogative, and still would not accept the Covenants—he made it clear that he would rather lose his crown than
lose his soul—thus the Scots would give him no support. If he
had agreed to their terms they would have defended him against
all comers. As it was, they struck a bargain to hand him over to
the English Parliament, on the express condition that his life
should be spared—and that the English should pay £500,000 due
to the Scottish army for services rendered. (The original amount
was much greater than this.) An Act to this effect was rushed
through a dubiously representative Parliament in Edinburgh. The
English Parliamentary forces reluctantly paid over £200,000 sterling, and in return received the captive king on 28th January,
1647.

> Two hundred thousand pounds, a royal summe,
> Is now the ransome of a King become;
> The King deliv'red then, but not made free;
> From bad unto a worse captivitie . . .
> But here is comfort in his great distress,
> The King of Kings himself was sold for less.[2]

One last effort to save Charles was made by some of the Scottish
nobility. The Earls of Lanark, Lauderdale and Loudon, visited
him at Carisbrooke Castle on the Isle of Wight, and there on
27th December 1647, they made with him a compact known as
"The Engagement."[3] According to this, they were to find an
army for him, and in return he would agree to establish Presby-

[1] *Montrose*, 1928, pp. 292ff.
[2] Sir Henry Spottiswoode in *The Spottiswoode Miscellany*, ed. James Maidment,
The Spottiswoode Society, 1844, pp. 180f.
[3] For text of this document see S. R. Gardiner, *Constitutional Documents of the
Puritan Revolution*, pp. 347-52.

terianism in England for a period of three years. As a result, the
Marquis of Hamilton, leader of the Engagers, raised an army of
10,000 men and invaded England. Opposed by Cromwell, whose
New Model Army had meanwhile won ascendancy in England,
he was routed by him at Preston in August 1648. Charles's last
effort had failed.

The Engagement had had the support of only a section of the
Scots. A majority of the Estates were for it, with the notable exception of Argyle. Due in some measure to the dying Gillespie's
influence (he was Moderator of the 1648 Edinburgh Assembly),
the Church opposed it, which opposition greatly strengthened and
encouraged their brethren in England. The ordinary people, for
their part, were war-weary after Montrose's campaigns, and justifiably sceptical of any agreement which Charles might enter into.
The Engagers, having relinquished all thought of military action
in Scotland, sued for peace, leaving the management of affairs in
the hands of their enemies. The latter then proclaimed that all
Engagers were debarred from holding office till they made a public profession of repentance. The result was farcical. "All churches
were upon that full of mock penitents," narrates Burnet, "some
making acknowledgments all in tears, to give more credit with the
new party."[1]

Meanwhile, in England, the league with Scotland was considered to have come to a natural end now that its immediate
objective had been achieved. The English, having won their fight
with the assistance of the Covenanters, renounced the Solemn
League and Covenant. Its terms admittedly were wildly impracticable so far as England was concerned, but they had nevertheless
been accepted, and the fact of this defection was ever after regarded as a breach of faith by the staunchest Presbyterians—indeed, as apostasy, and as a falling away from an enduring Cove-
mant with the Almighty Himself. "Shall they escape," exclaimed
John M'Clelland in the words of Ezekiel 17: 15, "shall they break
the covenant and be delivered? words which I dare apply to
England, I hope, without wresting of Scripture . . . the matter
was civil, but the tie was religious . . . England's covenant was
made not with Scotland only, but with the high and mighty
God. . . ."[2] Similar interpretations are frequently found in Covenanting literature, and led them, for example, to attribute the
Great Fire of London in 1666 to the burning of the Solemn
League and Covenant in the metropolis.

This defaulting of the English served to increase the zeal of the

[1] *History of His Own Time*, 1809, Vol. I, p. 59.
[2] Letter to Lord Kirkcudbright, dated 20th February, 1649, quoted by J. Howie,
Scots Worthies, 1902, p. 199.

Scots. Led by the Marquis of Argyle—now convinced Covenanter, sworn foe of Montrose, and anti-Engager—they induced the Scottish Parliament, a week before the death of Charles I, to pass the Act of Classes.[1] This is an important point to which frequent reference will be made throughout this volume. Law Mathieson refers to it as "the worst and wildest of many such Acts—all of them incoherent, vague, prolix, redundant, and confused, and all of them testifying to that negation of statesmanship, which consists in postponing every ulterior consideration to the end immediately in view."[2] The Act excluded from all civil and military posts all who were hostile to the Covenants. By this measure a large number of ministers was deposed, or, as Covenanting terms expressed it, "the ministry was notably purified". The act was soon formally repealed, and when Charles II invaded England in August 1651,[3] most of the Scots supported him.

Charles I was executed by the English on 30th January, 1649. The man who, according to Burnet, "minded little things too much," and who had "too high a notion of the royal power," showed up better in the face of death than he had done in life. "So ended the best of princes," lamented Henry Guthry, "being cut off in the midst of his age, by the barbarous hands of unnatural subjects."[4] Even the Covenanting historian James Kirkton deals with Charles kindly, then concludes: "People generally think his greatest unhappiness was he mistook wilfulness for constancy, his condescensions alwayes coming too late, granting unprofitably to his people today that which would have abundantly satisfied yesterday, and the next day that which would have satisfied this day, but all out of time."[5]

Covenanters and Royalists alike in Scotland were profoundly shocked by the news. The Scots, though they had fiercely opposed him in defending their liberties, and though he was in their eyes a tyrant, had handed him over to the English only after express assurance had been given that his life would be spared. Thus, for the second time, the English had broken their word—not only their word, but the written terms of the Solemn League which had pledged them to defend and uphold the king.

---

[1] For text see *Acts of the Parliaments of Scotland*, Vol. VI, part ii, pp. 143–7.
[2] *Op. cit.*, Vol. II, p. 107.
[3] See Chapter IV.
[4] *Memoirs*, p. 303.
[5] *The Secret and True History of the Church of Scotland*, ed. C. K. Sharpe, 1817, pp. 46f.

CHAPTER III

THE EARLY COVENANTING WRITERS

THE PREVIOUS CHAPTER TOLD HOW CHARLES'S PLAN TO OVER-
awe the Presbyterians was thwarted, and discussed the
general political implications of the National Covenant. We
have seen the reason for the Solemn League and Covenant with
England, and traced the events which culminated in the death of
the king. We should now deal more particularly with the political
principles which made the Scots take the stand they did against
the absolutism of Charles I, in so far as this touched upon their
religious conscience.

For this purpose we go back to the year 1637, when George
Gillespie first came before the public eye at the age of twenty-four.
His father was minister at Kirkcaldy, and was what the language
of the day termed "a thundering preacher." George, who was
"dull and soft-like," according to his mother, was educated at the
University of St. Andrews and intended for the ministry, but
an apparently insurmountable difficulty both held up his further
progress towards that goal and strengthened his determination
not to compromise with anything which ran counter to his religious convictions. Gillespie wanted to be a minister, but he was
convinced that the prelatic system of church government was a
mere human invention and not of divine institution. Since no one
at that time could be admitted who had not received Episcopal
ordination, Gillespie was constrained to postpone his plans for a
time, and we find him acting as chaplain to Lord Kenmure, and
afterwards as chaplain and tutor in the household of the Earl of
Cassillis. At the former residence he met Samuel Rutherford, with
whom he was before long to be closely identified in matters vital
to Church and State.

It was at this period also that Archbishop Laud sent to Scotland
that Prayer Book previously mentioned which was overwhelm-
ingly rejected by the people. Gillespie's first work, printed in
Holland, then appeared anonymously—a well-timed and representative protest entitled *A Dispute against the English Popish
Ceremonies obtruded upon the Church of Scotland* (1637). Scholarly,
lucid and biting, it countered every kind of argument employed

by the Episcopalians, and completely demolished them. No answer was ever attempted by the hierarchy. The book's significance is sufficiently attested by the fact that within a few months of its publication a proclamation of the Scots Privy Council commanded all copies of it that could be found to be called in and burned by the common hangman; the decree alleged that the work had "stirred the hearts and affections of the subjects from their due obedience and allegiance."

In this work we find reiterated, as we shall find it so frequently in the mouths of the Covenanters, the firm opposition of the Reformed Church of Scotland to two principles: the authority of the civil power in spiritual matters, and the prelatic superiority of one minister over others. This opposition, consistently maintained to this day, involves the necessary corollary that a thoroughgoing Presbyterian Church (or any holding similar tenets) can never be completely relied upon by civil rulers who wish to use it as a mere engine of state for their own political ends.

Now that he had come into the public eye, Gillespie was not allowed to remain in comparative obscurity. In open defiance of the authority of the bishops, the Presbytery of Kirkcaldy on 26th April, 1638, took it upon itself, despite the disapproval of the Archbishop of St. Andrews ("maugre St. Andrew's beard," in Baillie's words), to ordain him and induct him to the parish of Wemyss. (From this time till after the Restoration Presbyterian ordination was the regular practice in Scotland.) Thereafter, for the rest of his brief life he was incessantly occupied in all the great measures of that momentous period of his church's history. Before we discuss Gillespie's later work, we should examine several of the utterances of contemporary Covenanters.

After the signing of the National Covenant in February 1638, the Covenanters were faced with the necessity of hammering out into a systematic form the principles of the Reformed Church of Scotland in relation to the State; and more especially now, against the opposition of a monarch who regarded them as rebellious subjects. Alexander Henderson pointed the way in a sermon preached at St. Andrews in March 1638, in which he declared: "Whenever ye are enjoined to do anything by any man . . . forget not this dignity and power that God has over you, and that ye are the people of Jesus Christ; and therefore no man ought to enjoin anything to be done by you, but that for which he has a warrant from God. There is a great controversy now about disobedience to superiors, and the contempt of those who are in authority; but there is not a word of that, whether God be obeyed or not, or if He be disobeyed by any . . . Try anything that they [i.e. the magistrates] impose upon you, before ye obey it, if it is warranted by God or not; because God is the only superior over you." This is a typical statement of the Covenanting position regarding civil matters.

Yet that was comparatively moderate language, at a time when the whole kingdom was ablaze with excitement and indignation against the king. Even Henderson, however, dignified and courteous as he was, who had difficulty at times in curbing his more extreme colleagues, took a stronger line when, as Moderator, he spoke at the General Assembly in Edinburgh in August of that year. Towards the close of his discourse he addressed himself to the Earl of Traquair, the king's Commissioner, saying: "We beseech your Grace to see that Caesar have his own, but let him not have what is due to God by Whom kings reign. . . ."

A few months later the Glasgow Assembly met, and we find George Gillespie, despite his youth, taking a leading part in the revolutionary changes which were enacted there. He was invited to preach at one of the sessions, a singular honour to one so young. Robert Baillie tells of the first recorded utterance of Gillespie on that subject which he was to make peculiarly his own: "After a sermon of Mr. Gillespie," records Baillie, "wherein the youth very learnedly and judiciously . . . handled the words, 'The King's heart is in the hand of the Lord,' yet did too much encroach on the King's actions; he [i.e. the Earl of Argyle] gave us a grave admonition to let authority alone, which . . ." (and Baillie surely continues with tongue in cheek) "we all religiously observed as long as the Assembly lasted."[1]

In March 1641 the Earl of Loudon, another Covenanter, addressed Charles I in London. He craved the king's protection in defence of religion, liberty, and the cause of the Church and kingdom. More specifically, he spoke of the laws of God, and the power of the Church, saying: "We must distinguish betwixt the Church and State, betwixt the ecclesiastical and civil power . . . yet there is so strict and necessary a conjunction betwixt them as the one cannot firmly subsist and be preserved without the other, therefore they must stand and fall, live and die together."[2]

George Gillespie became one of the ministers of Edinburgh in 1641, a position which he retained for the rest of his life. In 1643 he was one of the Scottish Commissioners at the Westminster Assembly, and there distinguished himself by his fluency, learning, and clarity of thought. As we will be dealing more fully in this chapter with Gillespie's later work, we might cite briefly one famous example taken from the proceedings of that Assembly, which will show more clearly than any explanation the kind of man he was.

[1] *The Presbyterian's Armoury*, Vol. I, p. xviii.
[2] J. Howie, *Scots Worthies*, p. 271.

During the debate on church discipline, the Presbyterians found themselves opposed by the two other parties—the Independents and the Erastians. The former, who held what was adjudged to be the untenable position that the Church had no power of excommunication, soon retired from the debating floor. The Erastians, though admitting such a power, placed it in the hands of the civil authority. One of their leaders, "the learned Selden," held forth at great length with a staggering display of minute rabbinical lore, striving to demonstrate that Matthew 18: 15–17, the passage under dispute, contained no warrant for ecclesiastical jurisdiction, but concerned the ordinary practice of the Jews in their common civil courts.

Even the most erudite and able of the divines present were in no hurry to encounter such a formidable opponent. Samuel Rutherford, the story goes, turned to Gillespie and said: "Rise, George, rise up, man, and defend the right of the Lord Jesus Christ to govern by His own laws, the Church which He hath purchased with His blood." With every appearance of reluctance Gillespie rose, gave first a summary of the previous speech, stripping it of all its cumbrous learning and reducing it to simple language. Then steadily, point by point, he completely refuted it, proving that the passage in question could not be interpreted or explained away to mean a mere reference to a civil court, and that the Jews both possessed and exercised the right of spiritual censures. The effect of Gillespie's speech was so great as not only to convince the Assembly, but also to astonish and confound Selden himself, to whom Gillespie was a veritable *enfant terrible*. The Erastian leader is reported to have exclaimed in bitter mortification: "That young man, by this single speech, has swept away the learning and the labour of ten years of my life."[1]

The champion, against English opposition, of the place of the elder in the kirk, and of the Presbyterian system of church courts, Gillespie was still a young man when he died, two years after piloting the Confession of Faith[2] through the Assembly. Before discussing his chief work, we should note the words of another Covenanter, Archibald Johnston of Wariston, in a speech made before this same Westminster Assembly, a speech in which there are echoes of the later Covenanting position:

> That is before you which concerns Christ and these kingdoms . . .
> which will be the chiefest means to end or continue these troubles. . . .
> I am convinced they have a higher rise, from and for the highest end,

[1] R. Wodrow, *Analecta*, 1834, Vol. III, p. 110.
[2] For general comments on the Confession, and some observations on its lasting influence, see the Introduction in G. S. Hendry, *The Westminster Confession for Today*, 1960.

the setting up of the Crown of Christ in these islands . . . until King Jesus be set down on His throne, with His sceptre in His hand, I do not expect God's peace . . . in these kingdoms. . . . Christ lives and reigns alone in His Church, and will have all done therein according to His Word and will, and that He has given no supreme headship over His Church to any Pope, King, or Parliament whatsoever. . . . We hear much of the breach of privilege and of the Covenant in relation to the civil right. Let us remember . . . the Covenant begins with the advancement and ends with the enlargement of the kingdom of Christ. . . . All laws contrary to the will of Christ are acknowledged to be void in His Kingdom. . . . There is no authority to be balanced against His, nor posts to be set up against His, nor Korahs to be allowed against His Aarons. . . . Is it so small a thing to have the sword, but they must have the keys also?

Assertions that Christ was the only universal bishop and head of the Church had been made in the First Helvetic Confession (1536), and reaffirmed in the French Confession (1559), the Scots Confession (1560), and the Belgic Confession (1561). On another occasion Johnston stated tersely: "We must not edge away an hem of Christ's robe royal." Scotland was coming to an age, adumbrated in the reigns of James VI and Charles I, when it would be faced with the question, no longer on a mere academic level: how much power are you to give a king? Unlimited power? But what if he is a tyrant—does this make any difference? Answers were given to these questions by George Gillespie and Samuel Rutherford at a time when the issue was little more than a theoretical one. Their descendants, after the Restoration of the Stuart dynasty in 1660, were confronted with a tyrannical king—and thus with the necessity either of compromise, or of sticking by those principles of religious freedom which had found their inspiration in the heyday of the Covenant movement.

In 1644 Gillespie published his *One Hundred and Eleven Propositions Concerning the Ministry and Government of the Church*, a discussion of the perennial problem of the civil power's duty in reference to the Church. This matter had been brought into sharp focus, both because of the Covenanters' relations with Charles I on the one hand, and also as a result of their dealings with the English Erastians at the Westminster Assembly on the other. Following Bilson and Hooker, who had advocated such principles half a century earlier, these Erastians made Christ's kingdom something altogether spiritual, mystical, invisible, and insisted that questions such as the external government of Christ's house belonged to the civil power. This theory they claimed to have derived from Constantine.

Among the seventeenth-century Scottish theologians there was some difference of opinion about the civil power—not that Caesar should not be given what is legitimately his (the Covenanters were most punctilious on that point), but in the determination of what precisely pertains to Caesar. Thus we are frequently met with such statements as the following, which at first sight appears to be a defence by Gillespie of the rights of the civil power. "The reformed churches believe also, and openly confess," he says in number 40 of his *Propositions*, "the power and authority of emperors . . . kings . . . princes and dukes over their dominions, and of other magistrates or states over their commonwealths and cities, to be the ordinances of God Himself appointed as well to the manifestation of His own glory, as to the singular profit of mankind: and . . . we must not only suffer and be content that those do rule . . . but also love them, fear them, and with all reverence and honour embrace them as the ambassadors and ministers of the most high and good God, being in His stead, and preferred for the good of their subjects, to pour out prayers for them, to pray tribute to them, and in all business of the commonwealth *which is not against the Word of God* to obey their laws and edicts." The sting is, of course, in the tail, where a few simple words (our italics) effectually annul what had until then seemed to be a promising panegyric.

Despite all their differences in the practical application of their doctrines, the Covenanters were agreed on one point: that they should enlist the aid of the civil power to impose ecclesiastical decrees. This had earlier been seen when the Church leaders would have had the signing of the National Covenant made compulsory on all. This weak spot in the Covenanting position was to some extent offset by the fact that its advocates were conspicuously free of the ecclesiastico-political ambition which often motivates such an attitude; an ambition and a motive, moreover, which we shall find when we come to discuss the Episcopal hierarchy of the following reign.

But the Covenanting leaders did believe in literally "compelling them to come in." James Durham put their viewpoint clearly when he said that the civil ruler may order subjects "to keep the Ordinances." This, he adds, "is but a constraining of them to the means whereby religion worketh, and a making them, as it were, give God a hearing, leaving their yielding and consenting to their own wills, which cannot be forced; yet it is reason that, when God cometh by His ordinances to treat with a people, that a magistrate should so far respect His glory and their good as to interpose his authority to make them hear."[1]

---

[1] *A Dying Man's Testament to the Church of Scotland*, 1659, Part III, p. 231. One might seek a parallel in the compulsory church parade only recently abolished in the British Army.

That the means is condoned by the end is an argument which must always be suspect; in any case it is a most dubious justification for an aggressive evangelism. The necessary counterpart of these Covenanting views was intolerance towards other ways of religious thinking. That because two men think differently neither need be wicked was to them both unacceptable and incredible. That, however, was all too often the religious outlook of the age. The Church of Scotland was still in a state of siege, and the shadow of Rome was a perennial bogey often espied behind the Episcopal vestments. That there was, however, some substance in the Scots' apprehension can be seen in the information given by a converted Jesuit, Father Abernethy, who in 1638 supplied the names and addresses of eighteen priests living secretly in Scotland.[1]

In addition, we must consider the Covenanting attitude in the light of the rise of Anabaptists and other Antinomians in the latter years of Charles I—"fantastical men," according to Gillespie, "who, under pretence and cloak of Christian liberty, would abolish and cast out laws and judgements. . . ."[2] That statement would find many analogies from the early centuries of the Christian Church. Calvin, moreover, had been similarly plagued in Geneva. Small wonder that the Presbyterians felt themselves in danger from the unorthodox and clamped down heavily upon them. Indeed, remarks MacPherson, "their vigour in controversy was so great that sometimes, fearing lest those whom they had laid low might yet have breath left in them, they returned to the fray, and were guilty of the folly of performing works of supererogation by slaying over again those they had already slain. . . ."[3]

In his sermon to the House of Commons in 1644, Gillespie similarly ruled out liberalism in religious thinking: those who "cry up that detestable indifferency or neutrality abjured in our solemn covenant, insomuch that Gamaliel (Acts 5: 38–9) and Gallio (Acts 18: 14–17), men who regarded alike the Jewish and Christian religion, are highly commended, 'examples for all Christians,' and as men walking by the rules not only of policy, but of 'reason and religion.' "

So the Covenanters called in the aid of the civil magistrate, and pointed out to him his duty to "suppress, by corporal or civil punishments, such as by spreading error or heresy, or by fomenting schism, greatly dishonour God, dangerously hurt religion, and disturb the peace of the kirk." But while they allowed the civil power to share in the government of the Church, the Scottish

---

[1] R. Baillie, *Letters*, 1775, Vol. I, p. 78.
[2] *Propositions*, No. 39.
[3] *The Doctrine of the Church in Scottish Theology*, 1903, p. 23.

theologians were unanimous in maintaining that there is only one Head of the Church, and that He is Head over every aspect of it. There is no vestige of Erastianism here. In all things the Church is subject to Christ Jesus, all things having been created not only by Him, but for Him. As Christ is the Head of the Church, so too He is the only Head. There is no delegated authority: neither Pope nor civil magistrate can stand in His place, either as regards the Church as a whole, or as regards the individual. Once acknowledge the complete sovereignty of Jesus Christ in a life, and there is no room left for such enactments of the civil authority as violate His Lordship. He is not Lord at all if He is not Lord of all. There can be no compromise.

Under the domination of Rome and Scottish Episcopacy, the two jurisdictions had not been clearly delineated. Ecclesiastics were allowed to exercise authority in both spheres, and to judge in civil as well as in church cases. Right from the beginning, however, the Presbyterian Church had consistently opposed all such blurring of this distinction, and insisted that her ministers participate in civil affairs only in emergency, and never without the express permission of the Church. This rule, made in the Second Book of Discipline, was specifically confirmed by the General Assembly of 1638.

Second, and complementary to the above, the Reformed Church in Scotland was equally resolved to prevent statesmen and others not having Christ's mandate from giving judgment or exercising authority in things ecclesiastical. They were jealous of encroachment on either side. Magistrates and ministers each had a distinct and independent jurisdiction; in their respective provinces each owed no subordination to the other. Thus the present-day Covenanter, opposed to the Established Church of Scotland on other issues, would find much more to object to in the Church of England. The latter, unable to stress the royal prerogative to the same extent as it did in Stuart times, now invests that prerogative in the more abstract "State". Bishops are appointed by the State, and twenty-six of them (including two archbishops) are members of the House of Lords. Dean Stanley asserted, indeed, that "the religious expression of the community should be controlled and guided by the State."[1]

In 1646 came Gillespie's chief work. Published in London, it was launched upon the world with one of those fantastic appellations so popular with theologians of that era: *Aaron's Rod Blossoming*. Once described as "the chef d'oeuvre of Scotch ecclesiastical theology," this remarkably able work dealt with the Erastian controversy—and apparently was the last word on the subject, if

[1] "Address at Sion College," in *Essays on Church and State*, p. 344.

we can assume that from the fact that not one of the learned
Erastians of the time even attempted to answer it. Selden's dis-
comfiture, it may be, had not yet been forgotten. We feel a certain
sympathy towards them, for in its original form this work ran to
some 300 pages of closely-reasoned argument. Like the painfully
systematic theologians of nineteenth-century Germany (and a
remnant even in our own day), Gillespie did not believe in shoddy
or incomplete work—whatsoever his hand found to do, he did it
with his might.

This volume meets the objection that to grant unlimited power
to ecclesiastical courts is to grant power which properly belongs
to Parliament. He shows that Presbyterian church government is
the least arbitrary, and the most fitted for a limited monarchy, of
all the forms of ecclesiastical rule. The distinction between civil
and ecclesiastical government, and, indeed, all other relevant
questions, are fully debated and discussed from Scripture at great
length.

Gillespie makes an interesting point in this work, one which
may be a defence of the early Reformers. He insists that he is far
from saying that the Christian magistrate should not meddle with
matters of religion:

> In extraordinary cases, when church government doth degenerate
> into tyranny, ambition, and avarice, and they who have the managing
> of ecclesiastical power make defection and fall into manifest heresy,
> impiety or injustice (as under Popery and Prelacy it was for the most
> part;) then, in such cases (which we pray and hope we shall never see
> again), the Christian magistrates may and ought to do divers things
> in and for religion, and interpose his authority in divers ways, so as
> doth not properly belong to his cognisance, decision and administra-
> tion ordinarily . . . for extraordinary diseases have extraordinary
> remedies. . . .[1]

Whether this is indeed an apology for the Reformation in Scotland, it falls strangely from the lips of Gillespie. Just as in our own
time the term "a Christian country" is bandied about very loosely
and we impose a tacit ban on enquiry as to what precisely is meant
by it, so the designation "the Christian magistrate" somewhat con-
fuses the issue. Apart from problems of terminology and practical
implication, Gillespie himself elsewhere, in speaking of the respective powers of magistrates and ministers, had made the interesting
statement: "Neither are those powers mingled one with another,
or less distinguished, where the magistrate is a Christian than
where he is an infidel."[2] That is a difficult point. If, for example,

---

[1] *Aaron's Rod*, p. 85.
[2] *Propositions*, 79, 80.

both Caesar and people are Christian, what is the significance of Caesar's claims? Surely there is a sense in which the division of authority into spiritual and secular destroys the meaning of both. The problem, moreover, is perhaps greater when Caesar is a Christian than when he is not.

But it is easier to cite objections than to evolve consistent theories; and the explanation of any seeming confusion in Gillespie's work possibly lies in the fact that he was arguing from a theoretical point of view, yet with an eye on the swiftly-moving political developments of his day. We need not lay too much emphasis on what Gillespie himself describes as an extraordinary disease, and we find him once more on safe ground in his later work thus: "As we do not deny to the magistrate anything which the word of God doth allow him, so we dare not approve his going beyond the bounds and limits which God hath set him. And I pray to God [and this remark shows penetrating insight] that this be not found to be the bottom of the controversy, whether magistracy shall be an arbitrary government, if not in civil, yet in ecclesiastical things?"[1]

Thereafter we come upon that section of Gillespie's work which spoke to the condition of the later persecuted Covenanters and was used by them in their own defence. What Gillespie asserted here in general terms became relevant and particular when the martyrs came right up against the tyranny of Charles II and his ministers—and found themselves forced to propound questions and make concrete explanations for their stand in the face of a very concrete king. Said Gillespie: "If it further happen (which God forbid) that the magistrate do so far abuse his authority, that he doth straitly forbid what Christ hath ordained, yet the constant and faithful servants of Christ will resolve and determine with themselves that any extremities are rather to be undergone that they should obey God rather than men . . . being ready in the meantime to render a reason of their practice to every one that demandeth it, but specially unto the magistrate."[2]

George Gillespie was essentially a man of peace at a time when peacemaking was not one of the chief preoccupations of the Covenanters. He was no lover of intrigue, in contrast to his brother Patrick, Principal of Glasgow University. (The latter was to be calumniated as the first, perhaps the only, minister in Scotland who publicly prayed for the Lord Protector, with whom he was a great favourite.) The writings of George Gillespie can only be fairly considered against the background of their almost necessarily controversial contents and his own chronic ill health. Some-

[1] *Aaron's Rod*, p. 124.
[2] Ibid., pp. 98f.

times in personal relationships, and occasionally even in public debate, he is not seen at his best. "Too rash a youth in his determinations,"[1] concluded Robert Baillie. A certain irascibility of temperament (a feature by no means absent from modern General Assemblies of the Kirk) led to vitriolic language now and then, and, like Rutherford, Gillespie defies precise analysis.

At other times he could be more level-headed than some of his colleagues; it was he who warned against the danger of hot tempers, while at the same time realizing the difficulty of "how to keep off from splitting either upon the Charybdis of pertinacity and tenaciousness, or upon the Scylla of levity, wavering, and scepticism."[2] Yet this was the man who could say of John Coleman, an English critic of Scottish Presbyterian claims: "The Lord was pleased to remove him by death before he could do what he intended to do."[3]

The sting of Gillespie's arguments was not forgotten in official quarters. The Restoration Parliament, at the beginning of 1661, twelve years after his death, brought his tombstone from the churchyard, and, on a market-day (shades of the Romans!), had it "solemnly broken" with a hammer by the hands of the public hangman at the Cross of Kirkcaldy.

We have already met Gillespie's friend, Samuel Rutherford, who was described by an English merchant as "a little fair man who showed the loveliness of Christ." The writings of Rutherford complement those of his colleague at this epoch-making point in the history of the Scottish Church. In him is found the fullest expression of the political thought of seventeenth-century Scottish Presbyterianism. Looked upon at first as the spokesman of the left wing, Rutherford came with the turn of events to be regarded as the representative of the whole Covenanting party. Dr. James Walker suggests that Rutherford had some similarities with Bernard of Clairvaux, but this most complex and colourful character of all Scottish theologians quite eludes satisfying description.

Born in 1600 at the little border village of Nisbet, about four miles from Jedburgh, Rutherford early displayed such talent that his parents destined him for the ministry. In 1617 he went to Edinburgh University, where he took his Master's degree in four years—no mean feat for that age. After two years as Regent of Humanity, an alleged moral misdemeanour (of which we have no sure details) led to his demission of that office. Many responsible

---

[1] *Letters and Journals*, Vol. I, p. 152, but see also p. 451 for Baillie's unstinted praise of Gillespie.
[2] *Miscellany Questions*, 1649, heading of Chapter X.
[3] *Aaron's Rod*, Preface.

scholars have attributed this to a conspiracy on the part of the Episcopal party.[1] He took to the study of theology, and in 1627 was inducted to the parish of Anwoth on the Solway Firth, with which his name is always now associated. Though Episcopacy had been the national church polity since 1612, Rutherford was inducted "without giving any engagement to the Bishop." Nine years passed. Anwoth was a far-scattered parish, but Rutherford knew his people; not a child but was called by name. At three o'clock each morning he rose to pray. It was said of him, indeed, that he was always visiting the sick, always praying, always preaching, always writing and studying. "Many a time," said one of his congregation, "I thought he would have flown out of the pulpit when he came to speak of Jesus Christ." The young pastor suffered a grievous blow in the loss of his wife and two little children. "It is, I know," he wrote, "hard to keep sight of God in a storm," but his faith never faltered, and the experience enabled him to help others in trouble.

About this time the doctrines of Arminius began to spread to an alarming extent in Scotland among the Episcopalian party. Of prelacy generally Rutherford spoke with typical Presbyterian contempt, describing it as "the fifth element and the sixth finger in the hand, and therefore unlawful."[2] He viewed with the utmost anxiety the promulgation of these dangerous tenets, and both spoke and wrote vigorously against them and against the Episcopal system, particularly in his *Exercitationes Apologeticae pro Divina Gratia*,[3] published in Amsterdam in 1636. The result of this book was a summons before the Court of High Commission, on the motion of Sydserff, Bishop of Galloway. After a three-day trial, Rutherford was deprived of his pastoral office, forbidden to preach in any part of Scotland under pain of rebellion, and confined within the town of Aberdeen during the king's pleasure. This was in July 1636.

Eleven months later he wrote: "I am the first in the kingdom put to utter silence." He remained in Aberdeen, at that time a town of about 9,000 people, for eighteen months of "dumb Sabbaths." He did not like it. "Northern love is cold," he complained, ". . . the town consists either of Papists or of men of Gallio's naughty faith."[4] The latter is probably a reference to the Aberdeen Doctors whose lasting influence is probably reflected in

---

[1] See, for example, W. M. Campbell, *The Triumph of Presbyterianism*, 1958, pp. 73f.
[2] *A Peaceful and Temperate Plea*, 1642, p. 311.
[3] Oddly enough, this work was evidently not known in Utrecht until 1668. In that year Robert McWard brought it to the notice of Essenius and Voetius, who arranged for its immediate publication.
[4] *Letters of Samuel Rutherford*, ed. A. Bonar, 1891, LXVI.

the fact that Aberdeen still has proportionately more Episcopalians than any other Scottish city.

Our previous chapter dealt with Laud's ill-starred Prayer Book
and the rising of the Scottish people against it, leading to the
signing of the National Covenant in February 1638. When that
happened, Rutherford hastened down from the north to add his
name with the rest. One result of the Edinburgh Assembly of
1639 was his appointment as Professor of Divinity in the University of St. Andrews.

Rutherford was the author of various controversial works, and
it is important for our understanding of Covenanting thought to
draw particular attention to the most notable of these. This work
appeared in 1644, and was called *Lex Rex, or, The Law and the
Prince; a Dispute for the Just Prerogative of King and People*, a volume
which gives Rutherford a recognized place among the early
writers on constitutional law. It was written originally in answer to
a treatise by John Maxwell, the excommunicated Bishop of Ross,
entitled *Sacro-Sancta Regum Majestas, or, The Sacred and Royal
Prerogative of Christian Kings*, in which Maxwell tries to prove that
the royal prerogative of kingly authority is derived alone from
God; and it demands an absolute and passive obedience of the
subject to the will of the sovereign.

Rutherford's answer caused a great furore. What he did in effect
was to call Scotland to a Holy War which would rescue England
from the tyranny of Episcopacy, and bring her to the true (i.e. the
Presbyterian) religion. Henry Guthry, afterwards Bishop of Dunkeld, tells that every member of the 1645 General Assembly at
Edinburgh "had in his hand that book lately published by Mr.
Samuel Rutherford . . . stuffed with positions, that in the time of
peace and order, would have been judged damnable treasons; yet
were now so idolized, that whereas in the beginning of the work,
Buchanan's treatise, *De Jure Regni apud Scotos*, was looked upon
as an oracle, this coming forth, it was slighted, as not anti-
monarchical enough, and Rutherford's *Lex Rex* only thought
authentic."[1]

Lex Rex is the plea of the Covenanters for the majesty of the
people; for the truth that the law, and no autocrat on the throne,
is king; for the creed that limitless sovereignty is the property of
God alone. This was directed generally against Stuart absolutism,
which held that by a "free monarchy" is meant that of a king who
is above the law and not bound by any bonds of constitutional
obligation. Such a king would be free to modify or overrule, to
dispense with or set aside, the law. On such a view the words of
Robert Burns, referring to Edinburgh, would be true in a sense

[1] *Memoirs*, 1748, p. 177.

the poet did not intend, when he spoke of it as the place "where oft beneath a monarch's feet sat legislation's sovereign powers."

Thus Rutherford, whose theories might still be regarded in some quarters as "advanced", deals with the pressing question of absolutism. Is the king above the law? Can he modify or dispense with it? Can the people legitimately resist him in defence of it? As a first step towards answering these questions, Rutherford discusses the origin of government. Government in general, he asserts, is from God, and is by His authority. But the particular form of government is by the voluntary choice of men; and "the aptitude and temper of every commonwealth to monarchy rather than to democracy or aristocracy is God's warrant and call to determine the wills and liberty of the people to pitch upon a monarchy *hic et nunc*, rather than any form of government, though all the three be from God."[1]

Moreover, Rutherford makes the familiar distinction between the king *in concreto*, the man who is king, and the king *in abstracto*, the royal office of the king—a distinction which the later Covenanters were always careful to observe. He supports this by citing Knox's *History of the Reformation*, thus: "There is a great difference betwixt the authority, which is God's ordinance, and the persons of those who are placed in authority."[2] The kingly office is from God, but the people are the true rulers, not any individual James or Charles. (Humanly speaking, that is. The people rule in the sense that theirs is the power to choose who shall rule.) They can delegate authority to this representative or that, selecting whom they please.

It follows, then, that as the people have this sovereignty, they have a right to modify or limit, and in case of a tyrant, to recall the power already given. They can take it to themselves again, if the conditions on which they bestowed it are disregarded and broken. This is curiously reminiscent of the limitations which certain of the Conciliarists would have placed upon the power of the Pope more than two centuries earlier.

The king, beyond all doubt, has his special dignity and his stately privileges; but the commonwealth is more excellent than the king. Is not the pilot less than the passengers, the physician less than the patients? (Rather surprisingly, Rutherford does not pursue this by citing the point previously made by the unknown author of *Vindiciae contra Tyrannos:* that while a people can subsist without a king, no king can exist without a people—thus the people are superior to their king.) He who by his very office, continues Rutherford, is obliged to expend himself, and in the last

[1] *Lex Rex*, Question III.
[2] Vol. I, p. 168.

resort to sacrifice himself, for the safety of those who are called his subjects, must in reality be inferior to them. If they invest him with honours and prerogatives, they keep to themselves natural prerogatives and honours which they can never surrender.

Moreover, Rutherford affirms that the people are to "suffer much before they resume their power." From one who in another context advises the taking of "men's feud for God's favour," this is a significant and salutary limitation, for it offsets the tendency which we shall find in some of the Covenanters towards an easy suffering for righteousness' sake—making martyrs of themselves on the slightest provocation. Gillespie had made a similar point in *Aaron's Rod*. There is no more pernicious doctrine than this, and Rutherford was careful to speak against it. The bigot who "on principle" consistently makes disobedience to Caesar an obligation to God, and bolsters it up with appropriate scriptural texts—sometimes arbitrarily interpreted—does Christianity great disservice. "Woe to him who is led by vanity," said Fénelon, "he runs the risk of a futile martyrdom."[1] We find the same warning repeated from the lips of Alexander Peden: "You that are people of God, be not too forward upon suffering, except ye be sure that He call you to it."[2] Sir James Stewart of Goodtrees, a prominent Covenanting layman, suggests that God never calls to suffering "when he giveth a fair way of preventing it."[3] Even James Renwick, often regarded as one of the most fanatical Covenanters, makes the same point: "Ye should not cast yourself into needless calamities, ye should not take sufferings upon you, before they be laid upon you."[4]

Scottish Reformed teaching regarding the obedience owed by the people to the civil power states that the power of the king is restricted, and that his authority has bounds within which it ought to be kept. These tenets were upheld by Knox, Buchanan and Melville, despite the opposition of the Stuarts. To these early theological writers and thinkers the principle was crystal clear: there were laws that set bounds to royal rights. Rutherford points out that the king is trustee for the people whom God, by their own choice, has committed to him. He is to administer the law, not to make, break or dispense with it, nor to enforce his own private interpretation of it. Interpretation of the law is the business of the civil judges who are the king's public officers (not his

[1] *Letters to Men*, 1886, p. 41.
[2] Editorial note in J. Kirkton, *op. cit.*, p. 152. "Peter was too forward," suggested Peden. "Stay man, says Christ, till once I bid thee; and I trow Peter got the braid of his back, to learn him more wit in the time to come."
[3] *Jus Populi Vindicatum*, 1669, p. 277.
[4] *The Church's Choice: A Sermon on Canticles i.7*, 1687.

private servants), responsible directly to God alone for their administration of the law.

Monarchy, asserts Rutherford, is the worst of all possible forms of government—in which conclusion he is at variance with other scholars.[1] Elsewhere in *Lex Rex* he qualifies this by saying he does not rule out monarchy as in certain circumstances being the best form, but, he adds, "the question to me is most problematic."[2] It can conduce towards absolute power, and absolute power is contrary to nature, irrational, and unlawful. It is tyrannical to claim it, and beyond the right of the people to grant it, for they have to answer to the King of kings.

In matters unlawful, obedience can be refused by the people. "When the king defendeth not true religion," declares Rutherford, "but presseth upon the people a false and idolatrous religion, in that they are not under the king, but are presumed to have no king and . . . have the power in themselves."[3] While we might hesitate to endorse possible interpretations of "false and idolatrous religion" at the hands of the seventeenth-century Presbyterians, we could do worse than take the statement at its face value. It is a lesson which is not so antiquated as to be uncalled for in our own age. Whatever their faults, our Presbyterian forefathers were true conservators of divine rights and duties in the matter of civil government and citizenship.

Just as the people cannot yield their liberties irrevocably to the king, so too they cannot give them up to Parliament—that is, neither to one man nor to many. The power of Parliament, like that of the king, is fiduciary. If it abuse that power, the people can annul its acts. Since the king's power is from the people, it is for the people to say what the limits are of the power with which they entrust their rulers, to resume that power if need be (though Rutherford does not specify how this is to be done, and whether, for example, armed rebellion is justifiable to achieve it), and to hold it within the bounds of law as long as the trust lasts. Thus the king's is no irresponsible lordship. If the people are the cause, the king is the effect—they make, as well as choose, a king. Family constitutes no claim to the throne.

The cause of the people in all countries is the same, according to Rutherford, and it is the duty of one country to go to the aid of another. This very probably is in part an apology for the Solemn League and Covenant between England and Scotland, which had

[1] Jean Bodin, for example, in his *Six Books of a Republic* (1576), says that "monarchy is unquestionably the noblest form of sovereignty" (pp. 292ff.). Aristotle admits monarchy, but only when the monarchy is superior in ability to all the rest taken together (cf. Susemihl and Hicks, *The Politics of Aristotle*, 1894, p. 44).

[2] *Lex Rex*, Q. IX.

[3] *Ibid.*, Q. XIV.

been arranged in the year previous to the publication of *Lex Rex*. It could similarly be regarded as a defence of the later invasion of William of Orange, in 1688.

There are limits to freedom, however, continues Rutherford: that people, as a collective entity, should have their way, is not to say that the component parts may do and think as they will. Rutherford is vulnerable here. What constitutes "a collective entity"? Do the people ever really speak "with one voice"? Where are you to stop, forget theory, and begin the very mundane but necessary task of counting heads? What majority is needed? Rutherford's position is built upon a practically impossible hypothesis. The Covenanters in 1638 had tried to make it obligatory on all to sign the Covenant. If that had been rigidly enforced, you could speak of a nominal unanimity, but you would have "cheated," so to speak, because some of the people had been coerced. While we would disclaim any attempt to draw an analogy between the Covenanters and some authoritarian rulers of the twentieth century, the latter also have discovered the propagandist and utilitarian advantages of the "rigged" election, though their motives are political, and not at all religious.

Buchanan had dealt slightly more satisfactorily with this problem.[1] Meeting the objection that the people is "a monster of many heads" full of rashness and inconstancy, Buchanan replied that he did not mean that legislation should be entrusted to the multitude, but that selected men of all ranks should meet the king in council; after which their proposals should be referred to the whole people, who must agree to any decisions taken. Thus Buchanan apparently looked for some form of plebiscite; yet he does not enlarge on the issue, and after frequent vague references to "the whole people" he descends to admitting that he means "the greater part." This section of the work then tapers off into a not-too-convincing discussion of the superiority of a majority of quality over a merely numerical majority.[2]

In such comparatively unsatisfactory treatment is reflected the dilemma of the later Covenanters when, persecuted in the time of Charles II, they tried to adapt such views as Rutherford's in their opposition to a much more successfully absolute monarch than Charles I had been. But this was the age of theory, and we have accordingly dealt with the theoretical basis of the Covenanting position. Its practical application will confront us later.

We should not leave *Lex Rex* without making mention of a few

[1] *De Jure Regni*, pp. 246 ff.
[2] This is very much akin to the view expressed by Marsilius of Padua in the fourteenth century—cf. *Defensor Pacis* 1:12:3, discussed in Gewirth's biography, 1951; cf. too L. Sturzo, *Church and State*, 1939, p. 142.

of its axioms which were to prove most relevant to Scottish history during the ensuing forty-five years:

> The law is not the king's own, but is given him in trust . . . the king may not dispose of men as men, as he pleaseth . . . my life and religion, and so my soul, in some cases, are committed to the king, as to a public watchman, even as the flock to the feeder, the city to the watchmen, and he may betray it to the enemy. (Q. XVII)
>
> Power is a birthright of the people borrowed from them; they may let it out for their good, and resume it when a man is drunk with it. (Q. XV)
>
> A limited and mixed monarchy, such as in Scotland and England, seems to me the best government, when Parliaments, with the king, have the good of all the three. This government hath glory, order, unity, from a monarch; from the government of the most and wisest, it hath safety of counsel, stability, strength; from the influence of the commons it hath liberty, privileges, promptitude of obedience. (Q. XXXVIII)

Much of this doctrine has become the constitutional inheritance of most countries in modern times, but it can readily be seen why the Stuart kings took such a marked dislike to it. In that age the author narrowly escaped, and the book itself did not escape, the hands of the public hangman. Yet its theories were substantially the same as those which, in the previous century, had appeared in Scotland with George Buchanan. They were continued through the generation after Rutherford, as we shall note later, by various manifestoes and dying "Testimonies" of the Covenanters, down to that Revolution of 1689 which incorporated so many of them in its Settlement.

But Rutherford's treatise is much longer, much more logical, much more learned, than other writings on the subject. In tone it is strongly anti-Roman, and it is careful to point out that views of constitutional monarchy were held long before the advent of the Jesuit Monarchomachs,[1] and owed nothing to the latter. *Lex Rex* nevertheless is not an inspiring work: it has, as Alexander Whyte remarked, as much emotion in it as the multiplication table. As we hew our way through the 600 tediously pedantic pages with their minute detail, their syllogistic method, and their apparent heedlessness at times to the inevitable consequences of their teaching, we find it difficult to believe that this is the author of what have been called the most seraphic letters in the whole of Scottish literature. Rutherford was indeed, in his own phrase, "a man of extremes." *Lex Rex* was reissued in 1648 as *The Pre-eminence of the Election of Kings*, and in 1657 as a *Treatise of Civil Polity*, this latter

[1] Cf. L. Sturzo, *op. cit.*, p. 248.

showing that the same political maxims held good for Protector and king alike.

In the same year as his *Lex Rex* was published, another work appeared from Rutherford's pen, entitled *The Due Right of Presbyteries*. Here the author teaches unequivocally that the civil magistrate has directly spiritual and supernatural ends. This opinion he was led to modify, however, and quite another view is taken in his *Divine Right of Church Government* (1646) after he had passed through the Erastian conflicts of the Westminster Assembly. "It is true," he says,

> that I have said the intrinsical end of the magistrate is a supernatural good, but 1. That I speak . . . to Socinians and such as exclude the magistrate from all meddling with religion, or using of the sword against heretics, apostates and idolaters. 2. That I understand only of the material end, because the Prince, punishing idolatry, may *per accidens*, and indirectly, promote the salvation of the Church by removing the temptations of heretics from the Church; but he doth that, not in order to the conscience of the idolater, to save his soul (for pastors as pastors do that) but to make the Church quiet and peaceable. . . . But all this is but to act on the external man by worldly power.[1]

In 1649 the principle of toleration in religion was beginning to be broached in England, and, in a modified form, to find acceptance there. Earlier there had been a tendency in this direction by the early Congregational societies, but it was probably the Quakers who first recognized and approved the possibility of religious freedom. Rutherford rushed to the rescue in that same year with *A Free Disputation against Pretended Liberty of Conscience*. The seventeenth century gave a markedly churlish response to the idea of toleration in religion,[2] and Rutherford has many plausible things to say against it: it is against Scripture and common sense to have two religions side by side. It is outrageous ecclesiastically; it is sinful civilly.

This was one of the few points on which Anglicans, Roman Catholics and Presbyterians were agreed. To Rutherford himself the issue was clear. "Indulgence in non-fundamentals," he asserts, "not in facts, is a vain distinction . . . false teachers in both cases may justly be put to death."

But Rutherford does not hold that the magistrate is to punish false religion as religion. He rather strongly maintains that the civil

---

[1] *Divine Right*, p. 592.

[2] See the chapter entitled "The Fiction of Toleration," in P. S. Belasco, *Authority in Church and State*, 1928, pp. 214–37; cf. "Testimony against Cromwell's Toleration by the Ministers of Perth and Fife," in *Brown's Collection*, 1783, pp. 89ff.—Samuel Rutherford was one of those who signed his name to this essay.

magistrate never aims at the conscience. The magistrate, he urges, does not send anyone, whether heretic or murderer, to the scaffold with the idea of producing conversion or other spiritual result, but to strengthen the foundations of the civil order. Modern analogies to these ideas would not be hard to find.

Such views of the function of the civil magistrate are a part of the whole ecclesiastico-political theory of the sixteenth and seventeenth centuries, and were intimately connected with their more religious notions of the magistrate. The latter was God's vicegerent in that he stood on a special level above the officers of the Church. This status, however, affected only the external man, and did not apply to a man's soul and conscience. This whole line of argument, echoes of which we have already found in Gillespie, strikes an unreal note, built as it is upon the assumption that the magistrate is himself a God-fearing man, that he, as it were, knows the rules, and has a due awareness of what is involved in being God's vicegerent.

Rutherford, moreover, does not recognize the existence of religious minorities: they have no place in his scheme of things; it does not constitute a problem for him. In this he differed from Richard Hooker who, half a century earlier, had conceded a strictly limited liberty of conscience—though not its exercise—a view substantially in accord with Sir Thomas More's Utopian dream. Yet that Rutherford the surprising had a great vision of the unity of the Christian Church is seen in the motto adopted for his *Due Right of Presbyteries*: "Who is she that looketh forth as the morning, fair as the moon, clear as the sun, and terrible as an army with banners?"

For the more popular government of Independents and others in church matters he expresses contempt. For that reason his name is pilloried for ever among the Forcers of Conscience in Milton's famous sonnet, and doubtless his *Free Disputation* fully deserves the condemnation expressed in the poet's words:

> Dare ye for this adjure the civil sword
> To force our consciences that Christ set free,
> And ride us with a classic hierarchy,
> Taught ye by mere A.S. and Rutherford? . . .
>
> When they shall read this clearly in your charge—
> New Presbyter is but Old Priest writ large.[1]

But Samuel Rutherford is not now remembered chiefly as pro-

---

[1] In this quotation from "On the New Forcers of Conscience under the Long Parliament," "A.S." is Dr. Adam Stewart, apologist for Presbyterianism, and professor first at Sedan, then at Leyden.

fessor or political theorist, or even as Covenanter. His name lives because of his *Letters*. They have been decried as wild and extravagant, and their metaphors held to be in questionable taste. Calling Rutherford "both a very learned and an utterly uncultured man," Law Mathieson describes Rutherford's spiritual raptures as "of the grossest and most indecent kind."[1] Yet here surely is the language of the spirit against which no earthly yardstick can be laid. Spurgeon called them the nearest thing to inspiration in the whole range of evangelical literature. Richard Baxter, a protagonist of the writer in other matters, said: "Hold off the Bible, such a book as Mr. Rutherford's *Letters* the world never saw the like."

Some cavil about their literary value. A church historian of the nineteenth century, whose own learned tomes are boring and seldom read, comments loftily: "We cannot ascribe much merit to his style." But when someone brings us good tidings of a loved one, do we rebuke him for grammar or enthusiasm? To Rutherford, Christ was all. "O, how rarely do the needle-eyed schoolmen write of Christ!" he laments, "how subtle and eagle-eyed seem they to be in speculations . . . touching His grave-linens, what became of them when He rose from the dead, and the chestnut colour of His hair, and the wood of His Cross . . . and the adoring of anything that touched His body!"

"Some have written me," he wrote on another occasion, "that I am too joyful of the Cross, but my joy overleapeth the Cross— it is bounded and terminated in Christ." Rutherford constantly stresses the urgency of the Gospel, and the importance of finding Christ early in life. "Like a fool," he tells, "I suffered my sun to be high in the heavens, and near afternoon." No one was to imitate him, loitering on the road too long: "Lose your time no longer," he insists; "flee the follies of youth; play the merchant, for ye cannot expect another market-day when this is done." He stresses the fleeting nature of earthly things in writing to Lady Kenmure: "Build your nest upon no tree here, for ye see God hath sold the forest to death."

In 1661 the Restoration Government called in all copies of *Lex Rex* as a work poisonous and treasonable; its author had six months earlier been cited to answer the charge of treason, and only fast-failing health prevented his ultimate encounter with the royal hangman. Just before the end in his beloved St. Andrews, he was asked what he thought now of Christ. "I shall live and adore Him," he replied, then was heard whispering again and again, "Glory to Him in Immanuel's land!" So the little fair man died, as storm clouds were gathering over Scotland and the first

[1] *Op. cit.*, Vol. 2, p. 224.

Covenanters were paying the penalty on a scaffold in Edinburgh.

It is difficult to assess at its true worth the great service rendered by these Covenanting theologians in the first half of the seventeenth century. It was the unspectacular half: it boasted no martyrs or scaffold speeches. It was not a time when Covenanters felt they had to "perish, stoned and blinded in the desert, that men unborn may see." This is not, of course, to suggest that the early Covenanters would not have died for their faith if circumstances had been different. Nevertheless, theirs was a mighty contribution to the cause of Scottish liberty, for the right of the people in government, and the independence of the Church in discipline and worship. Presbyterianism was a democratic organization—albeit qualified in that age by a disfiguring intolerance of outlook, which view they shared with Episcopalians and Roman Catholics. But Presbyterianism was the channel in which ran the religious life of the nation. It was important to vindicate the right of the people to choose their own form of church government, and to assert the inherent independence of the Church to run its own affairs in its own way.

This unhappily involved the belief that those who differed with them on religious issues were wrong. Even fellow-Presbyterians of independent mind were careful to keep their objections to themselves. Not until Robert Leighton became a bishop did he (an erstwhile Presbyterian) raise his voice against the Covenanters. The Church of Rome, placed in the position of the stricter Covenanters, could scarcely have been more inflexible in the assertion of Divine Right on its own behalf. On one view we can concede that the Covenanters were forced to this position by the political developments of the age, for the real problem of the Reformed Church, the crux of the matter, was not in the last resort one of the royal supremacy, nor did it concern the right of a people to rebel. It was a problem of authority. Wherein did authority lie?

The Church of Rome's answer was, as ever, clear-cut and uncompromising, which tremendous psychological advantage it has consistently exploited to this day. The answer of the Anglicans was rather less lucid. The Church of England came to identify itself with the doctrine of the Divine Right of Kings, possibly because it was the only answer which dealt equally well with the opposition of Rome on one hand, Puritanism on the other—and at the same time ensured the English Church's position in the State. "Thus it fell out in England after the Reformation," observed Robert McWard, "that the same, if not a more exorbitant, power taken from the Pope was transferred and settled on the Crown."[1]

[1] This, McWard considered, was perhaps a change for the worse, "the Pope being at least in show a Church man" (*The True Nonconformist*, pp. 467, 471).

Wrote Bishop Jewel in Elizabethan times: "We publicly teach, that princes are to be obeyed as men sent by God; and whosoever resists them resists the ordinance of God. And this is well to be seen both in our books and in our preachings."[1] Moreover, Archbishop Laud declared in 1626: "The office and person of a king is sacred and cannot be violated by the hand, tongue, or heart of any man, that is, by deed, word, or thought; but 'tis God's cause, and He is violated in him."[2]

But there were other issues now which the Covenanters had to consider. The excesses of the Anabaptists on the Continent had brought home to the Scots the perils of anarchy or of complete individualism. Hitherto for them, as for the sixteenth-century Protestants, the great authority which superseded Pope and Church was the Bible. But that presented difficulties too, for the Anabaptists could justify their beliefs from scriptural texts—and the Devil himself was word-perfect on Scripture when it suited him.

So the Covenanters held the Divine Right of Presbytery—a tenet which fitted in very well with their Calvinistic tradition—a tenet which was, moreover, to land them in serious trouble when it came up against a king who, this time with Parliament at his back, held quite another theory of Divine Right.

---

[1] *The Apology of the Church of England*, 1843, p. 331. For a summary of Church of England thought on the subject in Jewel's time, see "The Doctrine of the Prince and the Elizabethan Episcopal Sermon," *Anglican Theological Review*, XLV, January, 1963, pp. 83–92.

[2] Quoted by M. S. Bates, *Religious Liberty: An Inquiry*, 1945, p. 171.

CHAPTER IV

DEVELOPMENTS UNDER THE COMMONWEALTH

T HE EXECUTION OF CHARLES I WAS REGARDED IN SCOTLAND with horror and resentment; indeed, the immediate reaction was to make the Scots, with few exceptions, the adherents of the dead king's son, who had fled first to Jersey before going on to The Hague. When the General Assembly had its next meeting, it adopted an address to him, protesting that "we do from our hearts abominate and detest that horrid fact of the Sectaries against the life of your royal father, our late sovereign." During Charles's exile in Holland, the Duke of Hamilton (who had succeeded to the title after his brother's execution in March 1649) and the Earl of Lauderdale were his chief advisers on Scottish affairs.

Three months after the king's death, the Commonwealth under Oliver Cromwell was officially set up in London, but before that, on 5th February, Charles II had been proclaimed at Edinburgh as king, not only of Scotland, but of Great Britain and Ireland. Had the announcement of his accession concerned Scotland alone, the Scots would have stood on firm ground, and Cromwell would have had no legitimate reason for protest and action against them. As it was, Charles was thereafter by the Cromwellians consistently called "King of Scots."

An odd stipulation was included in his recognition by the Scots. Charles was not to be allowed to exercise the kingly power in Scotland till he "should give satisfaction for religion and peace." This involved the acceptance of both Covenants, and the swearing of an oath to establish Presbyterianism in all his dominions. In order to secure his acquiescence, a deputation of ministers and laymen waited on him in Holland with these terms. Charles refused to accede. In the first place, the conditions were, not unnaturally, unpalatable to him; and, moreover, he had decided to try his luck in Ireland. For some time, therefore, negotiations were suspended while he dangled for the support of the Irish Roman Catholics.[1]

It is not difficult to appreciate the quandary in which the young man found himself in the face of the Scottish demands, especially

[1] For the situation in Ireland, see W. L. Mathieson, *op. cit.*, Vol. II, p. 110.

as his attitude was not to be determined by religious scruples such as were the very life-blood of the Scottish leaders. Charles simply had none. For him the issue was partly a personal one, but even more so was it political. It was personal, because he wished to stand by Montrose, who implored him not to perjure himself by submitting to the Scots. It was political, because he saw the wisdom of trying to conciliate the Covenanters. Bound up with the latter issue was the hope that he might induce them to abandon the Act of Classes, made just before the death of Charles I, by which both Royalists and Engagers were prevented from joining the Covenanters in the king's service. For that reason Charles rejected the initial approach of the Commissioners while, among his other schemes, he worked towards a general reconciliation of Scottish parties.

But situated as he was, there could be only one outcome. In vain did Montrose sketch for Charles the history of the Covenant movement, from "its justifiable beginnings to its impossible end." In vain did he point out that the Covenanters insisted on the king's giving up his own private form of worship (surely an unconsciously ironic touch), "yet they made it a ground of rebellion against your royal father that they but imagined he intended to meddle with them after the like kind."[1] Montrose's arguments were doomed to failure, because they presupposed in Charles a religious character and moral principles which were conspicuously absent in that nineteen-year-old youth. In the Marquis of Montrose, a true Royalist, yet with no belief in Divine Right or bishops and with little interest in ecclesiastical disputes (though he had at one time taken the Covenant), Charles had a servant of whom he was totally unworthy.

Before long, however, Cromwell and his New Model Army had shattered the king's hopes of success in Ireland, and the royal dreams faded before reality and the necessity of a stark choice when negotiations were resumed with the Scots in January 1650. No prevarication was possible now. Either he must take the Covenanters on their terms, or he must abandon for the present, perhaps for many years, all hope of restoration.

The first Charles had preferred to die rather than sign the Covenant, on which condition the Scottish army would have come to his aid in England. No trace of any such fervent religious feeling characterized his son. He was prepared to swallow the Covenant at a gulp, to give himself the chance of possessing a crown which he had never yet worn. In the process, while negotiations at The Hague were continuing with the Scots Commissioners, he sacri-

[1] J. Buchan, *Montrose*, 1928, p. 288.

ficed to the hangman's noose the faithful Montrose, who desired to continue the royal cause at home.

It is sometimes forgotten that Montrose did an incredibly difficult thing for that age: he remained loyal to his Church as well as to his king. In anticipation of death he declared:

> The Covenant which I took, I own it and adhere to it. Bishops, I care not for them. I never intended to advance their interest. But when the king had granted you all your desires, and you were every one sitting under his vine and under his fig tree, that then you should have taken a party in England by the hand, and entered into a league and covenant with them against the king, was the thing I judged my duty to oppose to the yondmost.[1]

Montrose's letter on "Sovereign Power" further clarifies his position thus: "And thou, seditious preacher, who studies to put sovereignty in the people's hands for thy own ambitious ends—as being capable, by thy wicked eloquence and hypocrisy, to infuse into them what thou pleasest—know this, that this people is more incapable of sovereignty than any other known." It seems evident that this shaft was directed at Rutherford and his known anti-monarchical views.

Betrayed by Neil Macleod of Assynt, Sheriff-Depute of Sutherland, the thirty-eight-year-old fugitive marquis was executed on 21st May, 1650, and his head stuck on top of the Tolbooth in Edinburgh. There it stayed until after the Restoration, when Charles ordered that the remains be reverently collected and given state burial. Macleod was at that time arrested because of his part in Montrose's downfall. Lodged in prison, he "struck up to a high pitch of vice and impiety, and gave great entertainments," and in the process so ingratiated himself with so many people that finally in 1674 he was "found clean by ane assyse" and released.[2]

Meanwhile, Charles's triumph was still ten years off, and he was in dire straits. Every allowance should be made for his position, for a prince in exile has the most unenviable of roles. During his time on the Continent, Charles had been forced to degrading shifts to live at all, much less maintain the dignity compatible with his status. Supplies had reached him only by uncertain and fitful remittances from fickle allies whose main motive seems to have been the securing of his potential future support. Under such circumstances the taking of a distasteful oath which would change his position may have seemed a small price to pay. Perhaps he overestimated his power to win over the Scots (Charles had an engaging way with him), and so beat down the unreasonable terms which he was now driven to accept.

[1] M. Napier, *Memoirs of the Marquis of Montrose*, 1856, Vol. II, p. 787.
[2] Cf. G. Burnet, *op. cit.*, Vol. I, p. 176.

He found the Scots Commissioners obdurate. One of them, Alexander Jaffray, who later had a change of heart, wrote of this interlude:

> . . . being again sent there by the Parliament, in the year 1650, for that same business, we did sinfully both entangle and engage the nation and ourselves, and that poor young prince to whom we were sent; making him sign and swear a covenant, which we knew, from clear and demonstrable reasons, that he hated in his heart. Yet, finding that upon these terms only, he could be admitted to rule over us (all other means having then failed him) *he* sinfully complied with what *we* most sinfully pressed upon him:—where, I must confess, to my apprehension, *our* sin was more than *his*. . . .[1]

Even so, that the king did not give way without some qualms is seen, both in the fact that he sailed from Holland without having subscribed to the Covenants, and also in a minor addition which was made to his acceptance of them on board ship at the mouth of the Spey in June 1650. Charles had tried to have inserted the condition that he would not do anything against the laws of England, but the Commissioners would have none of it. They were determined to leave neither loophole nor room for ambiguity in the wily Charles's interpretation of their terms.

Moreover, all the Royalists and Engagers who had accompanied him from Holland were to leave Scotland, with only nine exceptions, none of whom was to be permitted to exercise a position of the greatest influence—most of them, indeed, were at first excluded from Court altogether. (This ban was later relaxed.) The measure was due probably as much to fear of the nation as to fear of the king, for the news of Charles's landing had evoked a great demonstration of loyalty in Edinburgh.

Nor were the Scots finished with him yet. On 16th August, 1650, at the ancient capital of Dunfermline, he was forced to subscribe to a paper in which he admitted the error of his father's ways, the idolatry of his mother (Henrietta was a Roman Catholic), and the sinfulness of himself.[2] At first he had objected that if he accepted this he could never again look his mother in the face, but when told there was no other way "he resolved to swallow the pill without farther chewing it." All this seems incredible to modern ears; even in that age there were some who guessed the value of Charles's vows and who publicly and privately depreciated them. Hugh Binning, for example, was one of a band of Covenanters who later considered themselves unjustified in supporting

---

[1] *Diary*, 1833, p. 32. This diary is generally interesting as showing the contemporary development of Quakerism in Scotland.
[2] R. Wodrow, *History of the Sufferings*, Vol. I, pp. 66ff.

Charles, without additional security's being provided for the maintenance of their religious principles, and unless some adequate restraint were imposed upon the exercise of the royal authority.[1] We shall see in the following pages that Binning's dread of arbitrary power was only too well founded. Others there were, however, who in oddly perverse fashion seemed to go to excessive lengths to concoct still more humiliating oaths for Charles to consent to. Thus he was made to say, among other things, that he had not sworn to the Covenants "upon any sinister intention and crooked design for attaining his own ends;"[2] that he would not tolerate popery or prelacy or error; and that he would establish Presbyterianism in England.

On 1st January, 1651, there was enacted the last coronation in Scotland, and the only one under exclusively Presbyterian auspices, featuring neither holy oil nor papal benediction. Charles dutifully held up his right hand and swore the following oath which we give here for purpose of future reference:

> I, Charles, King of Great Britain, etc., do assert and declare, by my solemn Oath, in the Presence of Almighty God, the Searcher of Hearts, my Allowance and Approbation of the National Covenant, and of the Solemn League and Covenant, above written, and faithfully oblige myself to prosecute the Ends thereof in my Station and Calling; and that I for Myself and my Successors shall consent and agree to all Acts of Parliament enjoining the National Covenant and Solemn League and Covenant, and fully establishing Presbyterial Government, the Directory for Worship, Confession of Faith, and Catechisms, in the Kingdom of Scotland, as they are approven by the General Assemblies of the Kirk, and Parliaments of this Kingdom; and that I shall give my royal assent to Acts or Ordinances of Parliament passed, or to be passed, enjoining the same in my other Dominions: and that I shall observe these in my own Practice and Family, and shall never make Opposition to any of these, or endeavour any change thereof.

It is difficult to believe that even the most dyed-in-the-wool Covenanter really accepted the king's professions at their face value. John Livingstone, for one, is known to have pleaded for delay, because he realized the hypocrisy of Charles in accepting the Covenants "without any evidence of any reall change in his heart, and without forsaking former principles, counsells, and company."[3] Another Covenanter, Walter Smith, voiced the judgment of the following generation when he attributed contempor-

---

[1] Binning outlined his case in *An Useful Case of Conscience*, 1693.
[2] *Apologetical Relation*, pp. 65f.
[3] *Records of the Commission of the General Assembly*, Scottish History Society, 1896. Vol. II, p. 437.

ary evils to the fact that "after the removal of the late king, both
Church and State have agreed to proclaim and bring home and set
up this man Charles II, who is now both an idol and a tyrant, to
rule over a Christian people in covenant with God, while by many
evidences he was known to be a heart-enemy to God and godliness, and, in all his oaths and declarations, a mocking hypo-
crite. . . ."[1]

The king's irreligious disposition more than justified the objection. Someone has said that he stood aloof, not in the least per-
plexed as was the ass in the old story, but supremely indifferent,
between the two bundles of hay—atheism and popery. Others
have expressed the opinion that Charles was a secret Catholic at
this time. The possibility, which does not flatter the Roman
Church, has never been confirmed beyond any doubt. Even old
Samuel Pepys, scarcely numbered among the Puritans himself,
admits that Charles cared for nothing but his pleasures. On one
occasion, after protesting that he was no atheist, Charles added
that he could not think that God would make a man miserable just
for taking a little pleasure out of the way.[2] What kind of a lasting
alliance could such a personality make with the narrow, intractable
Covenanter with his rigidly biblical code of ethics? When Charles
visited St. Andrews on one occasion, Samuel Rutherford, ever the
opportunist, improved the shining hour by subjecting him to "a
speche in Latin, running mutch upon what was the dewty of
kings."

We may question the consistency of the Scottish agreement
with the king at this juncture. They had denounced the Engagement of 1648 as an infringement against "our neighbour nation of
England," but the Scottish compact with Charles II laid itself open
to a similar charge.

This early phase of Charles's dealings with Scotland and the
Scots has been discussed at some length because of its vital importance in the understanding of future events and of the literature
of the Covenanting period. It is to this era that we must later point
back again and again when faced with the bewildering problem of
accounting for the misery and persecution to which Scotland, and
particularly the men of the Covenant, were exposed during the
twenty-five years when Charles II acted as absolute ruler of the
country from 1660—a policy which was continued for three more
years when James VII succeeded his brother. There is a sense in
which the conflict was inevitable. "Given a Divine law of the
Bible on one hand," comments Thomas Carlyle, "and a Stuart
king, Charles I or Charles II on the other; alas, did history ever

[1] P. Walker, *Six Saints of the Covenant*, 1901, Vol. II, p. 71.
[2] G. Burnet, *op. cit.*, Vol. I, p. 128.

present a more irreducible case of equations in this world?"

The situation in Scotland about this time is not unfairly gauged by a quaint old English broadside entitled, "Old Sayings and Predictions verified and fulfilled, touching the young King of Scotland and his gued Subjects." This contains a caricature on Charles's submission to the Scots. The king's nose is held to a grindstone by a Scots ecclesiastic, whilst "Jockie", a layman in a blue cap, turns the handle. At the side of the picture are the words:

> This Embleme needs no learned exposition,
> The World knows well enough the sad condition
> Of regall power and prerogative,
> Dead and dethroned in England, now alive
> In Scotland, where they seem to love the Lad
> If hee'l be more obsequious than his Dad,
> And act according to Kirk principles,
> More subtile then were Delphick oracles:
> For let him lye, dissemble, kill and slay
> Hee's a good Prince that will the Kirk obey.
> . . . .
> Turne Jockie turne (for gold will turn thy heart,
> And make thee to renounce in Christ a part)
> The grindstone to make sharp thy Levite Laws,
> Or else t'abate the edge of regall Cause
> And privilege. And Jockie for thy paines
> Great treasures, pleasures, offices and gaynes
> Shall be thy large reward when England's wonne.[1]

But far from England's being won, Scotland itself was lost to Charles when Cromwell achieved his "crowning mercy" by defeating the king's armies at Worcester in September 1651, after a campaign which need not concern us here. That monarch departed into exile in France with convictions about his erstwhile kingdom and its people which were to shape his attitude towards them after the Restoration—and indirectly to pave the way for what is perhaps the most tragic, certainly the most thrilling, story in Scotland's fight for spiritual independence.

After Cromwell's victory there ensued in Scotland that curious episode known in British history as the Commonwealth and Protectorate—really a military dictatorship so far as Scotland was concerned, with the land governed by the English General Monk on behalf of the Lord Protector. Scotland and Ireland were joined with England for Parliamentary purposes, and after having only 5 representatives in June 1653 out of 140, Scotland by 1656 achieved the right to send 30 out of 460 to the united Parliament.

[1] The poem is reproduced in full in the *Catalogue of Satirical Prints and Drawings in the British Museum*, i. 448. For the caricature see Wright's *History of Caricature and Grotesque*, p. 369.

This body maintained a form of government, but was denied the power thereof, for Cromwell was very much of a dictator. It may be noted that Cromwell had earlier shown himself a match for the Covenanters in dialectic. He played the Scots at their own game by quoting against them their own limitations on the royal power, giving illustrations from Mariana and Buchanan. Bound to defend the true religion as they were, Cromwell held, the Scots were discharged from their avowed loyalty to the king when the latter proved an enemy to that true religion.[1]

It is beside our present purpose to speak of the history of that remarkable era when, on the whole, the Scots knew peace, order and justice to a degree never enjoyed under their own native kings. There was little Covenanting literature during Cromwell's supremacy—one might almost say that its *raison d'être* had departed with the temporary eclipse of the Stuarts—but we must note various ecclesiastical developments. During the years 1650–60 we see the beginnings of a serious discord within the Presbyterian ranks—an "infatuating and ruining distemper" which was to hasten the fall of the national Church. To understand how there came to be two main factions on the ecclesiastical scene we go back to consider a decree of the Estates in December 1650.

In that month the Estates ordered Robert Douglas to convene the Commission of the General Assembly in Perth, the chief reason for which was to obtain a judgment whether it was lawful to reinstate those formerly purged from the army by the Act of Classes.[2] The Commission agreed that it was lawful to reinstate all but a small minority. This was known as the first Public Resolution. In March 1651 the Commission was asked to judge of the lawfulness of admitting to the Committee of Estates those persons formerly debarred but who were now, after satisfaction given, admitted to the Covenant. On this occasion the Commission was more guarded, but it eventually replied by desiring Parliament to admit to the Committee all save a few "pryme actors against the State." This was the second Public Resolution.

Those who upheld these decisions were henceforth known as Resolutioners, and they were for the most part moderate Presbyterians and moderate Royalists. Yet even they, at this stage, were still in favour of the measure that Presbyterianism, according to the terms of the Solemn League and Covenant, should be forced upon England and Ireland. Only slowly and unwillingly did they begin to confine their efforts to the preservation of the national religion in Scotland.

Those who disagreed with the decision to join forces with the

[1] G. Burnet, Vol. I, pp. 56f.
[2] *Supra*, p. 37.

so-called Malignants were named Protesters or Remonstrants. The latter, most of whom came from the south-west, condemned the Resolutions as "involving ane conjunctione with the malignant partie in the land." Thus in 1650 the Protesters rejected Charles as king till he had given proof in his heart as well as with his lips that he approved the Covenants. As he was never likely to afford them that satisfaction now, the Protesters stood in irreconcilable opposition to his government.

Before the beginning of the Scottish campaign which ended in such disastrous fashion on Worcester field, the schism in the Scots ranks had been further accentuated. Taunted by Cromwell, perhaps justifiably, with upholding the Arch-Malignant himself in the transparent guise of a Covenanted king, the army of the Covenanters, assembled under the leadership of Johnston of Wariston and James Guthrie, minister of Stirling, was zealously purged by the removal of all men "of a scandalous conversatione, and of a questionable integrity and affection in the cause of God".[1] It is reckoned that from one of the best armies Scotland has ever mustered some 5,000 men were cast out as a result of this procedure which aimed at an army of saints. (Cromwell, too, thought himself on the side of the angels, but his confidence in divine help did not lead him to deplete his earthly forces.) Rash the Covenanters might have been, but their action was nevertheless consistent. If they are condemned as unpractical, the condemnation must begin with the Solemn League and Covenant of which their action was the legitimate and logical result.

Enthusiasm for the Covenants tended to be no longer national but sectarian, because the Resolutioners were beginning to have doubts about the action of the extremists. Men were thus already losing sight of the original purpose of the National Covenant as the protest of a whole realm against the absolutism of the king, and that of the Solemn League as standing for the Reformation of religion by those who were firm believers that the true Church should be Presbyterian.

The strict Covenanters have often been criticized for their intolerant suppression of dissentients at this stage. However, to be fair to them, extant records make it clear that the country was being threatened with a repetition of that moral decadence which, more than a hundred years before, had so exercised George Wishart and John Knox, and been one of the chief causes of the Scottish Reformation.[2]

This view of the situation has not gone unchallenged. The historian Kirkton, speaking of the Commonwealth era, tells of "the

[1] *Calendar of State Papers*, 1858, Vol. 2, p. 324.
[2] See, e.g., A. Jaffray, *op. cit.*, p. 120.

great successe the word preached hade in sanctifying the people of the nation." It was claimed that swearing was largely abolished, and that over much of the country there was scarcely a family which did not have family worship. "I verily believe," adds Kirkton, "there were more souls converted to Christ in that short period of time, than in any season since the Reformation, though of treble its duration."[1] Law agrees, and attributes this to the fact that ministers were now preaching the Gospel alone, instead of preaching up "Parliaments, armies, leagues, resolutions, and remonstrances which was much in use before."[2]

Some seven or eight thousand English soldiers garrisoned Scotland with chief strongholds at Leith, Ayr, Stirling, Perth and Inverness. Money was brought into the country (but evidently remained to a large extent in the hands of the occupying army), peace was maintained, justice done, and according to Burnet, vice was suppressed and punished.[3] Men had their ears torn off for drinking the king's health, witches and warlocks were burnt, and in July 1657 seven gipsies were scourged through the capital and banished from Scotland. The citizens of Edinburgh groaned under the high degree of taxation needed to support the alien army, but flocked to pay threepence each to see a dromedary ("ane heigh great beast") and a turnip-faced baboon which an enterprising individual had imported into the country.

Nevertheless the Restoration Parliament, when it came to legislate in 1660, was to find it necessary to pass an Act condemning "the abominable sins of drunkenness and all manner of cursing and swearing," and to impose the usual sliding scale of fines on offenders. James Guthrie bemoaned the wickedness in the land at this time, and attributed it partly to the admission of Charles II "to the full exercise of his power, and the crowning him, notwithstanding the new discoveries of his adhering to his former principles and ways, and of many warnings to the contrary."[4]

Yet whatever the moral condition of the land, it is clear that the Commonwealth and Protectorate brought to Scotland some eight years of peace. James Guthrie seems to express bewilderment at Cromwell's régime in *The Great Danger of Backsliding and Defection from Covenanted Reformation Principles* (1651) in saying that "though the Lord has assisted England to put down the Popish, Prelatical and Malignant Party . . . yet to this day we know not what is set up instead thereof, either in doctrine, wor-

---

[1] *Op. cit.*, pp. 54f., 64f. Kirkton thought it no bad thing that General Assemblies were suppressed at this time, for they "seemed to be more sett upon establishing themselves than promoving religion."
[2] *Memorials*, ed. C. K. Sharpe, 1812, p. 7.
[3] *Op. cit.*, Vol. I, p. 83.
[4] *Causes of the Lord's Wrath against Scotland*, 1653, pp. 6, 55.

ship, discipline or government, but a high toleration of all things contrary to the Gospel of Jesus Christ."

Cromwell's attitude towards the Covenant and Presbyterianism generally may be judged from the fact that the General Assemblies of the Kirk were suppressed. This was partly due also to the fact that many of the leading ministers had strong Royalist affiliations. The Assembly which met at Dundee in July 1651 hurriedly dispersed on hearing of the approach of the English soldiers. Another one met at Edinburgh in July 1653, with David Dickson as Moderator. Colonel Cotterall marched in and demanded by whose authority the Assembly had met. "Sir," said Dickson, "you ask by what authority we sit here; we sit, not as having authority from any power on earth, but as having power and authority from Jesus Christ; and by Him, and for Him, and for the good of His Church." The Colonel was not impressed. He ordered them all out, and the Assembly was closed for many years to come. An attempt was made to meet in Edinburgh in July 1654, but Cromwell's commander broke it up before the Assembly was constituted.

Apart from this one significant measure, however, which left synods, presbyteries and kirk sessions undisturbed, the Protector was inclined to leave the Kirk to itself, torn as it was by a dissension which it was rather to his interest to encourage than to subdue. Such dissension did no good to Presbyterianism in England, as a leading Presbyterian minister in London pointed out in a letter to Samuel Rutherford in January 1657. "The sad differences amongst the Presbyterian brethren in Scotland which your letter to me suggesteth," wrote Simeon Ash, "are no lesse greivous to your Presbyterian friends here, than joyous to such who both on the right and left hand doe with detestation decrye the Presbyterian Government."[1]

Changes and new developments in this era are both constant and bewildering. It will therefore help our understanding if we look once again at the respective attitudes of the two main parties in the Church under this new régime. The Resolutioners were opposed to the English Sectaries (a designation which, used by most historians, seems to have included a most miscellaneous group: Independents, Anabaptists,[2] Arminians, Antinomians, Ranters, Seekers, and others), and in sympathy with the exiled king. The Protesters, on the other hand, still regarded any truck with Charles as criminal, and they were in opposition to the majority of the clergy, whom they accused of placing loyalty to

[1] *Consultations*, I, p. 288.
[2] On this point see J. Scott, "Baptists in Scotland during the Commonwealth," *Records of the Scottish Church History Society*, Vol. III, 1929, pp. 174-85.

the king above the rights of Christ in His Church. These Protesters refused to pray for the king, and patterned their manner of worship after the somewhat austere mode of the Sectaries—worship characterized by preaching and praying at great length and with great fervour.

They were accustomed to meet in large gatherings comprised of ministers, elders and church members, and to condemn whatever was not of their way of thinking (such groups are yet with us), defying the enactments of the General Assembly itself, before the suppression of that court. Obviously their attitude as confirmed anti-Royalists brought them into a somewhat uneasy alliance with the Cromwellians, and this fact gave the Protesters a measure of influence in Church and State. It would appear that they could have had more power, for in 1654 Cromwell offered to put the Protesting minority in control of ecclesiastical affairs in Scotland.[1] This tempting offer was rejected by the bulk of the Protesters, and we should mark the reason for their refusal to co-operate with the Protector—they felt that the invitation constituted an encroachment by the State on the jurisdiction of the church courts.

This seems a convenient point to look briefly at the life and opinions of James Guthrie, whom Cromwell called the "short man who would not bow." The spokesman of the stricter Covenanters, Guthrie was the only one of them who, during Cromwell's rule, published any work on the political implications of the Covenanting position. He was born about 1612, the son of a gentleman landowner in Angus. At first, through the influence of his father, he favoured Episcopacy, and his youth showed evidence that he was "prelatic and strong for the ceremonies." He admitted this himself at his trial in 1661, saying: "I was not honoured to be of those who laid the foundation in this kirk and kingdom. I am not ashamed to give glory to God, in acknowledging that until the year 1638, I was treading other steps. . . ."[2] Guthrie went to the University of St. Andrews, and the friendship of Samuel Rutherford, Professor of Divinity there, was probably responsible for much of the change which took place in his religious ideas at that time. We have no clear picture of what happened. We do know that when he left St. Andrews, it was for the ministry of the Presbyterian Church. He signed the Covenant in 1638, and when he did he added: "I know that I shall die for what I have done this day, but I cannot die in a better cause."

His first charge was at Lauder in Berwickshire, where he was ordained in 1642. In 1646 he was a member of the Scottish delega-

[1] Cf. J. Kirkton, op. cit., p. 56.
[2] R. Wodrow, op. cit., Vol. II, p. 171.

tion which met Charles I at Newcastle to give him a letter from the General Assembly, which pressed the claims of Presbyterianism and the Solemn League. He preached before Parliament in January 1649, and ten months later was inducted to the first charge at Stirling. Guthrie was acquainted with James Sharp (later Archbishop), whom he regarded shudderingly as one destined for a terrible career.

Guthrie warmly championed the cause of the Protesters, denounced the lukewarm policy of the Resolutioners, and protested that the principles of the Covenant should be maintained; that the Malignants should not be admitted to places of trust; and that the king's authority should be limited by a free Parliament and a free Assembly. Like John Knox, there was no tempering of the tongue with Guthrie. Burnet declared his language to be "indecent and intolerable." Guthrie and his Stirling colleague, David Bennet, were cited to appear before the king at Perth in February 1651, because of some things said in the pulpit in the royal presence. After some delay they arrived, but only to hand in a Protestation declining the king's judgment in matters of doctrine. For this act of defiance Guthrie was imprisoned in Perth, Bennet in Dundee. The former, moreover, deputed by the Commission of Assembly to excommunicate the Earl of Middleton, for good reason, proceeded to carry out the sentence in opposition to Charles's specific instructions. The king never forgot that. That Middleton was his favourite at the time probably counted less with him than the fact of his command's being ignored. Charles did not like to be ignored.

Under the Protector in Scotland we find Guthrie in a very different role. The Protesters refused to abandon those principles of constitutional government to which they had subscribed in the Covenant. As a result, Guthrie defended the king's right from the pulpit, in the presence of the Protector's dreaded officers, and maintained it in public disputation with Hugh Peters, Cromwell's chaplain. Royalist tendencies in a man like Guthrie appear anomalous, but his stand on this matter was probably based on that Covenanting principle which upheld the office of the king, while at the same time withholding support from King Charles II.

The people of Stirling, a town where feelings ran high, were not kind to Guthrie. Those who were Royalists disliked him for his criticism of the king; the Resolutioners and men of political expediency, who felt the lash of his tongue for their vacillation, found his forthright stand abhorrent; the Sectaries, who often commandeered the local pulpits as a sounding-board for their wild theories (under the protection of the English army), found obnoxious his thundering denunciations of religious toleration and his unwillingness to accept the *status quo*. From what we know of Guthrie, the role of Ishmael was not likely to have worried him. As there was at one point some likelihood that he would be invited to preach before His Excellency, Guthrie had carefully prepared a sermon, the matter of which can be guessed from his text: "Shall the throne of inquity have fellowship with thee, which frameth mischief by a law?" The invitation to preach was not forthcoming. Cromwell knew his man.

In 1653 Guthrie's main work, *Causes of God's Wrath against Scotland*, was published. While much of it is concerned only with theological matters and interpretations, several pointers are given regarding his attitude to events of the day. On behalf of the Protesters he spurned all suggestion of compromise, thus: "We judge it but the effect of the wisdom of the flesh and to smell rankly of a carnal politic spirit to halve and divide the things of God for making peace amongst men."[1] In these words we get the crux of the Covenanters' consistent refusal during the following two reigns to budge an inch from their adherence to the Covenants. In this stand of the Protesters even a modern Royalist writer, Dr. Law Mathieson, judges that they were upholding those principles which hitherto had been dominant in the Presbyterian Church in Scotland.[2] Moreover, they maintained that no necessity, however urgent, could justify the State in employing any but approved Covenanters in its defence.

Writing about the Solemn League and Covenant, Guthrie said: "The duty of defending and preserving the King's Majesty's Person and authority is joined with, and subordinate to, the duty of preserving and defending the true religion. . . ."[3] He is even more outspoken in his allocation of blame for the situation which provoked the heavenly wrath upon Scotland, declaring: "An arbitrary government and an illimited power was the fountain of most, if not all of the corruptions both of King and State; and that it was for restraint of this, and for their own just defence against tyranny and unjust violence (which ordinarily is the fruit and effect of such a power) that the Lord's people did join in the Covenant, and have been at the expenses of so much blood, travails and pains in these years past."[4]

Cromwell tolerated Guthrie with admirable good humour, and allowed freedom of speech to him in his zeal for defending "the true religion." In his attitude toward religious toleration Cromwell belongs in the nineteenth rather than in the seventeenth cen-

[1] *Causes*, p. 81.
[2] *Politics and Religion*, Vol. II, p. 169.
[3] *Causes*, p. 54.
[4] Ibid.

tury. Guthrie's other antagonists, Charles II and the Resolutioner party, nursed their wrath against him and the Protesters. The king soon had an opportunity for vengeance. After the Restoration, James Guthrie headed a band of twelve Protesters who met together and drew up an address of congratulation to the king. This reminded Charles of his Covenant obligation, and asked him to "fill all places of trust, not only in Scotland, but in England and Ireland, with those who had taken the Covenant and were of known affection to the cause of God."[1] For a Protesting manifesto, its tone was comparatively reasonable, though it showed its authors' distinctive lack of religious toleration.

However, it appeared treason most foul in the eyes of the Committee of Estates which was at the time entrusted with the affairs of Scotland, and was proclaimed a libel, containing "many particulars reflecting upon his sacred Majesty, the government of our neighbour Church and kingdom of England, and the constitution of this present Committee—and many other things directly tending to seditions, raising of new tumults, and, if possible, rekindling a civil war amongst His Majesty's good subjects." On 23rd August, 1660, 100 years to the day after the Reformation had been confirmed by the Scottish Parliament, the petitioners were seized, except for one who escaped, and flung into prison. When Guthrie left it, it was for the scaffold, as we shall read in the next chapter.

During the Commonwealth, Guthrie's strong language naturally aroused the opposition of the more moderate ministers to an increasing extent, and both the future restoration of Episcopacy in Scotland and the decline of Presbyterianism in England were greatly facilitated by the presence of such factions in the Presbyterian ranks. An interesting comment is made on the situation by Hector Macpherson: it was, he remarks, "the unnatural coalition of Royalism and moderate Calvinism against the extremist elements typified in Cromwell and the 'sectaries' which made the Restoration possible."[2] Yet these same Moderates were remarkably reticent during the Protectorate about expressing any vocal opposition to Cromwell, as indeed were some of the Protesters. Thus Walter Smith, in describing God's dealings with the Kirk from 1649 to 1681, dismisses the Protectorate in a very offhand way and in few words: "During the Protectorate there was so little done for God by either Church or State, but a door kept open for his [Charles's] return to tyrannize and set up his heathenish laws and government, which . . . hath since been our snare and our scourge."[3] It is evident that the animus of the Presbyterians was not

[1] J. Brown, *Apologetical Relation*, pp. 70–6.
[2] *The Covenanters under Persecution*, 1923, p. 19.
[3] P. Walker, *op. cit.*, Vol. 2, p. 72.

actively directed against Cromwell. Yet the man who could appreciate and promote John Owen never came to any real understanding with the unbending intellectual pride of the ministers; it was in exasperation towards them that he addressed his deathless words when he besought them, "in the bowels of Christ, think it possible that you might be mistaken."[1]

Oliver Cromwell died on 3rd September, 1658, the seventh anniversary of Worcester field, and after the somewhat ineffectual eight-month attempt of his son Richard to carry on the government,[2] the English troops, "those badges of our slavery," were withdrawn from Scotland after some negotiations, and Charles II returned—this time as actual ruler of both England and Scotland. Life for him in the interval had been anything but easy, as Kirkton here shows:

Indeed his exile was very comfortless to himself, for, in France, first he was coldly entertained by his nearest neighbours and relations, and thereafter shamefully banished, and partly upon Mazarine's base pick. In Colen he quickly found himself a burdine to his host, and thereafter became the publick object of his dishonour, the boys in the city making a solemn anniversary mock pageant to the scorn of the king without land. And when he was driven back to seek shelter and rest in the Spanish Netherlands, where he made his longest abode, yet was he still hunted by his enemies, betrayed by his servants, and most unsuccessfull in all his attempts, besides his continual sorrow for his losse, his fear from his hazard, and the poor shift he was constrained to make among strangers for his supply.[3]

Now that he was back in London, it is significant to recall his attitude towards Scotland. It must primarily have been recalled as the land where he had led such an intolerable life of dreary repression; where there was not a woman "fit to be seen" (his own words), and where it was a sin to play the fiddle. He may have remembered one fast day when he was obliged to sit through six successive sermons. "I was there myself," Bishop Burnet feelingly comments, "and not a little weary of so tedious a service." Perhaps Sir Walter Scott's accounts of Covenanting diets of worship might not have been so exaggerated as we sometimes thought![4]

[1] See his *Letters*, ed. T. Carlyle, 1871, Vol. 3, p. 18 (Letter CXXXVI).

[2] It is somehow surprising to discover that Richard Cromwell lived on in discreet retirement for a further fifty-four years. "And so without any struggle he withdrew," comments Burnet (*op. cit.*, Vol. I, p. 115), "and became a private man. And as he had done hurt to nobody, so nobody did ever study to hurt him: a rare instance of the instability of human greatness, and of the security of innocence."

[3] *Op. cit.*, p. 57.

[4] We think especially of Kettledrummle's statement in *Old Mortality*: "The sermon had fifteen heads, each of which was garnished with seven uses of application, two of consolation, two of terror, two declaring the causes of backsliding and of wrath, and one announcing the promised and expected deliverance."

Charles conceived a great hatred for Presbyterianism, for it made him feel that he ought to apologize almost for ever having been born. "Rebel for rebel," he once wrote to Clarendon, "I had rather trust a Papist rebel than a Presbyterian."[1]

Constantly in our investigation we are driven back to consider the larger issues, the wider canvas on which the scene is displayed. There we find the key to all the differences between king and kirk —the fact that religion was not with him the serious matter it was with them, or as it was later with James VII from a Roman Catholic viewpoint. Charles regarded religion merely from the political aspect and from that of ease and personal convenience. Clarendon remarked that the "ill-bred familiarity of the Scots divines" had given him (Charles) a distaste for Presbyterianism. But apart from this altogether, the national religion of Scotland constituted for Charles a dangerous encroachment upon the royal prerogative. How well he had recognized this fact was seen after the Restoration.

Moreover, since his shaky tenure of the Scottish throne a decade before, the Protesters had become even more extreme. *They* were on the side of the angels; *he* was one of the worst of the "treacherous and lecherous" House of Stuart. He was, with some qualification on the point of expediency, in favour of a measure of religious toleration; to them, that was unthinkable, for they believed that the most wicked of all the wicked things done by Cromwell during the Protectorate was his establishment of "that hellish toleration" —which, however, did not extend either to Episcopalians or to Roman Catholics. It did extend to other bodies—to the Baptists, for example, and to the Brownist movement which had its Scottish beginnings in Edinburgh about 1584, and which had received a a great impetus during the latter years of Charles I by the advent of adherents from England and Ireland, from which latter country many of them had been expelled by the prelates. The Quakers also had been much encouraged during the Protectorate, and John Nicoll in his Diary tells us that "in the month of January 1655, and in sundry other months preceding, and many months following, there rose up great numbers of that damnable sect of the Quakers; who, being deluded by Satan drew away many to their profession, both men and women alike, sundry of them walking through the streets all naked except for their shirts, crying: 'This is the way, walk ye into it.' "[2] James Guthrie says that within about sixteen years they increased from "scarce . . . ten" to "sundry ten thousands."[3]

[1] W. C. Mackenzie, *Life and Times of John Maitland, Duke of Lauderdale, 1616–1682*, 1923.
[2] See excerpt in J. G. Fyfe, *op. cit.*, p. 180.
[3] "Some Considerations," in *Faithful Contendings Displayed*, p. 496. See on this subject A. Jaffray, *Diary*, 1833, pp. 44ff., 149.

Charles always lamented that common and ignorant persons were allowed to read the Scriptures, holding that such liberty caused the rise of "all our sects, each interpreting according to their vile notions, and to accomplish their horrible wickednesses." The Protesters, on the other hand, were proud of basing their beliefs on the Word of God. Their theme song might well have been expressed in the words of Robert Burns's *Imaginary Address of Robert the Bruce at Bannockburn*:

> That all the world may see
> There's nane in the right but we,
> Of the auld Scottish nation.

Yet in one respect at least, the attitude of the Protesters could be regarded as logical enough. Years before, in the early days of the Covenant movement, the Earl of Traquair, the king's Commissioner, was told by the Covenanting Earl of Loudon that "they knew of no other bands between a king and his subjects but those of religion and the laws. If these be broken, men's lives are no longer dear to them: boasted [threatened] we shall not be; such fears are past for us."[1]

It was this theory which the Covenanters unswervingly held; it was on this foundation that they lived their lives; it was with this protestation on their lips that they died justified, the victims of that impossible Stuart theory of the Divine Right of Kings. The manner of their living and dying we shall read in the following pages.

[1] T. McCrie, *Sketches*, 1846, Vol. I, p. 220.

CHAPTER V

THE RESTORATION AND THE FIRST MARTYRS

SCOTLAND REGAINED HER INDEPENDENCE AT THE RESTORA-
tion of Charles II in 1660, as a result of developments in
England which need not concern us here. His accession was
proclaimed at London on 8th May, and at Edinburgh six days
later. He entered London on 29th May. In Scotland the national
pride was boosted once more, for the people considered themselves freed from the supremacy of a foreign government. Charles
was greeted in Edinburgh, according to a contemporary diarist,
"with all solemnities requisite . . . and takins of joy for the advancement and preference of their native king to his crown. . . .
Whereat also there was much wine spent, the spouts of the foun-
tains running and venting out abundance of wine, placed there
for that end; and the magistrates and councillors of the town being
present, drinking the King's health, and breaking numbers of
glasses."[1] Oliver Cromwell and the devil, in fireworks, pursued
each other on the Castle Rock till both blew up in a thousand fly-
ing sparks. The king had come home!

The process of disenchantment was soon to begin. "As for the
freedom we were restored unto," remarked Sir James Stewart of
Goodtrees, "we are yet ignorant of it."[2] After all the transient
manifestations of jubilant enthusiasm had died away, one thing
could clearly be seen: that no possible policy of the new Government would satisfy all parties in the State, no legislative measures
serve to reconcile the different factions in the Kirk. The first ominous portent of things to come was made clear when a Parliament
of Royalist sympathizers was gathered together in Edinburgh. The
Earl of Middleton, a crafty and treacherous but able man who was
always ready to emulate the renowned Vicar of Bray, was made
the King's Commissioner in the Scottish Parliament, and commander of the army in Scotland.

Our previous chapter referred to the Protesters, who were the
extremists of the Covenant movement. On the other side were the
Resolutioners or Moderates, who had sanctioned Charles's coro-

[1] Diary of John Nicoll in J. G. Fyfe, p. 181.
[2] *Jus Populi*, p. 129.

79

nation as King of Scotland in 1651, and who were disposed to accept him now if he would guarantee Presbyterianism as the national polity, without rigorous insistence on his obligation to take the Covenants as a general guide to kingly legislation. As with the Protesters, there were degrees of strictness within the Resolutioner party, and no rigidly clear-cut line can be drawn between these two parties. It is nevertheless true to say of the large majority on either side that it regarded the other, not as merely differing in opinion, but as being almost of a differing religion. Of the Malignants, Hugh Binning had said earlier: "We are persuaded many of that party, who have been so deeply involved in blood guiltiness and barbarous cruelties, should neither have lives nor liberties secured to them: because they ought not to be permitted to live."[1]

Since most of the ministers were Resolutioners, they, in common with the ordinary people of the land, were ready to welcome the king on his return. Soon, however, these very ministers were to find themselves, in Wodrow's words, "ill handled for their hearty concern in the Restoration."[2] This was partly because of the gradual realization of the king's ecclesiastical policy, partly because of the disillusionment which spread over the Scottish people as a whole when they began to understand the king's true character. The ministers were not blameless, for before Charles had decided on his policy for the Church of Scotland, Robert Douglas and four of the other leading Resolutioners reminded the king of his Covenant-oath which pledged him to "the principles of the Church of Scotland . . . fixed for the provision and maintenance of lawful authority."[3] This was all very well, but—which *was* the Church of Scotland? Who were authorized to speak on its behalf? Were Protesters or Resolutioners the true Kirk? In Glasgow and in Deer, for example, each party had a presbytery, and each claimed sole legality.

Also influencing the situation was a further factor which seemed at first sight to favour the Resolutioner party: the National Covenant was now twenty-two years old, the Solemn League seventeen. A new generation had grown up in Scotland for whom the Covenants were only a memory, with nothing of their former glories and associations. There was also little left of the traditional attitude towards these bonds on the part of those who were not Protesters. Gone, for the most part, was that pride which had motivated the subscribers of 1638, and which had caused Alexander Henderson to say of the functions of government and order

---

[1] *An Useful Case of Conscience*, 1783, p. 43.
[2] *Op. cit.*, Vol. I, p. 62.
[3] Ibid., Vol. I, pp. 22f. (n.).

in the Reformed Church of Scotland, that here was "a superiority to tyranny . . . a parity without confusion and disorder . . . a subjection without slavery."

Robert Douglas, though himself a staunch Presbyterian, even went so far in April 1660 as to write to James Sharp, the representative in London of the moderate Presbyterians (who in fact was advancing no one's cause but his own), that "this new upstart generation have no love to presbyterial government; but are wearied of that yoke, feeding themselves with the fancy of episcopacy, or moderate episcopacy."[1] They soon had ample opportunity of sampling the Episcopal system.

Yet Douglas himself had no illusions about Episcopacy. Preaching before the Synod of Lothian on 1st May, 1660, he recommended the combination of king and kirk, and effectively thus demolishes James's conviction about "no bishop; no king":

Shall kings, which are God's ordinance, not stand, because bishops, which are not God's ordinance, cannot stand? The government by presbytery is good, but prelacy is neither good in Christian policy or civil. Some say, may we not have a moderate episcopacy? But 'tis a plant God never planted, and the ladder whereby antichrist mounted his throne. Bishops got caveats, and never kept one of them, and will just do the like again. We have abjured episcopacy, let us not lick it up again. Consider the times past, how unconstant men have proven, like cock-boats tossing up and down; leave them, and come into the ship, walk up to the way of the covenant; and if this be not the plank we come ashore upon, I fear a storm come and ruin all.[2]

It is not easy at this stage to distinguish the various streams of thought during these first two years after the king's homecoming, but one thing is clear: throughout that period there were signs of a change in the original meanings of "Resolutioner" and "Protester," and a word on this will help avoid future bewilderment. Many of the Resolutioners were not averse from, and some even believed that the people wanted, an Episcopal system. On 29th May, 1662, for example, the people of Linlithgow staged a pageant. On top of an arch, disguised as an angel of light, they placed the devil with the inscription, "STAND TO THE CAUSE." Underneath was a litany:

> From Covenants with uplifted hands,
> From Remonstrators with associate bands,
> From such Committees as governed this nation,
> From kirk commissions and their protestation,
>   Good Lord deliver us.

[1] R. Wodrow, op. cit., Vol. I, p. 21.
[2] Ibid., p. 62.

At the back of the arch was another figure, clothed with a religious habit, with *Lex Rex* in one hand, Guthrie's *Causes of God's Wrath* in the other. Strewn all around were ecclesiastical and civil acts passed during the previous twenty-two years. Above this figure appeared the words: "REBELLION IS AS THE SIN OF WITCHCRAFT."

The Protesters were from now on regarded as those who continued to hold the general name of Covenanters—although this too is in some ways a misleading appellation, in that many of those who had at one time taken the Covenants were now unprepared to adhere to them, either from conviction or as a result of persecution. We shall use the term "Covenanter" now only in reference to those who continued to press the Covenant obligations upon Church and State. The meaning of "Protester" (a term applied to those who had opposed the Public Resolutions of 1650–1) now broadened to include all who fought against the ecclesiastical system of the Government during the reigns of Charles II and James VII. All who came into the general category of strict Covenanters—especially the Cameronians or Hill-Folk whom we shall meet later—were successors of the original Protesters, and were sometimes called by that name.

Another factor which had to be reckoned with by the Government at the Restoration was the perennial problem of the Erastian element in the Kirk, with which Knox and Melville had had such trouble. There was no point on which the Presbyterian conscience was more sensitive than this (as we saw in discussing the writings of Gillespie and Rutherford), and Episcopacy was identified in their minds with the crudest variety of Erastianism. In this connection we should remember that the Covenant, as a matter of historical fact, invoked the aid of the State, and only turned against the State when the State turned against the Covenant.

This, then, was the ecclesiastical state of the parties when the thirty-year-old king returned. Charles saw that a complete restoration of church affairs as they had been in his father's time would be a most difficult undertaking, and that the very attempt to carry out such a policy might well result in a renewal of strife. It was, after all, the Scottish revolt against the Prayer Book which had compelled Charles I to call the Long Parliament, and had led to all his subsequent misfortunes. His son, during his brief occupation of the Scottish throne after the execution, had taken the Covenant. He had no thought of being bound by it now, no desire "to mind his former engagements to God and his people" (as Patrick Walker nicely puts it), but he had learnt his lesson, and judged it more discreet not to attempt the reintroduction of the offending Prayer Book. Despite all differences of opinion, therefore, despite any changed attitude to the Covenants on the part of the new generation, the Presbyterians at the Restoration were still the dominant force in Scottish politics, and the chief problems of the Restoration Government were religious problems.

There was yet another factor to be considered: if the character of Presbyterianism had changed, so also had the character of monarchy—or, perhaps more accurately, men's attitude towards the monarchy. The monarchy that was restored was by no means the same as that which had been destroyed, for at least three reasons. Charles I, a king, had been tried and punished like any other man; the experience of Cromwell's novel Commonwealth and Protectorate had revolutionized political thought in Britain; and, probably most important, there had been taking place all over Europe for some time past a change and development in men's ideas, the result of which was that the value and rights of the individual were being increasingly asserted.

It is one mark of the shrewdness of Charles II on his return (doubtless one of the features which made Horace Walpole describe him as the only genius of the line of Stuart[1]), that he saw this fact more clearly than did most men of his time, and yet contrived to pursue his own policy in spite of it. A salutary sense of limitations, coupled perhaps with a sense of humour, saved him from the folly of pushing to its logical or illogical conclusion the theory of Divine Right which was so characteristic of his ancestral house. Yet that even his moderation in this direction was unacceptable to the dissenting Scots we shall see in the course of the following chapters. Charles, as a result, felt himself compelled to adopt more drastic measures.

Thus we have, on the one hand, traces of an inherent caution in his dealings with the Kirk on his return. Some have suggested, although it appears doubtful, that Charles had no intention of restoring Episcopacy in Scotland for several months after his arrival (in England such a restoration had been made at once). It is more likely, however, that Charles was merely being circumspect. This would tie up, moreover, with his known resolve "not to go on his travels again"—to lie, if necessary, to pander, or prevaricate or bribe (and Charles thought that all men could be bought)—to do anything, in fact, which would serve to further that resolve.

But there is, on the other hand, a very different, and much more significant and sinister note in the whole of Charles Stuart's policy in all his governing—an innate selfishness which determined him to have his own way in his own affairs. This might be

[1] "James II," in the *Catalogue of the Royal and Noble Authors.*

considered a dangerous tendency in a monarch who is bound to rule constitutionally. Thus any canniness which he might have felt it politic to display in his dealings with the Presbyterians in Scotland at first was in the end more than offset by a very different memory: that it was Presbyterianism which had dethroned his father, and that that same Presbyterianism, unless rigidly controlled, might deal with him similarly. In the light of future events, no one could dismiss such reasoning as being wildly unwarrantable.

Finally, we should note one more ominous factor. Before his restoration, Charles had written to the English Parliament, promising that bygones would be bygones, and that he would take no action against any except those who had been concerned in the execution of his father—a vow which he kept, perhaps because he found it expedient to do so. No such promise was made at the same time in the case of Scotland. The importance of this omission was soon to be underlined.

During the previous century the advocates of despotic government in France had found that in order to achieve their ends it was necessary to exterminate the Protestants. Charles II in Scotland, similarly faced with the problem of a religious minority which was a potential source of trouble, seems to have whole-heartedly endorsed that dictum. He determined to make an example of some of the Covenanting leaders—and, incidentally, to square a few old scores against personal critics.

From this point onwards much of the Covenanting literature is comprised of protests, declarations and dying testimonies, scrupulously written down and combined in various volumes, often curiously named, by contemporary scribes. In addition to this literature, we shall see how the writings of Gillespie and Rutherford apply to the later Covenanting era, and how their theories fared when political developments gave scope for their application.

Charles's first action was taken against the powerful Presbyterian Marquis of Argyle. The king detested him, both because of his Covenanting affiliations, and because Argyle had long inveighed against Charles's immoral life—and Charles never forgave mention of such details about which any with the slightest claim to gentility would have been reticent.[1]

Argyle hurried to London to do honour to the newly-returned king and was promptly clapped in the Tower. Sent under guard to Scotland, he was indicted as a traitor on what now look suspiciously like trumped-up charges. Among the fourteen articles of the

---

[1] Forneron's *Court of Charles II* (1897, Vol. II, p. 293) gives a list of thirteen illegitimate children of Charles who grew up.

indictment, his "compliance with Cromwell's government" was ostensibly the chief ground of condemnation—though, as Argyle himself pointed out, that was "the epidemical fault of the nation" at that time. Moreover, Sir John Fletcher, the King's Advocate who so fiercely led the prosecution against the accused, and many of the judges, had similarly collaborated with the Lord Protector. It was of no avail. Argyle was tried and condemned to death. He received the sentence of death upon his knees, and said: "I had the honour to set the crown upon the king's head, and now he hastens me away to a better crown than his own."[1] Some friends devised his escape from Edinburgh Castle, but after their plans were far advanced Argyle changed his mind lest he be considered to "disown the good cause he had so publicly espoused." To some ministers who came to comfort him in prison, he prophesied with uncanny accuracy: "Mind that I tell you, my skill fails me, if you who are ministers will not either suffer much, or sin much; for though you go along with those men in part, if you do it not in all things, you are but where you were, and so must suffer, and if you go not at all with them, you shall but suffer."[2]

On the scaffold the speech which Argyle made was gracious and eminently reasonable. There were no recriminations, no blame cast on particular individuals. "I could die like a Roman," he declared, as he left his cell for the last time, "but choose rather to die like a Christian." Addressing the crowd of spectators who had assembled, this proto-martyr of the Covenant said: "I was real and cordial in my desires to bring the King home, and in my endeavours for him when he was at home. I had no . . . accession to his late Majesty's murder . . . I shall not speak much to these things for which I am condemn'd, lest I seem to condemn others. . . . But whatever they think, God hath laid engagements on Scotland, we are tyed by covenants to religion and reformation; those who were then unborn are engaged to it . . . and it passeth the power of all Magistrates under heaven to absolve a man from the oath of God . . . it's the duty of every Christian to be loyal; yet . . . religion must not be the cock-boat; it must be the ship: God must have his, as well as Caesar what is his, and those are the best subjects that are the best Christians."[3] When Argyle stopped speaking the axe fell. "As he was a very great support to the work of refor-

---

[1] R. Wodrow, *op. cit.*, Vol. I, p. 150.

[2] John Howie, in introducing Michael Shields's *Faithful Contendings Displayed* in 1780, observes: "By a minute observation of the church militant, thou wilt find that she has been often reduced unto this sad dilemma, *Sin or Suffer.*"

[3] Sir G. Mackenzie, *Memoirs of the Affairs of Scotland*, 1821, pp. 42ff. (Mackenzie, later Lord Advocate, had been one of Argyle's defence counsel). We should note that, in common with the trend of most Covenanting literature, there is no question of Caesar's *not* having what is lawfully his.

mation," comments James Kirkton, "so it was buried with him in one grave for many a year."[1]

James Guthrie was executed later that same week, with William Govan, a Protester soldier who was said to have been an attendant on the scaffold at Charles I's execution. The latter charge was never proved. Sir George Mackenzie suggests that Govan's guilt "was that he brought to Scotland the first news of the king's execution, and seem'd to be well satisfied with it."[2] Guthrie had for some time anticipated his end, because he had always been an outspoken advocate of religious liberty in the face of royal tyranny. Not long before his execution a Perth minister said to him, "We have a Scotch proverb, 'Jouk [duck] that the wave may go over you.' Will ye jouk a little, Mr. Guthrie?" "Mr. Pollock," returned Guthrie gravely, "there is no jouking in the cause of Christ." Perhaps no utterance is more typical of the attitude of the more extreme Covenanters under persecution.

Guthrie's offence officially was that of declining the king's authority in ecclesiastical affairs—an authority which had been specifically renounced by James VI in 1585 when he had declared that "he, for his part, should never, and that his posterity ought never, to cite, summon, or apprehend any pastor for matters of doctrine . . . but avoucheth it to be a matter purely ecclesiastical, and altogether impertinent to his calling."[3] It will be readily recalled that James himself did not adhere to that promise.

The real charge against Guthrie was, of course, his excommunication of the Earl of Middleton ten years earlier. During the course of his trial the minister of Stirling, who had fought for so long against so many different enemies of the Covenant, declared: "My conscience I cannot submit, but this old crazy body and mortal flesh I do submit, to do with it whatsoever you will, whether by death, or banishment, or imprisonment, or any thing else; only I beseech you to ponder well what profit there is in my blood; it is not the extinguishing me or many others, that will extinguish the Covenant and work of reformation since the year 1638. My blood, bondage, or banishment will contribute more for the propagation of those things, than my life or liberty could do, though I should live many years."[4] He further maintained, both at his trial and on the scaffold, that the conduct of the Government was such as to release its subjects from their debt of obedience.

Both Guthrie and Govan faced the gallows fearlessly and with great equanimity. Eating his last meal before execution, Guthrie

[1] *Op. cit.*, p. 104.
[2] *Memoirs*, p. 51; cf. R. Wodrow, *op. cit.*, Vol. I, pp. 193ff.
[3] J. Brown, *An Apologetical Relation*, p. 53; cf. R. Wodrow, *op. cit.*, Vol. I, p. 168.
[4] R. Wodrow, *op. cit.*, Vol. I, p. 172.

noticed some cheese on the table—a delicacy hitherto forbidden him for health reasons. Said he cheerfully, "Give me a good piece of it, for *it* will not now be my death!" He summed up his own position by declaring from the scaffold: "I durst not redeem my life with the loss of my integrity." Nearly three centuries later, at the inaugural address on the unveiling of the Guthrie Monument at Stirling, it was said that the charges against him amounted to freedom of the press, freedom to hold public meetings, to defend constitutions, to defend conscience, and have a free church.

The Government thus made examples of a fair cross-section of the opposition in Scotland—a nobleman, a minister, and a commoner—perhaps *pour encourager les autres*. Regarding his ecclesiastical policy, the king's course of action seems to have been determined mainly by the nobles, most of whom hated what they regarded as the tyranny of the Kirk and saw in Charles a kindred spirit. Like many of the people, they complained (and we know what they mean) that during Cromwell's rule the Kirk was so strict that they had not liberty enough to sin. The Earl of Eglinton as one example, was sentenced to the stool of repentance during public worship—the cynosure of all eyes! He responded by declining to sit anywhere else ever afterwards, because he thought it the best seat and himself the best man in the church.[1]

By the time monarchy was restored, many of the leading families were desperately impoverished, and eager to try any course that might recover the family fortunes. The way, they felt, might lie through the support of the king. For his part, Charles saw in them a valuable source of assistance; without them, indeed, it is questionable whether he would have been so ready to restore Episcopacy in Scotland, or whether his attempt to do so would have met with the success it did.

Yet we must keep in mind also a curious point, one which seems often to have been overlooked by historians of the period; that there was scattered here and there throughout the country an element of genuine royalism ("sentimental rather than reasoned," in John Buchan's words) which can be traced far back in the mists of Scottish history. This same romantic conception of kingship, found chiefly among the more mystical Highlanders, appeared again in the Jacobite rebellions of 1715 and 1745 on behalf of the exiled Stuarts—though, here, of course, there were other more important issues involved also. The Scots might murder their kings—and frequently did—but they were always very much aware of the status of kingship, always ready to distinguish between the officer and the office. We have found this stressed in the writings of Samuel Rutherford, and we shall find it repeatedly

[1] See G. Burnet, *op. cit.*, Vol. I, p. 273n.

when we come to consider the Cameronian writings of twenty years later.

Paradoxically, this royalism was to be found even among the extreme Covenanters, who were never quite able to rid themselves of the haunting notion of a Covenanted king, and who were always discerning enough to distinguish between principle and person. We shall hear in the next chapter, for example, how there was an uprising of the Western peasantry against the tyrannical policy of the king, and of how the rebels first denounced the king's legislation—and thereafter drank the king's health! Incidents such as these make this era of Scottish history difficult to understand and even more difficult to explain.

Charles decided, then, after a period of hesitation, on his plan for what Alexander Shields has called the Deformation of the Church of Scotland. The king's motive was not religious, but rather part of a secular reaction to his experience of Presbyterianism and Presbyterians, coupled with certain political interests. Charles I and Archbishop Laud had complained that there was no religion in Scotland, and forthwith had proceeded to fashion one after their own schemes and dreams; Charles II and Clarendon, in the following generation, had a very different complaint. They saw too much religion in the land for their taste, and proceeded to unmake it. "God preserve me," exclaimed the latter piously, "from living in a country, where the church is independent from the state, and may subsist by their own acts; for there all churchmen may be kings."[1] Andrew Melville would have approved of that last clause.

But these were ominous words. Even more ominous was the order of the Privy Council in June 1660 for the suppression of a proposed new edition of George Buchanan's *De Jure Regni apud Scotos*, as "very pernicious to monarchy, and injurious to his majesty's blessed progenitors. . . ." Yet, digressing for a moment, it is unfair to compare Laud with Archbishop Sharp, whom the king chose to carry out his ecclesiastical policy in Scotland. William Laud was a genuine enthusiast, however misguided we may consider him, for a certain ideal—someone has described him as the type who either dies a martyr or makes other martyrs; Sharp was an ambitious wretch who obtained power by duplicity and kept it by abject submission to his masters, punctuated by secret intrigues of his own whereby he tried to free himself from their yoke that he might pursue his own crafty schemes unhindered. Wodrow speaks of Sharp as one "whose great talents were caution, cunning, and dissimulation with unwearied dili-

[1] Sir G. Mackenzie, *Memoirs*, p. 56.

gence."[1] Sir James Stewart refers to him as the Arch-knave who was advanced to the primacy instead of to the gallows.[2]

Sharp played such a prominent part in the ensuing persecution that we should take a moment to comment further on him. Despite persistent rumour that he had strangled the child of his illicit union with a woman in St. Andrews, he was sent to London during the opening weeks of 1660 as the representative of the moderate Presbyterian party, in negotiations with General Monk. He was instructed to do his utmost, throughout that critical period, to ensure that the Kirk's lawful privileges were maintained under the new régime, to testify against "the late sinful toleration," to co-operate in the establishment of a system for the payment of ministerial stipends and to seek amendment of prevalent abuses involving stipends in vacant charges, and to press for the implementing of that Act of Parliament which had abolished patronage. He was also to negotiate for the recognition of the Solemn League and Covenant—if feasible, in England as well as in Scotland.

He embarked on a course of deception by sending back to Scotland progress reports which were, if not downright lies, at least dubious euphemisms. All the time he was "loosing the pins of Presbyterian government" and planning the restoration of Episcopacy with the Cavalier statesmen, and doubtless dreaming of himself in the Primate's robes. "Ere long we shall see him lay aside his Presbyterian Cloak, which covered but his Knavery, and put on his pontifical Gown."[3] So said one contemporary who had no illusions about him, and had earlier suggested that Sharp followed the Machiavellian principle which held that "religion is to be pretended but not intended."[4] This was the man whom Cromwell after an interview labelled an atheist, and who could write to Robert Douglas from Breda, where he had gone to see the king just before the Restoration: "I find the king very affectionate to Scotland, and resolved not to wrong the settled government of our church."[5] Sharp reiterates this in a further letter to Douglas dated three days later.

Even the king, though he was to use Sharp for his own ends, regarded him as "one of the worst of men," according to Bishop Burnet, who credited Sharp with "a very small proportion of

[1] *Op. cit.*, Vol. I, p. 101.
[2] *Jus Populi Vindicatum*, p. 128.
[3] Anonymous, *Life of Mr. James Sharp*, 1719, p. 89.
[4] Ibid., p. 59.
[5] R. Wodrow, *op. cit.*, Vol. I, p. 29. To be fair to Sharp, a letter from the king himself to Douglas, for communication to the Presbytery of Edinburgh, a few months later expresses a similar intention; cf. Wodrow, Vol. I, pp. 80f.

learning."[1] Sharp's character and conduct were long disputed, but they have now been finally determined adversely beyond reasonable doubt.[2] It is highly probable, however, that he did as much harm to Episcopacy by adopting it as he did to Presbyterianism by rejecting it. The anti-Covenanting J. H. Millar comments: "Had any other man than James Sharp been at the head of ecclesiastical affairs in Scotland its [Episcopacy's] triumph would have been assured."[3]

As it was, the Presbyterian cause suffered irretrievable damage for lack of adequate and faithful representation in London during a vital period. Indirectly contributing to this was a singular lack of co-operation with English Presbyterians by which the Scots expressed themselves disappointed. Three of the English leaders, Edmund Calamy, Thomas Manton and Dr. Reynolds, accepted the invitation to become royal chaplains. Sharp's letter dated 2nd June, 1660, to Robert Douglas is probably a fair guide to this aspect of the situation. "The influencing men of the presbyterian judgment," he advises Douglas, "are content with episcopacy of Bishop Usher's model, and a liturgy somewhat corrected, with the ceremonies of surplice, cross in baptism, kneeling at the communion, if they be not imposed by a canon, *sub poena aut culpa*."[4] It is not surprising that under these conditions the king listened, not to the true voice of Scotland, but to a time-serving and impoverished Scottish nobility, out of touch with other classes, bitterly hostile to the national Church, and seeking only its own gain. The outcome was inevitable. (This does not, of course, imply that Charles would not still have insisted on getting his own way had there been no Sharp and no pressure from the Scottish nobility.)

Parliament, which for obvious reasons the people of Edinburgh soon dubbed the "Drunken Parliament," began its sittings on the first day of 1661, ten years exactly from Charles's coronation at Scone. At the outset it procured the repeal of the Acts which in the last year of Charles I had re-established Presbyterianism as the religion of Scotland; and then an Act of Parliament rescinded without distinction all the statutes passed since 1633, in which year the first Charles had been crowned as Scottish king. This was known as the Act Rescissory.[5] Middleton and his friends, we are told, discussed this piece of legislation over their cups and, "when

[1] *Op. cit.*, Vol. I, p. 301.
[2] Cf. O. Airy, *Sharp's Letters*, 1900, Vol. II; R. Wodrow, Vol. I, pp. 5ff. Even Dr. Law Mathieson, a moderate Royalist, concurs in this unfavourable judgment on Sharp (Vol. II, pp. 185ff).
[3] *Scottish Prose*, 1912, p. 28.
[4] R. Wodrow, *op. cit.*, Vol. I, p. 33.
[5] For text see *Acts of the Parliaments of Scotland*, Vol. VII, pp. 86f.

they had drunk higher, they resolved to venture on it."[1] Some of the nobility argued against this Act, but they were overruled.

Even Lauderdale in London unsuccessfully represented the Act to the king as a dangerous precedent which showed that Middleton "understood not the first principles of government." Other legislation of this Parliament included Acts against consulters with devils, familiar spirits and witches; Sunday fishing; worshippers of false gods; beaters and cursers of parents; and—excessive drinking! This last Act is even odder when it is recalled that after the king's return James Kirkton wrote: "No body complained more of our church government than our taverners, whose ordinary lamentation was, their trade was broke, people were become so sober."[2]

It was declared that the power of establishing the model of church government was vested in the Crown, thus making the king head of the Church as well as of the State, and erecting him, according to James Kirkton, into a sort of pope,[3] albeit one without pretence of religion. The Privy Council issued in March 1661 a proclamation to say that it was the king's will that Episcopacy should be the form of church government, though the "present administration by sessions, presbyteries and synods" was meantime allowed. Like his grandfather, Charles II had evidently decided that Episcopacy agreed best with monarchy. Not surprisingly, a hierarchy was found to be more amenable to court influence than a free Assembly. Kirkton thus expands on the king's motives at this point:

> He knew well bishops would never be reprovers of the court, and the first article of their catechism was non-resistance. They were men of that discretion as to dissemble great men's faults, and not so severe as the presbyterians. They were the best tools for tyrannie in the world; for, doe a king what he would, their daily instruction was, kings could doe no wrong, and that none might put forth a hand against the Lord's anointed and be innocent. The king knew also he should be sure of their vote in parliament, desire what he would, and that they would plant a sort of ministers which might instill principles of loyalty into the people till they turned them first slaves and then beggars.[4]

However prejudiced a view this might be, the Presbyterians never-

---

[1] G. Burnet, op. cit., Vol. I, p. 163.
[2] Op. cit., p. 65.
[3] Ibid., p. 91. Kirkton possibly got this phrase from a statement of Archbishop Spottiswoode, Primate of Scotland during the First Episcopate some thirty years before. Said the Archbishop to a recalcitrant Presbyterian: "I tell you, Mr. John, the King is Pope now, and so shall be" (D. Calderwood, The History of the Kirk o Scotland, ed. T. Thomson, 1842–5, Vol. VII, p. 421).
[4] Op. cit., pp. 131f.

theless all too soon discovered how easily their Covenanted king could sacrifice his promises to inclination or self-interest. The protests which came from presbyteries and synods in many quarters of the land were of no avail.

One by-product of all this was that it softened somewhat the rivalry between Protester and Resolutioner, though this came too late to be of any use. Robert Douglas exclaimed: "Our brethren the Protesters have had their eyes open, and we have been blind!" and another Resolutioner leader, David Dickson, admitted: "The Protesters have been truer prophets than we."[1] Douglas, said to have been of royal descent ("though the wrong way," adds the gossipy Burnet), was a sort of walking concordance who "had the Scriptures by heart to the exactness of a Jew." Described to Cromwell by Lord Broghill in 1653 as "the leadingest man in all the country of Scotland," Douglas had after the Restoration been approached by Sharp who sought to enlist his support in the Episcopal cause. James Kirkton takes up the story where Sharp told Douglas that

> it was the king's purpose to settle the church under bishops, and that for respect to him his majesty was very desireous Mr Douglass would accept the archbishopric of St Andrews. Mr Douglass answered, he would have nothing to doe with it, (for in his private conversation he used neither to harangue nor to dispute;) Sharp insisted and urged him; Mr Douglass answered as formerly, whereupon Sharp arose and took leave. Mr Douglass convoyed him to his gallery door; and after he hade passed the door, Mr Douglass called him back, and told him, James, (said he,) I see you will engadge, I perceive you are clear, you will be bishop of St Andrews: take it, and the curse of God with it. So clapping him upon the shoulder, he shutt his door upon him.[2]

On 25th January 1661, the Scottish Parliament issued an "Act concerning the League and Covenant, discharging the renewing thereof without His Majesty's warrant and approbation." The Act declared that Covenant and the Acts relative to it "were no longer obligatory on the kingdom or lieges who were henceforth forbidden to interpose by arms or in any seditious way in religious or secular affairs . . . or to renew any Covenant or Oath without royal warrant." To guard against subversive activity, an oath to this effect had to be sworn by every person who assumed an office of trust in the land. Robert McWard, minister in Glasgow, protested against this Act as contrary to the oath of God. "As a proud member of this Church of Scotland, and an unworthy minister in it," he told the congregation of the Tron Church, "I do this

---

[1] R. Wodrow, *op. cit.*, Vol. I, p. 112.
[2] *Op. cit.*, pp. 134f.

day call you, who are the people of God, to witness, that I humbly offer my dissent to all acts which are or shall be passed against the Covenants, and work of reformation in Scotland."[1] The Government acted swiftly. Arraigned for sedition and treasonable preaching, McWard refused to renounce this view and was sentenced in July 1661 to perpetual banishment. He was the first of a group of exiles to settle in Rotterdam, where they founded a presbytery and indulged in dialectical sniping at the Stuart dynasty.

One outcome of this Act was the restoration of church patronage to loyal subjects of the king—that could mean only one thing: that it was vested in those likely to appoint Royalists to vacant charges. So at one stroke all that the Covenanters had fought for was swept away, and the whole existing system of the Scottish Church deprived of legal sanction. The Solemn League and Covenant was burned by order of the English Parliament; the National Covenant was ostentatiously torn by herald at the Mercat Cross of Edinburgh. By effecting this piece of legislation the king acquired a degree of power inconsistent with both Presbyterianism and Episcopacy, in that he might have abolished both at any time and have established any other religion arbitrarily. He thus violated one of the three great tenets of the Covenanters: that of the headship of Christ in the State. He was soon to violate the others: His headship over the individual Christian, and in the Church of God.

On 19th September, 1660, a proclamation had been made, calling in all copies of Samuel Rutherford's *Lex Rex* and James Guthrie's *Causes of God's Wrath*, as works poisonous and treasonable. Those who refused to comply were to be looked upon and treated as enemies of the king, and punished according to the Committee's discretion. On 17th October the hangman consigned them to the flames in Edinburgh. "It was much easier," comments Wodrow, "to burn those books, than to answer the reasonings and facts in them."[2] All this meant, in effect, that the king's prerogative was the new touchstone by which everything and everyone was judged. The day had come when, as Guthrie had foreseen, the choice was between loyalty to the king and spiritual integrity. Guthrie's book denied that the king had authority to try a man in respect of matters which were purely ecclesiastical, such as presbyterial acts and letters, preaching, and the discharge of his ministerial functions.

Samuel Rutherford, Principal of St. Mary's College, St. Andrews, had in March 1661 been cited by the Privy Council to answer the charge of treason. For some time the shadow of death had been hanging over him. When the order came from the

[1] R. Wodrow, *op. cit.*, Vol. I, p. 207.
[2] Ibid., p. 84.

Council, he said: "Tell them that sent you that I have got summons already before a Superior Judge and Judicatory, and I behove to answer to my first summons, and ere your day come, I will be where few kings and great folks come."[1] It will be readily recalled why *Lex Rex*, which had been reissued in 1648 and again in 1657, was held in such disrepute by the Royalists.

Some in the Council, though told that Rutherford was dying, maliciously proposed to have him removed from his college, and even carried the vote for that purpose. One of the few who stood up for him was Lord Burleigh. "Ye have voted that honest man out of the college," he told his fellows, "but ye cannot vote him out of heaven." To the callous reply that hell was too good for the old man, Burleigh replied: "I wish I were as sure of heaven as he is; and I would reckon my self happy to get a grip of his sleeve to hale me in, when Mr. Rutherford enters the gates."[2]

There was in Rutherford a healthy strain of self-criticism not always apparent in his colleagues. In his dying testimony he freely admits that the Covenanters had weak points, that sometimes church government had been concentrated upon to the detriment of the spiritual. "Afterwards," he remarks, "our work in public was too much in sequestration of estates, fining and imprisoning . . . in our Assemblies we were more bent to set up a state opposite to a state, than concerned with the meekness and gentleness of Christ."[3]

In September 1661 the Privy Council prohibited anyone not of "known loyalty and affection to his Majesty's Government" from being a magistrate or councillor in any burgh. Scottish bishops were appointed by the Crown, and at the end of 1661 four of them were summoned to London and given episcopal ordination—"a flower not to be found in a Scottish gardine," comments the ironic Kirkton.[4] The four were James Sharp, Andrew Fairfoul, Robert Leighton and James Hamilton. Sharp and Leighton were earlier subjected to "re-ordination"; Fairfoul and Hamilton had been ordained during the First Episcopate. Sharp was made Primate and Archbishop of St. Andrews, he having determined to "ride the ford where his predecessor [Spottiswoode] drowned."[5]

One cannot help noting a certain untidy patchwork about the application of Episcopal policies here. While Sharp and Leighton were re-ordained, and all four Scottish bishops were responsible for the later consecration of their colleagues, no re-ordination was

[1] J. K. Hewison, *op. cit.*, Vol. II, p. 94.
[2] P. Walker, *Six Saints of the Covenant*, 1901, Vol. I, p. 359.
[3] *Martyrs for the Truth*, p. 55.
[4] *Op. cit.*, p. 137.
[5] For details of the other bishops, with somewhat sardonic comments thereon, see R. Wodrow, *op. cit.*, Vol. I, pp. 236ff.

explicitly required of the conforming ministers.[1] Not even in the interests of ecumenicity would Episcopalians be found so accommodating today!

Ordinary meetings of presbyteries and synods were suspended until the details of the future church administration should be decided on by the new bishops. The mistakes of 1637 were for the most part avoided. The Prayer Book was not introduced; the surplice was not worn; there was no altar, no diaconate, no Episcopal confirmation. When the subject is examined closely, indeed, it will be found difficult to distinguish between Episcopal and Presbyterian church worship during the reign of Charles II. It would seem that the only exceptions to this were in the use of the Doxology, the Lord's Prayer, and the Creed—all of which had been customary before the days of the Solemn League. A Royalist writer, Sir George Mackenzie, who was Charles II's Lord Advocate in Scotland from 1678, says: "The reader will be astonished when we inform him that . . . our Church differed nothing from the Presbyterian, as regards Church services, except . . . the Doxologie, the Lord's Prayer, and . . . the Creed—all of which they rejected. We had no ceremonies, surplice, altars, Cross in baptism, nor the meanest of these things which would be allowed in England by the Dissenters, in way of Accommodation."[2] From such contemporary descriptions and from the information to be gleaned from church records, it would appear that the service was very little different from that which John Knox himself had prescribed. It has been suggested that Mackenzie and some of his colleagues took the firm stand they did by Charles's side because they saw in the events between 1642 and 1660 the terrible results of a divided authority in the State.

Concerning the government of the Church, a compromise was effected between the Episcopacy sponsored by James VI, which did not interfere with the local church courts, and the Laudian Episcopacy of Charles I's day, which excluded local ecclesiastical legislation. Presbyteries were to be allowed to meet, but no longer were they strictly free, for they were placed in close dependence on the bishops, who could summon or dismiss them at their pleasure.

Thus there were no traditional and ceremonial points in controversy between the Scottish Presbyterians and Episcopalians; indeed, the best and most moderate of each body observed intercommunion—in which practice seventeenth-century Scotland was more enlightened than the present-day. Robert Leighton, Bishop of Dunblane and later Archbishop of Glasgow, though he be-

[1] Some sort of Episcopal blessing was given, but we shall meet this point again in the next chapter.
[2] *Vindication of the Government of Charles II*, 1691, p. 9.

lieved that Episcopacy was the primitive form of church government as well as the most convenient, never doubted the validity
of his earlier Presbyterian orders.

It was the discipline and outward government of the new-
modelled church which stuck in Scottish throats. The Covenanters complained, not without reason, that a greater authority was
now given to the bishops than their predecessors had enjoyed—
and that it was an authority much more harshly exercised. Wodrow tried to show the great difference in extent of power assigned
to the bishops on the revival of their order, by describing those of
1612 as "pigmeys to the present high and mighty lords."[1]

The theory of Episcopacy was insisted upon far more rigorously
than had ever been done in the reign of Charles I. During that
time, the ministers had "maintained such a share in the administration that the bishops never pretended to be any more than their
settled Presidents with a negative voice upon them." But now,
Burnet states, the government of the Church in the several
dioceses was "declared to be lodged in the bishops, which they
were to exercise with the advice and assistance of such of their
clergy *as were of known loyalty and prudence*."[2] Now these were
words which could mean just what the authorities chose them to
mean, and their very evident ambiguity deceived no one. Burnet
deplored the lack of any reference to piety and learning as desir-
able qualifications in a pastor.

To aggravate the situation still further, some of the newly-
appointed bishops (there were eventually fourteen of them) were
men with former injuries to avenge, as well as immediate contempt and insult to withstand. Wodrow reckoned that since the
income of all the Scottish bishops added together did not exceed
that of the see of Winchester, avarice and ambition led to the
acceptance of such impoverished dioceses. "A weak temptation
goes far," Wodrow explains, "where there is a strong corrup-
tion."[3]

The new bishops and curates had been set up in the teeth of a
proud Presbyterian ministry which could not soon forget its late
supremacy. Bitter warfare ensued between the two factions in
certain parts of the country, and we find Bishop Leighton condemning persecution, which he described as scaling heaven with
ladders fetched out of hell, and entreating his Episcopalian colleagues not to imitate the severities of the Covenanters, and so to
justify the sarcasm that "the world goes mad by turns."[4]

[1] *Op. cit.*, Vol. I, p. 262.
[2] *Op. cit.*, Vol. I, p. 199. Italics ours.
[3] *Op. cit.*, Vol. I, p. 235, but cf. J. Kirkton, *op. cit.*, p. 135. This is one of the many
places where Wodrow merely echoes Kirkton.
[4] G. Burnet, *op. cit.*, Vol. I, p. 202.

So Episcopacy once more entered Scotland, under even yet more ominous circumstances than before, facilitated by the patronage of a dissolute Court and a Scottish Council of profligate nobles. It came represented by a Primate who was a traitor to the cause which he had professed to serve, and by petty legislators, both soldiers and judges, whose reputation and character in many cases effectively precluded them from the administration of impartial justice, and from the preservation of the peace which the country so badly needed. Worst of all, it came represented by Episcopal incumbents who were, in many cases, "hireling wolves whose gospel is their maw"—a terrible indictment, but one endorsed by friend and foe alike. It came, in Leighton's words, with such "cross characters of an angry providence that it seemed as though God Himself was against the bishops;" as for the king's ministers, adds Burnet, they "were almost perpetually drunk."[1]

Drunk or not, when Middleton (High Commissioner for Scotland) and his colleagues went to London, they were greeted warmly by the king as faithful ministers. The southern hierarchy was even more effusive: "in a very particular manner," relates Wodrow, they "caressed our Scots peers, for procuring them another national church among all the reformed, to bear them company in their prelatic way."[2]

A virtually totalitarian state was established, with the same characteristics that we know all too well today—the demand for absolute obedience, followed by illegal detention, the use of spies and informers, torture, and summary execution. Drastic fines were levied on hundreds of people who were suspected as sympathizers to the Covenants, but such was the unsystematic nature of the persecution that the offenders named included men long since dead, infants, minors, and people who never were.[3]

The Earl of Middleton eventually lost the king's confidence by the continual state of drunkenness in which he and his Council were wont to transact the business of the country. Moreover, Middleton had made the mistake of setting himself up against the powerful Lauderdale, in which encounter he came off second best. He was superseded in 1663 by the Earl of Rothes, a great favourite of the king, and died shortly afterwards as Governor of Tangier. Even Charles, merry monarch as he was, thought that several hours in the day should be devoted to sobriety.[4] Nevertheless, the young men of the upper classes soon realized the situation: if they were to hope for advancement, then, as one wit put it, "debauching was loyalty, gravity smelled of rebellion."[5]

[1] Vol. I, pp. 195, 197.
[2] Vol. I, p. 223.
[3] Cf. *Naphtali*, p. 192.
[4] G. Burnet, *op. cit.*, Vol. I, p. 198.
[5] J. Kirkton, *op. cit.*, p. 114.

D

CHAPTER VI

PRESBYTERIANISM OUTLAWED

IN MAY 1662 PARLIAMENT CONFIRMED WHAT HAD BEEN DONE BY
king and Council; thus within two years of the Restoration,
Presbyterianism ceased to exist in Scotland. Its supporters
came to attribute this to Sharp's duplicity, Resolutioner vacillation, and misguided loyalty to the House of Stuart. Nevertheless
Robert Douglas tended thus to exonerate the king at this time:

> I profess I blame not the king, for he was not well acquainted with
> our government; and for any acquaintance he had, he met with
> some hasty dealing: but our evil proceeded from ourselves; some
> noblemen thinking to make themselves great by that way, were very
> instrumental in the change, and being wearied of Christ's yoke, they
> promised unto themselves liberty, they themselves becoming servants
> of corruption. They thought they would have more liberty under
> that loose government, than under presbytery, which put too great
> a restraint upon their vices. And with them were ministers who loved
> the world, especially that Sharp. . . .[1]

Lay patronage, an accompaniment of the king's re-accession,
was to be one of the chief causes of the conflict between his
Government and the Covenanters, both ministers and people.
Popular election was revoked. All ministers ordained since 1649,
the year in which patronage had been abolished, were declared to
have no right to their benefice, stipend, manse, and glebe—and
their charges were proclaimed vacant unless they forthwith received presentation from the patron and collation from the bishop.
Collation included the episcopal pronouncement: "I do hereby
receive him into the function of the holy ministry." This necessarily threw doubt upon the validity of a man's Presbyterian
ordination.[2] University professors had to take an oath of allegiance
acknowledging the re-established episcopal polity.[3]

[1] R. Wodrow, *op. cit.*, Vol. I, p. 228.
[2] Ibid., p. 265; cf. Law Mathieson, *op. cit.*, Vol. II, p. 228, who refers to "the
monstrous absurdity . . . that there could be no valid ministry without bishops."
The whole position has striking parallels three centuries later—see, for example,
the Dissentient View expressed in *Conversations between the Church of England and the
Methodist Church*, 1963, pp. 59f.
[3] R. Wodrow, *op. cit.*, Vol. I, pp. 266f.

Such measures, of which Sharp disclaimed all advance knowledge, were regarded as tantamount to a plain renunciation of Presbyterianism and a submission to Episcopal authority. It was a tactical blunder which the exercise of a little wisdom would have avoided. Its terms were refused by all zealous Presbyterians—men who, if things had been put differently, might have been ready to live at peace under the Episcopal system without any direct acknowledgment of it.

By obeying the Government, John Brown wrote, the ministers "should quite undo and betray their posterity;" by resisting, they would be "keeping up some footsteps of a standing controversy." Brown continued: ". . . if there were but this much of a standing difference betwixt the people of God and the common enemies of Zion to be seen, posterity would in some measure be kept from being deceived, and would see the interest of Christ, not killed nor buried quicklie, but living though in a bleeding condition. . . ."[1]

In the north, where Episcopacy was strong and the Aberdeen Doctors had been influential, the order was generally obeyed. In the west and south, particularly in the district of Galloway, where the Protesters predominated, it was scarcely obeyed at all. Even in the north, however, there were misgivings and some families about this time rejected both Episcopacy and Presbytery, and adopted Quaker opinions which had been introduced into Scotland during the Protectorate.[2] Among this number were some who had been zealous supporters of the Covenant in bygone years; one of these was Alexander Jaffray, formerly Provost of Aberdeen and a member of Cromwell's United Parliament, who had been a member of the Commission sent to negotiate with Charles in Holland in 1649.

The ensuing persecution of the Covenanting party in the south and west was directed also against the Quakers in the north, though in a modified form. In connection with the Quakers there was another reason for the Governmental action: the sect was then still addicted to symbolic demonstrations which provoked Government and people, and constituted the kind of breach of the peace not unknown to residents of twentieth-century London.

The order to submit to Episcopal authority had instant repercussions. Andrew Fairfoul, Archbishop of Glasgow, had said he did not believe more than ten ministers would abide by conscience and give up their livings and manses. (James Sharp guessed twenty.) Andrew Fairfoul was wrong. Out of some 950 beneficed

[1] *An Apologetical Relation*, pp. 273f.
[2] Cf. G. D. Henderson, *Religious Life in Seventeenth Century Scotland*, 1937, pp. 105-7.

clergy in the whole of Scotland, about one-third were expelled from their charges during the winter of 1662–3.[1] Robert McWard says that of "600 who carried on the Public Resolutions, there were but about forty who withstood prelacy"[2]—which nevertheless gives some idea of the strength of the dissidents.

"I believe that there never was such a sad Sabbath in Scotland," said James Kirkton, "as when the poor persecuted ministers took leave of their people. The congregations not only wept, but howled loudly . . . as when a besieged city is sacked."[3] Even the Drunken Parliament was momentarily sobered by the extent of the expulsions, and extended until the first day of February the opportunity for the recalcitrant to submit. "What will these mad fellows do?" exclaimed the astounded Middleton in exasperation. Some of the more influential rebels were banished lest they should infect others in the ministry.

The Government was faced with the major problem of how to fill the parishes thus made vacant. Gilbert Burnet tells how as a youth of nineteen he was given a choice of benefices, and adds: "Though I was entirely episcopal, yet I would not engage with a body of men that seemed to have the principles and tempers of inquisitors in them."[4]

Hugh MacKail, a young minister who was among the ejected, and of whom we shall hear more later, said in his last sermon in Edinburgh that "the Church in all ages has been persecuted by a Pharaoh upon the throne, a Haman in the State, and a Judas in the Church"—a barbed truth which was never forgotten or forgiven by James Sharp. A party was sent to arrest MacKail on the day after his sermon was preached, but he escaped abroad, and four years were to elapse before the vengeance of an insulted prelate overtook him.[5]

John Livingstone, minister at Ancrum, refused to acknowledge the king's supremacy over all persons and in all causes, civil and ecclesiastical, and was sentenced to banishment. He was refused permission even to say farewell to his wife and family. Undaunted, he told the Council: "Well, although it be not permitted that I should breathe in my native air, yet I trust, what part of the world so ever I go to, I shall not cease to pray for a blessing to these

---

[1] Law Mathieson (*op. cit.*, Vol. II, p. 193), after carefully working through Scot's *Fasti*, puts the total number of deprived ministers at a maximum of 271, but this seems to be the lowest of the more responsible estimates. Wodrow quotes the figure as just under 400, Burnet as 350.

[2] *Earnest Contendings*, p. 124.

[3] *Op. cit.*, p. 150.

[4] *Op. cit.*, Vol. I, p. 217.

[5] See "A Relation of the Sufferings and Death of Mr. Hew MacKail," appended to *Naphtali*, p. 355.

lands, to his Majesty, and the government. . . ."[1] Livingstone lived in Rotterdam till his death ten years later.

Another of the ejected was John Brown of Wamphray, the first great Covenanting writer since the times of Gillespie and Rutherford. We find the latter referring to him thus about the year 1637 in a letter to one of his many correspondents: "Remember me to Mr. John Brown: I could never get my love off that man: I think Christ hath something to do with him." Yet we know little about Brown until he was in his fiftieth year. His name does not appear in any of the lists of members present at the celebrated Glasgow Assembly of 1638, nor does he seem to have taken any notable part in the public activities of the Church during the period between 1638 and 1660. In the latter year, with the return of Charles II, Brown was soon in trouble. He was one of the many who were "outed," and in May 1662 Parliament began a prosecution against him and eighteen other ministers who had with him been prominent in opposing prelatical and arbitary power. "Such a man," comments Wodrow, "could not easily now escape."[2] He was imprisoned in the Tolbooth of Edinburgh later that year, and then banished to Holland early in 1663. He was never again allowed to enter his native land—the same fate as had befallen Andrew Melville half a century earlier.

It was during Brown's exile, partly at Utrecht and partly at Rotterdam, that most of his works were written. According to J. H. Millar, John Brown "belonged to that gallant little band of ministers who, from the Patmos of Holland, denounced the Indulgences, deplored the lamentable lukewarmness of their countrymen in the good cause, and disinterestedly propelled the more zealous among them along the road which led to the Grassmarket and the gallows."[3] No one is in the slightest danger of putting Mr. Millar in any other category than that clearly indicated by his comment.

Before we discuss Brown's work, a little more should be said about political developments. Since not one of the expelled ministers took advantage of the extension of time offered, or went back, the Government adopted sterner measures.

Penalties were set for preaching or praying against the Episcopal government of the Church, and here we find another notable fact; that civil and ecclesiastical tyranny were so closely related that it was impossible for men to emancipate themselves from the latter without at the same time renouncing also the former—and thereby laying themselves open to punishment by the State. The

[1] J. K. Hewison, *The Covenanters*, Vol. 2, p. 162.
[2] *Op. cit.*, Vol. I, p. 141.
[3] *Op. cit.*, p. 28.

two Covenants were denounced as illegal by Act of Parliament, and everyone admitted to office of any kind had specifically to renounce them. That was the crowning blunder. It meant that if a Presbyterian was to remain such he must become a rebel. So he did become a rebel, in many cases. The suppressive measures employed by the State had the effect of preventing all chance of the Covenants' being gradually forgotten with the passage of time, and even endowed them with a new sanctity.

The Bishop's Drag Net Act imposed heavy fines on laymen for not attending the parish church. Curates would report nonconformists to the army, sometimes, indeed, to a private soldier. Wodrow summarizes the situation: "The soldier is judge, no witnesses are led, no probation sought, the sentence is summarily pronounced; and the soldier executes his own sentence, and he would not see the less to this, that the money, generally speaking, came to his own pocket; and very frequently the fine upon some pretext or other, far exceeded the sum liquidate by law."[1]

People continued, however, to assemble in secret to hear either their old pastors or violent young men who were ready to "preach to the times," and these conventicles (a name given by the Royalists) gradually increased in number and size. The services had at first taken place in private houses, and outside the hours of regular public worship, for the most part; but then as persecution increased, they were held on the moors and hills. Meetings for worship attended by more than five persons were declared to be conventicles, and a scale of fines was drawn up for those attending such gatherings.

The Government sent Sir James Turner to the west in September 1663 with a substantial military force, to gather all the fines imposed on the people for nonconformity, to break up conventicles, to live free of charge in the houses of the population, and by every sort of outrage to dragoon the so-called Whigs into submission. Masters were held liable if their servants or dependents were found at field-meetings;[2] landlords required farmers to bind themselves not to attend, and the tenant who broke his bond forfeited his possessions to the laird. Spies and informers were paid to ferret out information about Covenanters and conventicles. Additional troops were drafted in to enforce the governmental policy. Trained in the German wars, Turner's philosophy led him to take the view that it was required of him to be found faithful, irrespective of whom he served. Charles evidently approved, for he knighted Turner in 1662.

About this time the monument to Alexander Henderson in

[1] *Op. cit.*, Vol. I, p. 374.
[2] *Records of the Privy Council*, Vol. IV, pp. 197–200.

Greyfriars Churchyard was razed to the ground by order of Parliament. The inscription on the statue had borne some reference to the Solemn League, in the compilation of which Henderson had played a large part.

Charles and his Scottish Council, however, overreached themselves in their steps to suppress Presbyterianism. It may have been true that at the Restoration of the monarchy the Scottish people as a whole had no firmly-rooted objection to Episcopacy, a point on which historians disagree. It may have been even more significant that the Synod of Aberdeen—an area where Episcopal sympathizers were numerous—had virtually petitioned for its return.[1] Nevertheless the governmental policy against Presbyterianism was so misguided as to turn opponents into rebels, moderates into extremists, and prove anew the truth of Sir Thomas Browne's dictum that "persecution is a bad and indirect way of planting religion." The Episcopalian polity was now considered doubly odious: not only was it clean contrary to the Covenants, but it had deprived the people of their beloved pastors.

The basis of the Presbyterian position was not just an objection to Episcopacy *per se*—it issued even more from their reaction to the king's claim to supremacy over the Church. In their eyes Presbyterianism was the system of church government appointed in the Word of God, and Episcopacy was a mere human invention. They repudiated the claim of the king to settle the government of the Church. Christ was the sole Head, and on *His* shoulders was to be the government. Hence to them the establishment of Episcopacy was the setting up of a human device to replace a divine institution. The acknowledgment of the king's supremacy over the Church meant transferring a prerogative from the Crown of Christ to the crown of Charles II. Adherence to the Covenants, especially to the Solemn League (which, for the extremists, became the more important document),[2] was regarded by them as obligatory, both on account of the religious objects involved in it, and because of the oath which had been given. The Covenanting principles were summarized in the motto inscribed on their banners—"For Christ, His Crown, and Covenants."

It had been decreed that the Covenants were incompatible with the royal prerogative, and in the executions of the Marquis of Argyle and the Protesters Guthrie and Govan the Government had shown its hand in no uncertain manner. Charles II hated Scottish Covenants and Scottish sermons; and with Guthrie began

[1] J. K. Hewison, *op. cit.*, Vol. II, pp. 130f.
[2] This was because it virtually specified the Divine Right of Presbytery, which only an arbitrary interpretation could consider to be implied in the National Covenant.

that hanging of preachers which, nearly a century before, the Regent Morton is said to have considered "requisite" for the peace of the land.[1]

Various statements of the persecuted should now be recorded in the light of the developments described. William Guthrie, cousin of James, declared in August 1662: "Always I thought it had been true loyalty to the prince to have kept him in his own room and given him his own due; to have kept him subordinate to Christ and his laws subject to the laws of Christ. 'Fear God and honour the king;' I judged that had stood well in all the world, but there is a new generation now that has turned it even contrary, 'Fear the king and then honour God.' I never thought that was true loyalty. They make the rule all wrong that put the king in the first place; he will never stand well there."

In July 1663 Archibald Johnston of Wariston, Clerk to the Glasgow Assembly of 1638 and one of the framers of the National Covenant, was executed in Edinburgh. He had been obliged to flee from a wrathful monarch to what he thought was the safety of the Continent. There, he imagined, the King of England could not reach him. He was mistaken. After wandering for nearly two years in Germany and the Low Countries, he was rash enough to venture into France. Charles heard about it and got his agents to work. Wariston was traced to Rouen and seized, and the French king requested to sanction his extradition. Louis XIV, "to whose influence in part we owe many of the bloody measures, and destructive steps to good men and religion," agreed to deliver Wariston to the English king, despite the advice against it given him by many of his advisers.[2]

Bishop Burnet, who was Wariston's nephew, speaks of him as a man who "would often pray in his family two hours at a time, and had an unexpected copiousness that way," and one to whom Presbyterianism was "more than all the world." He was now charged in the Scottish capital with treason. During the Protectorate, according to one old writer,[3] Wariston in 1657 was "won over by the insinuating arts of Cromwell, and prevailed on to accept the office of Clerk-register at his hands. And this, together with his zeal for the Protesting cause was . . . the charge upon which he was condemned." Admitting his acceptance of such office, Wariston pointed out that even Daniel and Peter had been compelled to change their mind when circumstances warranted it. However, the real crux of the matter lay elsewhere. Wariston had been blunt

---

[1] McCrie's *Melville*, p. 69.

[2] For an account of the events leading up to Wariston's arrest in France, see *Lauderdale Papers*, Vol. I, p. 152; Law Mathieson (*op. cit.*, Vol. II, p. 178) says that the fugitive was in France for two years.

[3] *Martyrs for the Truth*, p. 75.

with Charles I, and even blunter with Charles II, whose Covenant obligations he continually emphasized. This was Wariston's mortal offence, for which he was hanged before a great crowd of spectators. For a time his memory was said to have been impaired through previous loss of blood at the hand of a royal surgeon in Hamburg, but he seemed to have revived surprisingly, and showed great composure at his execution.

On 13th August, 1663, in order further to limit conventicles, the Privy Council debarred the outed ministers from preaching, and from residing within twenty miles of their former parishes, six miles of Edinburgh or any cathedral town, or three miles of a royal burgh. This so-called Mile Act was a source of derision to Kirkton, who dryly points out that "no geographer in Scotland can find accommodation for 350 ministers, one only in one paroch . . . and keep all the distances in that proclamation."[1]

One might ask why the Scottish people were slow to combine against such outrageous government. This fact is perhaps chiefly explicable in terms of the old quarrel between Resolutioner and Protester. It was still smouldering, though it had lost much of its bitterness. The former had, under Cromwell's rule, developed traditions of loyalty to the House of Stuart and a great dislike of the men of the west. This kept them submissive after the Restoration and somewhat cooled their sympathy for the martyrs of Presbyterianism until it was too late. One party could refer to the other in Macbeth's words: "I could not say 'Amen' when they did say 'God bless us.'"

In 1665 there appeared a work by John Brown entitled *An Apologetical Relation of the Particular Sufferings of the Faithful Ministers and Professors of the Church of Scotland, since August 1660.* This treatise in twenty-three sections deals minutely with every aspect of the dispute between Crown and Covenant, and strongly upholds the righteousness of the principles and actions of the Covenanters, even to the point of justifying their resistance to their unconstitutional rulers. Brown refers to the "screwing up of the prerogative in civil matters many pegs above what was formerly," and to "the iniquitous acts and actings tending to the prejudice of the subjects as to their civil rights and privileges." He adds that where rulers have destroyed the spiritual rights and privileges of their subjects, "it is but a small matter to rob them also of what is their due as men and as members of the civil society." Brown, we will recall, was one of a growing band of Scots in exile for whom it was natural to deplore their loss of citizenship.

Yet we find also in Brown, as in Rutherford and Gillespie, the

[1] *Op. cit.,* p. 176.

condition laid down that rebellion is not something to be undertaken lightly or for trifles. Much of the later Covenanting literature, we may note in passing, is in fact based on these early theologians of the movement. Thus we find Michael Shields declaring in his *Faithful Contendings*: "Mr. Gillespie, and many others, have . . . left nothing for us to do, but to put our seals to what they have left on record."[1] Rebellion, according to Brown, can be justified only in cases of extreme necessity, "when religion, laws, lives and liberties, all that was dear to them as men and as Christians were in hazard."[2] Disobedience to a lawful monarch was no light thing to the Covenanters, to whom not the least of the biblical commands was Peter's injunction to submit to every ordinance of man for the Lord's sake.

Regarding that Act which made the king supreme in Church and State, by which "the clogs laid upon the king were knocked off," Brown did not overstate the position when he maintained that by this Act "the Church as to her ecclesiastical being is annihilated, and there is no more a Church as such, for that company is now metamorphosed into a formal part of the civil polity, and is like unto any other company or society of merchants, tradesmen, or the like."

In referring to tyranny generally, Brown is even more outspoken, thus: "God giveth no command to do evil, or to tyrannize; he [the magistrate] is not God's vicegerent when he playeth the tyrant, and therefore he may be resisted and opposed without any violence done to the office or ordinance of God . . . for it is only powers that are ordained of God that must not be resisted." This is a somewhat doctored version of Romans 13: 1 that is scarcely justifiable either on the text as it stands, or on the basis of the Covenanters' customary insistence upon Scripture as being the literal Word of God.

After making the same point as John Knox and Samuel Rutherford, that the person is to be distinguished from the office, Brown makes his apology for the Covenanters in these terms:

> They plead not for rebelling against the office, or resisting that which is God's ordinance: they did never intend to destroy magistracy, or to lessen the King's Majesty's just power and lawful authority, or to wrong the office in the least; and therefore all arguments of their adversaries taken from Romans 13: 1 or the like places, which speak against withstanding and opposing of the office and divine appointment of God are of no force against them and their cause. . . . What arguments speak well against resisting the office, or

[1] P. 70.
[2] *An Apologetical Relation*, p. 87.

the person duly and legally discharging the duties belonging to that office, will not conclude against resisting tyranny.[1]

All these were points which had previously been raised by earlier writers. What Brown introduced into the discussion was his systematic presentation of the case for armed rebellion and defensive war in general. On this issue Brown adopts a view which, secular and somewhat vindictive, takes up very low ground. He says: "It is necessary by the law of Nature that a man defend his life. And the reason is because God hath implanted in every creature inclinations and motions to preserve itself. Each are bound to love themselves better than their neighbours, for the love of themselves is the measure of that love which they owe to the neighbour." Then comes the dubious conclusion: "The law of Nature alloweth one rather to kill than to be killed, and to defend himself more than his neighbour."[2] Such theology as can be extricated from this utterance is not above suspicion; it is an extremist view, however, and it is questionable whether many of the Covenanters would have agreed unreservedly with Brown here.

It is noteworthy that he went to the Old Testament and the classical writers for support of his position, and he showed reluctance to have recourse to the New Testament. Covenanting apologists such as Brown, men whom we might have expected to share Tertullian's abhorrence of non-Christian sources, were paradoxically not above citing the writers of classical antiquity when it suited their purpose. Concerning rebellion, Brown had no scruple, and considered it even as a laudable enterprise. The discrepancy in his position, as we understand it, probably originates from that same preoccupation with the Old Testament. Brown built his argument here on a wrong hypothesis: that one should love oneself better than his neighbour. This is a theological point which we do not intend to pursue, except to suggest that it falls short of Jesus' teaching on the subject. From justifying rebellion to justifying assassination is no difficult step—we shall deal later with this point in discussing the action of James Mitchell, who attempted the life of Archbishop Sharp, and that of the fanatics who later were successful in a similar attempt.

Political developments, then, were soon to pose for the Covenanters a new ethical question of primary importance: in the face of a government whose agents were invested with summary and absolute powers, and who could shoot them down on sight without the formality of a trial (as happened later), were they justified in retaliating in like manner? This question was to come into

---

[1] *Op. cit.*, p. 86.
[2] Ibid., p. 86.

greater prominence in the succeeding years, and we dare not regard Brown as speaking for all his colleagues in his advocacy of extreme measures. He is found to be more representative when he defends the Covenanters against the charge of sedition, declaring: "There is a great difference between active disobeying of, rebelling against and violently with force of arms, resisting the lawful magistrate doing his duty and commanding just things warranted by the laws of God and the land, and disobeying his unjust acts and resisting his violent, tyrannical, oppressing, plundering, spoiling, and killing armies.[1]

The implication here is that the lawfulness of active resistance is dependent on the moral standing of the civil power; but such a view poses more problems than it solves, for it demands an impartial judge—an impossible requirement in this case. Your "impartial judge," as often as not, wants to be in the fight pushing with all the rest. Brown would doubtless find many supporters for his view that the character of authority should determine the extent of the subject's obedience, but ideas would differ radically as to what exactly was the character of the authority concerned.

Thereafter Brown lapses into a discussion of the ideal. In a truly Christian commonwealth, according to him, all laws should be "for the glory of God and the good of the souls of the subjects mainly, and for their external well-being only in subordination unto these great ends."[2] Moreover, he adds, "neither ministers nor others are bound at the magistrate's command to sin against God."[3] By "rulers" Brown meant not only kings but parliaments, the members of which he defined as "trustees intrusted by the people whose commissioners they are."[4] This is all very unreal. It is unreliably reported that Nero fiddled while Rome burned; Brown, overmuch addicted to Utopian dreams, an extravagance to which exiles are naturally susceptible, theorized in Holland while his colleagues in Scotland were suffering persecution and death.

Nevertheless the Scottish Council acknowledged the influence of this book by promptly proclaiming it seditious, ordering the public hangman to burn it at the Cross in Edinburgh, and attaching a fine of £2,000 Scots to any found in possession of it. Archbishop Sharp forwarded it to Lauderdale (the Scottish Secretary in London), at the same time unclerically styling it "a damnable book" which had fired the west and turned the country's grievance into a defiance of the Crown.[5] Mrs. James Guthrie and her

[1] *Op. cit.*, p. 153.
[2] *Jus Populi Vindicatum*, 1669, p. 69.
[3] *An Apologetical Relation*, p. 25.
[4] Ibid., p. 57.
[5] *Laing MSS.*, 9th February, 1666, p. 784.

daughter Sophia had a copy—probably a present from the author who vindicates Guthrie in it. The two women were summoned before the Council in 1666, refused to state what they knew about the work, and were banished to close confinement in one of the remote Shetland Islands.[1] Brown's book later convinced Thomas Forrester, curate of Alva, of the evils of Prelacy and led to his joining the Covenanting ranks.

Brown was the author also of a number of other works. His *Life of Justification* has been acclaimed as one of the most thorough discussions of that doctrine. Nineteenth-century Covenanters, however, recognized that his greatest work was *De Causa Dei contra anti-sabbatarios*. "Beginning from a far distance, like a captain attacking a strong fortress manned by the most powerful guns," says James Walker of Carnwath, "he toils slowly and steadily forwards, in a sort of zigzag way, withal overlooking no advantage, seizing and fortifying every point, that he may deliver his assault with success. The strength and resources of a modern author would be spent long ere this good man gets within range of his subject."[2] The result was the construction of what became the traditional Scottish attitude toward the Sabbath. Yet like every other Covenanting work of the seventeenth century, with the single exception of Rutherford's *Letters*, this book is virtually unknown today. Most such works were tinged with the spirit of the times, and it was a major tragedy for the Kirk that the talents of so many of her ablest sons were diverted into the field of barren controversy.

The wickedness committed in Scotland during the reigns of Charles II and James VII diverted sympathy more and more to the persecuted—not for their views, generally speaking, but for their sufferings. The era of oppression which ensued was the result of that attempt to foist upon the country a system of church government to which it was becoming resolutely opposed. "This plant," said Wodrow, "had for its root the king's supremacy, its stock was the bishop acting as the king's servant and depute, and the curates were its branches; and its fruit certainly could not be holiness, reformation, or the edification of the body of Christ. . . ."[3]

Robert Baillie, for example, Principal of Glasgow University, was a gentle scholarly man from whose works we have frequently quoted in the preceding pages. He tended to rebuke the enthusiasms of others, he believed in monarchy and in good government, and loved tradition as much as he hated radical schemes. He was a Covenanter, and lived just long enough to see destroyed the

---

[1] R. Wodrow, *op. cit.*, Vol. I, p. 236. There is some doubt as to whether the sentence was actually carried out.
[2] *Scottish Theology and Theologians*, p. 25.
[3] *Op. cit.*, Vol. I, p. 432.

hopes which his fellow-countrymen had built upon the Restoration. "I tell you, my heart is broken with grief," he wrote to Lauderdale in April 1661, sixteen months before he died.[1] Baillie was, as J. H. Millar has suggested, "a Covenanter with a difference."[2] He disliked Protesters, and referred at one point to James Guthrie's "restless and proud insolence."[3] Baillie was nevertheless swept into opposition—in spite of himself, it seemed. His life more than any other illustrates how the despotism of the Stuarts had a very different effect on the Scottish people from what was intended. Far from intimidating them, the ecclesiastical policy of Charles II served rather to breed loyalty to a religious faith which the king himself repudiated and tried to destroy.

Some further details are necessary at this state of the royal measures against the dissentients; of how they fought to preserve their spiritual liberties; and of how they became civil rebels in the process of protesting against the State's encroachment upon the life of the Church.

[1] J. K. Hewison, *op. cit.*, Vol. II, p. 155.
[2] *Scottish Prose*, p. 30.
[3] *Letters and Journals*, Vol. II, p. 445.

CHAPTER VII

THE FIRST REVOLT

THE FIRST OPEN CLASH BETWEEN KING AND COVENANTER
took place in November 1666. It was accidental that this
uprising shook the country at a time when the affairs of
England were still disrupted in the aftermath of the Great Fire.
The beginnings of the trouble were inauspicious. John M'Lellan
of Barscobe and three other outlawed Covenanters, after hiding
in the hills for some time, had come down into the village of
Dalry, near New Galloway, in search of food. There they rescued
an old man from some dragoons who had threatened to roast him
alive—and would evidently have done just that—because he had
refused to pay a fine imposed for not attending the parish church.
The Covenanters took the only action possible, and in the ensuing
struggle one of the soldiers was wounded. The three others thereupon gave up.[1] Gilbert Burnet denies the truth of this incident
which, he says, "was made out to beget compassion,"[2] but evidence suggests that he was mistaken in his rejection of the traditional version.

The damage had been done. Several hundreds of the western
peasantry needed just that spark. They had been deprived by the
dragoons, not only of religious liberty, but of the means of liveli-
hood itself. Word having spread like wildfire, they now drew together spontaneously, captured General Sir James Turner in his
night-gown at his headquarters in Dumfries, and held him captive
for about two weeks while they were on the march. Turner was
well treated by the rebels. His worst sorrow was the Covenanting
graces before and after meat: though himself a minister's son, he
complained that he was wearied with the tediousness and imperti-
nencies of their graces more than anything else. On one occasion,
after "one of the most bombastick graces that ever I heard in my
life," he remarked: "This grace did more fullie satisfie me of the
follie and injustice of their cause, then the ale did quench my
thirst."[3]

[1] R. Wodrow, *op. cit.*, Vol. II, pp. 17f.; J. Kirkton, *op. cit.*, p. 230.
[2] *Op. cit.*, Vol. I, p. 328.
[3] Cf. J. G. Fyfe, *op. cit.*, pp. 223ff., for an amusing account of Turner's captivity,
taken from contemporary diaries.

Turner, who had graduated at Glasgow in 1631, and later (1647) been Adjutant-General in Leslie's Covenanting army, was essentially in the tradition of Scottish mercenaries who participated in foreign wars. "I had swallowed without chewing, in Germaine," he says, "a very dangerous maxime which militarie men there too much follow, which was, that soe we serve our master honestlie, it is no matter what master we serve."[1] The words have a curiously modern ring.

At the Cross of Dumfries the Covenanters publicly drank the king's health and wished prosperity to his Government; for which, comments Wodrow, "they had very indifferent thanks."[2] Thereafter at Lanark they renewed the Covenant, denied that they rose against the king, complained of the oppression of their lives, asked for the abolition of episcopacy and the re-establishment of presbytery, and reiterated their loyalty to the throne.[3] That is an interesting sequence of events. The Covenanters were never forgetful of their duty of obedience in all reasonable things. There was no Antinomianism here. They not only regarded themselves as citizens of a heavenly country, but sought also to have the laws of the kingdom applied to their own land. It was said of William Guthrie, for example, that he could not understand a piety which was divorced from good citizenship. There are similar echoes of good sense here and there in Covenanting literature, showing that they regarded seriously their civic responsibilities centuries before Neville Figgis had written: "In regard to religion, the State as 'a power ordained by God' ought not to allow men so to use the great truth of freedom as to be false to the ends of civil society."[4]

Archbishop Sharp showed signs of panic, for this rebellion erupted at a time when he was in charge of the Government—Rothes had gone to London to assure the king of how well managed Scots affairs now were, and how the few stubborn fanatics left would be soon subdued. The rebels, having been joined by some preachers and a few gentlemen and officers of the Protesting party, marched, more as a gesture of despair than with any real hope, across the hills to Edinburgh. Their numbers never exceeded 1,100 horses and foot, according to Turner; *Naphtali* put them at a maximum of 900, with which estimate Kirkton agrees, but the consensus of opinion seems to suggest that there were more. It is possible that their numbers were eventually something in excess of 2,000 (one account says 3,000), but that this dwindled to less than half when they were disappointed of further support

[1] *Memoirs of his own Life and Times*, p. 14.
[2] *Op. cit.*, Vol. II, p. 18.
[3] G. Burnet, *op. cit.*, Vol. I, p. 329.
[4] *Churches in the Modern State*, 1913, p. 103.

from the population. Their effectiveness was further reduced by wretched weather, and by that internal dissension which has been the chronic malaise of Presbyterianism throughout its history.

Having found the east indifferent to their cause, they were headed off by the king's forces under Dalziel, forced to a battle they had not sought, and on 28th November, 1666, after some initial success, were cut to pieces on a steep hillside known as Rullion Green, on the slopes of the Pentland Hills about seven miles south of Edinburgh. Some of the fugitives were attacked by the country folk of Midlothian,[1] indicating that their hatred of Protesters may at that time have been greater than their hostility to Episcopalians. Burnet puts the Royalist casualties at five.[2] An inscription on the monument erected on the spot thus recounts Covenanting losses:

> Here and near to this place lyes the Reverend Mr. John Crook-shank and Mr. Andrew McCormick ministers of the Gospel and about fifty other true covenanted Presbyterians who were killed in this place in their own innocent self defence and defence of the covenanted work of Reformation by Thomas Dalzeel of Bins upon the 28 of November 1666. Rev. 12–11. Erected Sept. 28, 1738.

Many of the fugitives were captured by the king's men, or else were hunted down in their own west lands in the course of the following weeks. Others fled to Ireland. Colonel James Wallace, leader of the Covenanting forces at the battle, found refuge in Holland, where he died in 1678. The Archbishop of St. Andrews "caused celebrat the report of this Victory, with almost as many Guns from the Castle as there were men slain in the fields."[3]

The prisoners, who had been promised quarter, were crowded into the dungeon of the Haddock's Hole, part of the High Kirk of Edinburgh, and were barbarously treated; so much so, according to Alexander Shields, that "Turks would have blushed to have seen the like."[4] At the instigation of Archbishop Sharp, they were immediately tried and found guilty. When they claimed that they had surrendered on a promise of quarter, the Council with Sharp's warm support retorted that they had been pardoned as soldiers, but not acquitted as subjects. Casuistry of this type did nothing to endear the erstwhile minister of Crail to the Covenanters, as we shall see hereafter. Wodrow reports that when General Dalziel heard of this duplicity he "cursed and swore terribly, and said, were he to serve the king never so long, he should never bring in

---

[1] The Kirk Session Minutes of Penicuik includes the entry: "Dec. 9 1666 Disbursed to John Brown belman for making Westlandman's graves 3s. 4d."
[2] Op. cit., Vol. I, p. 331.
[3] Naphtali, p. 238.
[4] A Hind Let Loose, 1797, p. 137.

a prisoner to be butchered," and that even Sir George Mackenzie found the proceedings without legal justification.[1] (Later developments were to prove that such scruples were not typical of Dalziel.) Ten of the rebels were hanged on one gallows at Edinburgh, and their heads were cut off and fixed on the prison doors at Lanark because they had renewed the Covenant there. Thirty-five were taken to various parts of the south-west and hanged before their own doors.

Obscure and illiterate men as most of them were, and with their words on the scaffold hurried and interrupted by episcopal command, the witness they bore provoked the admiration and astonishment of the spectators. *Naphtali* gives an account of the Testimony they left, one point of which deserves attention. "We are condemned by men," they wrote on the day of their death, "and esteemed by many as rebels against the king (whose authority we acknowledge). . . ." Apologists for the House of Stuart are wont to bring this charge of rebellion against those who suffered under its rule. It is only true, morally speaking, if one first accepts the hypothesis that "the king can do no wrong," a hypothesis which in the following century Sir William Blackstone was still acclaiming as "a necessary and fundamental principle of the English Constitution."[2] We shall meet this point again. Those who took part in the Pentland Rising did so to point attention to their grievances. They did not plan to overthrow the Government; such a project would have required more than a thousand or two ill-equipped men, only a few of whom were professional soldiers.

The reign of blood had begun. Before it ended, if we are to believe the inscription of the Martyrs' Monument in Greyfriars Churchyard, Edinburgh, 18,000 people of all classes, young and old, and women alike, had died for their faith or had been banished from their native land, some to Holland, others to the plantations of the New World. (The figure cited is generally considered too high.)

Two leaders executed later, John Neilson of Corsack and Hugh MacKail, the latter a preacher who had taken no part in the battle, were tortured with the "boot" in the presence of the Council to make them reveal a supposed league with the Dutch. (Charles had entered into a dubiously justifiable war with Holland—punished, said the pious, by the Great Plague of 1665.) At Rotterdam was a colony of Scots exiles, and it was thought that the Dutch, working through them, might supply the dissidents at home with money and arms to encourage the rebellion for their own purposes.

[1] *Op. cit.*, Vol. II, pp. 38ff.
[2] *Commentaries on the Laws of England*, Book III, p. xvii.

Great efforts were made to secure a pardon for MacKail, a young man with influential friends, and it is believed by many that a reprieve was actually granted by the king, but held back by the vindictive Sharp who had never forgotten that MacKail had once dubbed him the Judas of the Church of Scotland. The charge of withholding the pardon has never been fully proved against Sharp, though evidence is strong in favour of it.[1] Gilbert Burnet accuses his namesake Alexander, Archbishop of Glasgow, of concealing news of the king's desire that MacKail should be pardoned.

The victim himself had evidently some inkling of episcopal duplicity, for at his execution he said: "I do partly believe, that the noble counsellors and rulers of this land, would have used some mitigation of this punishment, had they not been instigated by the prelates, so that our blood lies principally at the prelates' door. . . ."[2] Hugh MacKail is chiefly remembered for his 'Seraphic Song on the Scaffold":

> And now I leave off to speak any more to creatures, and begin my intercourse with God, which shall never be broken off. Farewell father and mother, friends and relations—farewell the world and all delights—farewell meat and drink—farewell sun, moon, and stars— welcome God and Father—welcome sweet Jesus Christ, the Mediator of the new covenant—welcome blessed spirit of grace, and God of all consolation—welcome glory—welcome eternal life, and welcome death.[3]

Rothes, the king's Commissioner in Scotland (1663-7), described the victims as "damd fules and incorrigeable Phanaticks," who might have saved their lives by renouncing the Covenant. The situation is succinctly put by Burnet: "Sharp governed Lord Rothes, who abandoned himself to pleasure. And when some censured this, all the answer that was made, was a severe piece of raillery, that the king's commissioner ought to represent his person."[4] The spirit in which Rothes worked is revealed in a letter he wrote to Lauderdale, thus: "This day in Council nine more of the rebels go to trial, so that next week they go to pot . . . if many of the prisoners had been soused it had been much better, and my trouble would have been much less."[5] He advised Lauderdale further that the people of the western shires would never be quiet until they be "totally ruined." To achieve this object he entered into an understanding with Sharp and several of the impecunious

[1] See, for example, an anonymous contemporary's *Life of Mr. James Sharp,* 1719, p. 164; and letter of Robert Wodrow to Mr. George Redpath of London in Wodrow, *op. cit.,* Vol. I, p. xix.
[2] R. Wodrow, *op. cit.,* Vol. II, p. 58 (editor's note).
[3] Ibid., p. 59(n).
[4] *Op. cit.,* Vol. I, p. 294.
[5] *Lauderdale Papers,* Vol. I, pp. 254ff.

nobles who held commissions in newly-raised regiments, to "ruin" the west country and divide the spoils.

Now that the chief enemies of the Government had been disposed of, and especially since many of the troublesome outed ministers had crossed the sea to Holland after the Pentland Rising, the more moderate among the clergy pleaded with the bishops to show a greater leniency towards the dissenting Covenanters, so that they might gain the affection of the people. Various concessions were suggested to make the system more palatable to them, notably by Robert Leighton. Most of the bishops seem to have been prepared to accept the proposals, but Sharp would have none of it, and derided Leighton's impracticable concessions to "beasts."

One of Sharp's chief critics had been Robert Blair, formerly minister at St. Andrews, who had been ejected and placed under house-arrest for a time, which confinement had affected his health. Just before his death in 1666 at Aberdour, he expressed himself thus: "O Sharp! Sharp! there is no rowing with thee; Lord open thine eyes, and give thee repentance and mercy, if it be Thy will . . . I would not exchange my condition, though I be now lying on my bed of languishing and dying, with thine, O Sharp, for thy mitre and all thy riches and revenues, nay, though all that's betwixt thee and me were red gold to the boot."[1]

Members of the Council were not above initiating prosecutions for their own gain. The Proprietor of Dullarg, William Martin the Younger, was later to find himself the victim of such tactics. Charged with being a Covenanter, a grievous offence, he was well aware that his innocence would not protect him from the avaricious Councillor who had turned thieving eyes on his estate. Thus he immediately transferred his property to the king. The outcome was revealing: the Council had nothing to gain from further proceedings against him, and the charge was withdrawn. Gilbert Monry of Carsphairn was fined fifty merks without any alleged fault. When he asked Sir William Bannatyne for an explanation, the other answered: "Because ye have gear, and I must have a part of it."[2]

Nevertheless, under the first two Restoration Commissioners in Scotland, the Earls of Middleton and Rothes, the bishops also played a prominent part in the administration. They favoured persecution, for the most part, regarding it as justifiable in the interests of king and Episcopacy. Robert Leighton, who might have been an exception, is the enigma of this period. Mystic,

[1] W. Row, *The Life of Mr. Robert Blair*, ed. T. McCrie, Wodrow Society, 1848, p. 493.
[2] A. S. Morton, *Galloway and the Covenanters*, 1914, p. 122.

ascetic and scholar, Leighton is fulsomely praised by Gilbert Burnet who thought that "he seemed to be in a perpetual meditation."[1] Leighton, formerly Principal of Edinburgh University, had grown tired of the Covenanters who, he discovered, "were not capable of large thoughts." His brother Elisha, as worldly as Robert was not, introduced him to the king. The result was that Leighton was nominated for a bishopric. He chose Dunblane, the smallest and poorest of the Scottish dioceses.

Robert Leighton condemned persecution, yet he passively acquiesced in it. Sir George Mackenzie states that Leighton, paradoxically enough, turned out to be more unpopular with the Presbyterians than any of his colleagues, because "he drew many into a kindness for Episcopacy by his exemplary life rather than debates."[2] It was said of the bishops generally, however, that they killed the bodies of the martyrs and the souls of the people. Morale slumped in the land. Even those who had formerly been hostile to the Protesting cause began to ask whether it could be a bad one for which the martyrs suffered so heroically—or a good one which resorted to such dubious methods to secure its triumph.

General Sir Thomas Dalziel, who had carried out his vow never to trim his beard after the execution of Charles I, had served in the Russian wars, from which fact he was called by the Scots "The Muscovy Brute." Doubtless it was there that he had learnt those methods which he now proceeded to apply to Scotland.[3] Agreeing with Rothes on the incorrigibility of the people of the west,[4] he took up the persecution. Some men he killed in cold blood; others he threatened to spit and roast. The households of those who absented themselves from the parish church were impoverished by quartering bands of soldiers on them. This phase was interrupted by internal quarrels among the personnel of the Scottish Council, and by Charles's difficulties in England which caused him to ease up on drastic action all over his domains.

In July 1668 an attempt was made upon the life of Archbishop Sharp by James Mitchell, a half-crazed "stickit minister."[5] Mitchell had been with the rebels at Rullion Green, and ever since had been hunted as a fugitive till it had affected his mind. He shot

[1] *Op. cit.*, Vol. I, p. 187.
[2] *Memoirs*, 1821, p. 161; cf. *Naphtali*, p. 301.
[3] Cf. R. Chambers, *op. cit.*, Vol. II, p. 484.
[4] Cf. Dalziel to Lauderdale, in *Lauderdale Papers*, Vol. I, p. 255.
[5] This is an old Scottish term from the days when it was difficult for a young preacher to obtain a parish. Many of them, as a result, engaged in teaching and other work, and such were known as stickit ministers. The official term was "licentiate" or "expectant." According to Sir George Mackenzie (*Memoirs*, p. 326), Mitchell was "a profligate fellow who for scandal and ill nature had been thrown out of the Laird of Dundas's household, where he serv'd as chaplain."

a pistol at Sharp as the latter was getting into his carriage in an Edinburgh street, but missed him and hit Bishop Honyman of Orkney instead. The cry at once arose that a man had been killed, and people began to rush to the spot; but when the word went round that "it was but a bishop," the crowd quietly dispersed. Burnet says he congratulated Sharp on his escape, whereupon the Archbishop "put on a show of devotion," and said his times were wholly in God's hands—"the single expression savouring of piety" that Burnet claims to have heard from Sharp's lips.[1]

Meanwhile the assailant had escaped in the confusion and remained undetected for several years. However, his crime had serious repercussions, and was responsible for further oppressive measures against the Covenanters generally. In England, Andrew Marvell's dislike of bishops led him to approve Mitchell's attempt, and he wrote Latin verses in praise of Scaevola Scoto-Britannus.

James Mitchell is noteworthy as being the first of the Covenanters to defend the taking of life, not on the battlefield, but by private individuals. He showed later from selected parts of the Old Testament, in the course of his defence of the attempted assassination, that "it is the duty of every Christian to the utmost of his powers and capacity, to destroy and cut off both idolatry and idolaters," and he specifically mentioned that the persecuting prelates should be put to death. Thereafter the principle of assassination was affirmed in several of the Covenanting works, such as *Martyrs for the Truth* and in the 1693 edition of *Naphtali*.

Some of the actual details of the persecution may help to a more intelligent grasp of the situation. In order to enforce subjection to the royal policy, the godliest folk in the land suffered, according to Kirkton, "by fyning, by imprisonment, by relegations, by selling for slaves, by banishment, by scourging, by stigmatizing, by bloody executions."[2] Even Sir Walter Scott, no friend of the Covenanter, registered his "unqualified detestation of the methods employed by the servants of the Government."[3]

Travesties of trials were conducted through the medium of the Court of High Commission which Sharp, against Lauderdale's advice, had caused to be revived in January 1664, with himself as its president. This Court, originally one of the devices by which James VI enforced his ecclesiastical policy, enjoyed almost absolute power, and could take immediate action without issuing a summons or examining witnesses. Accused persons could be dragged before it and compelled to answer questions, without knowing with what they were charged, and without being allowed

[1] *Op. cit.*, Vol. I, p. 389.
[2] *Op. cit.*, p. 198; cf. Sir J. Stewart, *Jus Populi Vindicatum*, 1669, pp. 6f.
[3] *Tales of a Grandfather*, Chapter 52.

to defend themselves. There was no appeal from its verdicts. It caused boys to be scourged, branded on the face with a hot iron, and then sold as slaves; it thought nothing of ordering women to be publicly whipped through the streets. Many left Scotland at this time and settled in Ulster, where they were welcomed and found religious liberty. The Court of High Commission continued for two years, till Lauderdale's influence with the king led to its suppression.[1]

The Protesters may have been bigoted and wrong-headed and provocative, but that was no justification for the savage fury with which the Government tried to bludgeon them into subservience. Age, rank and sex were not regarded. Some of the sufferers were humble people who

> . . . lived unknown
> Till persecution dragged them into fame
> And chased them up to heaven.

Some may have been stupid and deluded. Others were simple, honest souls, concerned only for the peace that passes all understanding, rejoicing that the shame which was theirs for Christ's sake would be soon over and followed by a better resurrection. To have submitted to the Government would for them have been a horrible apostasy. So they resisted, and the memorials which travellers can see to this day scattered throughout the hillsides of Galloway bear eloquent witness to the bitterness of the struggle.

Most precarious of all was the life of a field preacher. It was said of John Welsh, for example: "notwithstanding of all the threats of the state, the great price sett upon his head, the spyte of the bishops, the diligence of all blood-hounds, he maintained his difficult post of preaching upon the mountains of Scotland, many times to many thousands, for near 20 years time, and yet was alwayes kept out of his enemies' hands," even although Claverhouse "would have ridden 40 miles in a winter night" to apprehend him.[2] When the River Tweed was frozen, says one account, Welsh preached in the middle of the river, "that either he might shun the offence of both nations, or that two kingdoms might dispute his crime." Lauderdale reports thus on Welsh: "Indicted for treason . . . in 1661, and set at liberty on assurance of good behaviour. In 1666 was in the rebellion in the West and after the rebels were beaten was indicted for high treason, so it is lawful for any man to kill him without special authority for doing so."[3]

Sir George Mackenzie tells another side of the story which is not

[1] For an account of the Court's workings, see *Naphtali*, 1693, pp. 215ff.; cf. R. Wodrow, *op. cit.*, Vol. I, pp. 393f.

[2] J. Kirkton, *op. cit.*, p. 219.

[3] *Calendar of State Papers*, 1678, p. 428.

sufficiently dealt with by Covenanting writers: how the Episcopalian clergy in the west lands were continually harried and
robbed, so that they were distracted from their ministry, and impoverished also through the necessity of hiring guards to protect
themselves. Highwaymen were held responsible locally for the
offences, but Mackenzie blames the Presbyterian extremists "who
were known to think that all injuries done to Episcopalian ministers, were so many acceptable services done to God."[1] This might
not have been altogether untrue. "I have known some profane
people," remarks James Kirkton, "if they hade committed ane
error at night, thought affronting a curat to-morrow a testimony
of their repentance."[2] Finally, the situation became so serious that
by an Act of 30th November, 1669, parishes were made responsible for depredations committed against the clergy.

As the Government adopted extreme measures, so also the
Covenanters' outlook became correspondingly more extreme. In
1667 Sir James Stewart of Goodtrees and the Rev. James Stirling
published a manifesto which they called *Naphtali; or, The Wrest-
lings of the Church of Scotland for the Kingdom of Christ till 1667.*
Promptly condemned by the Scottish Privy Council as "a damned
book come hither from beyond sea" (Stewart was living in Holland at the time), its ideal was a theocratic State, rigidly moral,
fiercely intolerant. This book supplies a tediously full account of
the persecution of the Covenanters, in the form of "Testimonies,"
dying and otherwise. Each of these is a little story in itself,
making it impracticable to treat the book as a unity; yet it is in
the power of the whole that its importance lies. Holding that
"God grants the right and power of self-defence," it zealously
reaffirms the doctrine of tyrannicide which was the distinctive
teaching of George Buchanan's *De Jure Regni.*

All societies, governments and laws, announces *Naphtali,* are
subject to God. Serious infringement absolves people from subordination to such government. A king whose rule was against
God's law may be lawfully resisted. We shall have occasion later
to refer to some of the Testimonies. In common with similar
collections, *Naphtali* is not notable for a sane and balanced evalua-
tion of the historical incidents which it describes; it should be read
in conjunction with a healthy dose of Sir George Mackenzie's
Vindication of the Government of Charles II, published in 1691.

Sir James Stewart, one of the compilers of *Naphtali,* followed
it two years later with *Jus Populi Vindicatum,* after a rash Royalist
had essayed what he called a "Survey" of *Naphtali. Jus Populi* discusses the right of private individuals to defend "their lives,

[1] *Memoirs,* pp. 163f.
[2] *Op. cit.,* p. 163.

liberties and religion, against manifest oppression, tyranny and violence." In common with other such manifestoes, it stresses that the Covenants are "perpetually obliging . . . so long as Scotland is Scotland." Stewart holds that if the resistance of the Scots to Charles I was lawful, so also was the resistance to Charles II in defence of the same principles. His volume might be classed as a minor version of Rutherford's *Lex Rex* (it has the same meticulously legal approach, the same appeal to precedent supported by learned authorities), were it not that Sir James, freed on this occasion from the restraining influence of a clerical co-author, evinces in places a purely secular spirit reminiscent of George Buchanan and of some of the points made by John Brown of Wamphray. "The law and light of Nature," according to Stewart, "decrees that a man defend his life; men are not better than beasts in that respect." This is almost exactly Brown's position.

No man comes into this world with a crown on his head and a sceptre in his hand, Stewart points out. The people choose what form of government they like, and can alter or recall it when they will. We have discussed this point before in dealing with Rutherford's work. To hold, with Archbishop Sharp, that all men's lives were in the king's hand Stewart accounted ridiculous. "If the King's power be not absolute," he asserts, "then the people are not denuded of the power of self-defence."[1] Stewart then follows Buchanan in stating that when the ruler is a tyrant he forfeits his right to rule, and may be resisted, even by private persons. He cites as parallels the resistance made to their tyrannous rulers by the Maccabees, the Waldensians and others, and suggests that it was this very resistance which achieved religious liberty in certain Swiss cantons.

Stewart's work adds little that is new to the discussion; but we should note that the development since Buchanan's time, found particularly in *Naphtali* and *Jus Populi*, was that the appeal to the people was now an appeal against Parliament as well as against the king.[2] The latter book, so remarkably different from the former, and laying the basis of opposition to tyranny in "the law of Nature," is not much different from some of the writings of classical antiquity on the same subject—not so appealing, perhaps, in point of aesthetic taste or style, and (though prefaced by an "Epistle to the Christian Reader" and liberally sprinkled with biblical quotations) scarcely in parts more spiritual. For that reason it ought not to be regarded as typical of Covenanting literature. It lacks also the reiterated insistence of the latter on civil obedience, in so far as such obedience does not conflict with

[1] P. 170.
[2] See especially *Jus Populi*, p. 171.

God's Word, which we find in Stewart's fellow-Covenanters; for example in Alexander Shields's *A Hind Let Loose*. One reference to Christianity sounds, indeed, almost hostile: in answer to a possible objection that the primitive Christians did not resist tyranny, Stewart declares this irrelevant, on the basis that different circumstances necessitate different conduct.[1]

Nevertheless Stewart does make the point that "it is lawful, yea necessary, for every private person, whether the magistrates . . . give their countenance, concurrence, or consent thereunto, or not, to purge their hearts, and reform their lives, and to walk in all the ways of God's commandments."[2] The audacity of the whole work can be seen in true perspective when we recall that the author, the great legal authority of the post-Restoration Covenanters, was in exile in Holland. We may be forgiven for suggesting that open defiance is often traditionally associated with Dutch courage.

As though to confirm the verdict that this was a time of extremes, men pointed to the curates who replaced the ejected Presbyterian ministers. In character no less than in scholarship they were, with few exceptions, singularly unfitted to fill the role of those who had been deprived. Wherever the latter went, the people followed. Conventicles were held in private houses, in the fields, and on remote hillsides, giving their adherents the names of "Hill-Folk" and "Wanderers."

Of the curates Kirkton writes that "their most common politick profession was latitude and indifferency in opinions and questions, and this truely not because they thought so, but because hereby they were in best case to turn and serve the times without the reproach of inconstancy . . . if there were secret saints among them they did not appear."[3] Gilbert Burnet, who always considered himself "completely episcopal," designated the intruded clergy "a disgrace to their orders" and "the dreg and refuse of the northern parts."[4] Kirkton adds: "A gentleman in the north cursed the Presbyterian ministers, because (said he) since they left their churches wee cannot get a lad to keep our cows, they turn all ministers."[5] The same writer testifies that he heard curates swear like troopers in the streets of Edinburgh, and asserts that "no man will deny they wallowed in our gutters drunk in their canonical

---

[1] *Jus Populi*, pp. 294–305.
[2] Ibid., p. 176.
[3] *Op. cit.*, pp. 193f.
[4] *Op. cit.*, Vol. I, p. 221.
[5] *Op. cit.*, p. 160. Law Mathieson finds it necessary to point out that "the gentleman, doubtless, was joking." Alternatively this might be confirmation of a contemporary opinion quoted by C. K. Sharpe that Kirkton was "the everlasting comedian of the party" (ibid., p. 195(n.)).

gowns."[1] Writing to Lauderdale, the Earl of Tweeddale confirms
what the authors of *Naphtali* had called them: "scatterers and
devourers, not pastors of the flock."[2] Even Generals Turner and
Dalziel complained about having to collaborate with them.[3] In
his editorial note to this section of James Kirkton's *History*,
C. K. Sharpe quotes the following post-Revolution piece as
typical of Presbyterian invective against the Episcopalians:

> Jacobites, wicked sprites, hypocrites, by tongue and mouth,
> Ill inventors, earth's tormentors, curs'd dissenters from the truth;
> Blasphemous speakers, covenant-breakers, test-takers, filthy frogs,
> Perverse ones, Babel's sons, idle drones, and dumb dogs;
> Beggar bucklers, cheating trucklers, unclean cucklers, lustfull rams,
> Mammon curriers, butchering burriers, wolf worriers of the lambs;
> Pulpit jesters, state infestors, church pesters, by intention,
> Hellish kites, mothish mites, with your rites of Rome's invention;
> Beastly bodies, senseless nodies, venemous todies, nothing other,
> Priests of Baal, one and all, soon may you fall, with Rome your
>   Mother.[4]

At the same time it must also be recorded that a few of the
curates were well-qualified licentiates from the north who had not
hitherto succeeded in obtaining a charge under the Presbyterian
system. There were other exceptions. Burnet mentions especially
James Nairn and Laurence Charteris as learned men and faithful
pastors who carried out their ministry under the difficult days
of episcopal authority. "They both set me right," acknowledges
Burnet, "and kept me right."[5] Burnet thought highly also of
Henry Scougal of Aberdeen, Professor of Theology and author of
that great religious classic *The Life of God in the Soul of Man*, as a
minister of much piety and earnestness.

While Burnet was still minister at Saltoun, he issued a pamphlet
which contrasted the present régime with that of the primitive
Church. He accused the prelates of absenteeism, seldom preaching, preoccupation with affairs of State, arrogance, and theft of
church property. He charged many of the Episcopal clergy with
pride, simony, worldliness and pub-crawling. They inflicted upon
the people "long preachments" of "mean stuff," neglected the
Communion (which was celebrated only twice in Glasgow Cathedral during the twenty-eight years of the Second Episcopate),
were given to verbosity in prayer, and in Psalm-singing had a
predilection for "slow, long tunes." For this publication, which
he entitled *A Memorial of Diverse Grievances and Abuses in This*

[1] *Op. cit.*, p. 180.
[2] *Lauderdale Papers*, Vol. II, p. 207.
[3] G. Burnet, *op. cit.*, Vol. I, p. 296; J. G. Fyfe, *op. cit.*, p. 285.
[4] Editorial note in J. Kirkton, *op. cit.*, p. 199.
[5] *Op. cit.*, Vol. I, pp. 301ff.

Church, the twenty-three-year-old Burnet barely escaped deposition and excommunication on the proposal of James Sharp himself. The Archbishop did not appreciate Burnet's shaft that the low moral state of the land might be connected with the advent of the bishops. Wodrow, after remarking that the curates neglected the cure of souls, writes: "The prelates, strictly speaking, were Sine-cures, and few or none of them preached, save at extraordinary occasions," a situation which had been common also in the Scotland of the immediate pre-Reformation era. Burnet's *Memorial* delighted Lauderdale and his anti-episcopal friends, and it appears that even the king took some pleasure in reading it.

On a first cursory glance at the situation, a notable feature of this period is that neither Royalists nor Covenanters thought that men should be allowed to choose their own religion. The Royalists were Erastians who wanted to establish in Scotland the Church dependence on the State so characteristic of the southern kingdom. The Covenanters, on the contrary, wanted religious freedom to obey their own conscience, yet given that freedom, they would have withheld it from others whose conscience pointed a different course from theirs. But that would be a narrow and superficial view to take of the situation—almost a side-issue. A closer investigation reveals that the struggle between Charles II and the Covenanters was in reality one between spiritual despotism and spiritual independence, despite the dogmatic attitude of the Protesters. It is on this basis that we must consider it, remembering too that civil and spiritual liberty are irrevocably linked together. Just as there is an age-old problem of Church-State relations, there is also, as Hume demonstrated, "a perpetual intestine struggle, open or secret, between Authority and Liberty; and neither of them can ever absolutely prevail in the contest."[1]

How far can we regard Charles himself as responsible for the ensuing persecution of nonconformists in Scotland? The king would have had people believe that he was a persecutor against the grain—by compulsion rather than by temperament. Burnet tells us that a severe Act was passed by the Scottish Parliament in 1670 with which Charles was not well pleased: he asserted that bloody laws did no good, and that he would not have sanctioned it if he had known it beforehand.[2] The "bloody" law referred to would appear to be an Act against Conventicles, which read in part:

> Whosoever without licence or authority . . . shall preach, expound
> Scripture, or pray at any of these meetings in the field or in any house
> where there be more persons nor the house contains so as some of

[1] *Essays*, ed. Green, 1875, Pt. I, Essay V, i, 116.
[2] *Op. cit.*, Vol. I, p. 409.

them be without doors (which is hereby declared to be a field conventicle) or who shall convocate any number of people to these
meetings shall be punished with death and confiscation of their
goods.

Despite Charles's disclaimer, the repressive policy was maintained. One writer, indeed, reports that after Charles had heard in
full the debates concerning Scottish affairs on one occasion, he
said: "I perceive Lauderdale has been guilty of many bad things
against the people of Scotland; but I cannot find that he has acted
any thing contrary to my interest." Charles is still regarded by
many as having been a lazy, dissolute fellow who cared nothing for
the work of government, which he left to others. This may have
been a pose—or a sign of administrative wisdom. It is significant
that he always picked his agents carefully, and always controlled
the main lines of policy himself. Principles of religion and morality
he had none, but in practice he appears to have followed closely
the family theory of Divine Right, although he never talked about
it and never pushed the principle to extremes. In Burnet's view,
when he (Charles) talked freely, "he could not help letting himself
out against the liberty that, under the Reformation, all men took,
of enquiring into matters of religion: for from their enquiry into
matters of religion, they carried the humour farther, to enquire
into matters of State." Burnet adds that an oft-repeated statement
of Charles was that he "thought that government was a much
safer and easier thing where the authority was believed infallible,
and the faith and submission of the people was implicit."[1] It
would seem that Charles placed much faith in the maxim pro-
pounded by the great Strafford in his father's time, that reward and
punishment are the heaven-appointed agencies for the government of men.

The Covenanters, for their part, had no difficulty in assessing
Charles, and in a letter to friends in Ireland some of them put on
record ". . . his cruelty over the bodies of Christians in chasing and
killing upon the fields many without sentence, and bloody butcher-
ing, hanging, heading, mangling, dismembering alive, quartering
upon scaffolds, imprisoning, laying in irons, torturing by boots,
thumbkins, fire-matches, cutting pieces out of the ears of others,
banishing and selling as slaves old and young men and women in
great numbers; oppressing many others in their estates, forfeiting,
robbing, spoiling, pillaging their goods, casting them out of their
habitations, interdicting any to reset them under the pain of being
treated after the same manner. So for the continued and habitual
trade of these and many other acts of tyranny, we . . . do yet
adhere to our revolt from under the yoke of tyranny."[2]

[1] *Op. cit.*, Vol. I, p. 128.   [2] Quoted in M. Shields, *op. cit.*, p. 303.

CHAPTER VIII

THE FIRST AND SECOND INDULGENCES

IN 1668 SIR JAMES TURNER AND SIR WILLIAM BANNATYNE WERE tried for their atrocities and extortions, which proceedings constituted a tacit admission by the Government that things had gone too far. Both officers were dismissed the king's service, and Bannatyne was, in addition, banished from Scotland.[1] These two had set the example which their subordinates were not slow to follow. Minor officials had been equally corrupt and cruel, and had harried the Covenanters mercilessly. Informers had consorted with the rebels for the purpose of passing on information about future conventicles (Sharp had a finger in that pie); many had collected blood-money offered by the Government for notable dissidents whom the spies had succeeded in betraying. Against such a background it is astonishing to find that Andrew Lang tries to make a saint out of Turner.[2]

After two years during which the post of High Commissioner was vacant, the Earl of Lauderdale himself was appointed in 1669. The earl, who at one time had signed the National Covenant, was said to have been so stricken with remorse over the death of Charles I that he fought for Charles II at Worcester, where he was taken prisoner. Released just before the Restoration, Lauderdale was one of the few people to whom Charles II remained loyal for any length of time; and than him the king had no more faithful servant.

An ungainly man with a tongue too big for his mouth (which, narrates Burnet, "made him bedew all that he talked to"), he had few courtly graces. Learned in Latin, Greek and Hebrew, and no mean theologian, he could be oddly perverse, abject to superiors, high-handed with subordinates. Burnet calls him "the coldest friend and violentest enemy" he knew.[3] Lauderdale had after the Restoration advised Charles to retain Presbytery in Scotland, and cited the troubles which had overtaken the king's grandfather and

---

[1] For a full account of the proceedings against Turner from official sources, and a shorter but even more damning indictment against Bannatyne, see Wodrow, *op. cit.*, Vol. II, pp. 101ff.

[2] See *Blackwood's Magazine*, CLXXIV, July 1903.

[3] *Op. cit.*, Vol. I, p. 140.

father because of their resolve to establish Episcopacy in the land. Even when his counsel was ignored Lauderdale never concealed his dislike of Episcopal government.

His advent brought a change of policy towards the Covenanters. Although his position bound him to maintain the established ecclesiastical system, Lauderdale's jealousy of the bishops' authority was shown by his insistence on an Act which laid down the royal supremacy over the Church. He began by treating the recalcitrants more mildly, but an increase in the number of conventicles soon checked this lenient policy. He then resorted to the tactics of his predecessors, and imposed savage measures of repression, but when this also failed to subdue the rebels, he renewed his efforts at conciliation by a new approach which we shall discuss shortly.

During this time it was not unusual for Welsh or one of his colleagues to preach to an open-air assembly of several thousand people. Most of the ejected ministers, however, did not take part in field-preaching, which fact some Ayrshire ministers affirmed when summoned before the Council in 1669. William Fullarton, formerly minister at St. Quivox, was their spokesman. They admitted the God-given link between fearing God and honouring the king, adding that "none void of the first can rightly perform the second," but made it clear at the same time that the second was necessarily subordinate to the first. The Council seemed to listen not unsympathetically on this occasion, and finally dismissed them with a caution. "Indeed this year," records Wodrow, "conventicles were like the palm-tree, the more weights were hung upon them, the more they grew; and there were few presbyterian ministers in the west and south, but were preaching in their homes, and some in barns, and some few in the fields."[1] Nevertheless the Council issued another proclamation against conventicles in the west country, threatening heavy fines on landowners who permitted such.

Meanwhile in both England and Ireland there was a marked slackening of the persecution against nonconformists. A letter from a Presbyterian in Ireland to a Scottish colleague in April 1669 rejoices that "the sun seems to be fairly risen on this land" and that the Presbyterians had such liberty as was "in many places little less than when they had law for them." Ministers were being provided for vacant charges, meeting-houses built, says the correspondent, adding: "About a month ago, I had occasion to be at Dublin, where the sacrament of the Lord's supper was administrate publicly on the Lord's day, at the ordinary time, and some hundreds standing without, the doors and windows of a

[1] *Op. cit.*, Vol. II, pp. 124ff.

throng meeting-house being cast open; a public feast on the Thursday, two sermons on Saturday, and as many on Monday."[1]

A few months earlier, several meeting-houses had been built in London, and the king was said to have allowed Richard Baxter and some other nonconformist leaders to wait upon him, and to have told them that "he had been too long a king of a party, and now he resolved to be king of all his subjects."[2] The Scots had reason to be dubious about such royal pronouncements in the past, and many remained suspicious when the administration now tried new methods.

Despite some misgiving on the part of Robert Leighton (whom he later induced to accept reluctantly the Archbishopric of Glasgow), Lauderdale offered to the expelled clergy a Declaration of Indulgence in June 1669. The Government was naturally not prepared to turn out the curates—the only measure which would have restored full ecclesiastical peace among the ejected—but it offered to fill the still numerous vacant parishes with Presbyterian ministers, on the sole condition of their taking an oath to obey the law. This would mean that those who accepted the concessions held their charges, not by act of congregation, session, patron or bishop, but simply by the arbitrary will of the Government, on certain specified conditions. It was, as Law Mathieson says, "the introduction of a wedge of Erastian Presbyterianism into the heart of an Episcopal Church."[3]

This and succeeding Indulgences split the Protesting clergy much as the Public Resolutions had done in dividing the Covenanters of a former generation. Robert McWard was not hoodwinked, and referred to this cunning device intended to divide the faithful by separating "the Mad-cap Phanaticks (i.e. the truly tender and conscientious ministers and professors) from the moderate" (those liable to be "bewitched with this Court-charm").[4] James Renwick described the Indulgences in terms of the Machiavellian principle of *divide et impera*.[5]

The Covenanters generally were quick to recognize Lauderdale's offer as being the thin edge of the wedge (in this they were consistent), and both ministers and people, for the most part, regarded the offer as a snare of the evil one, an insidious way of getting souls to acknowledge prelacy unawares. A party catchword, straight from Scripture and therefore dear to the Covenanting heart, was "Touch not, taste not, handle not." As it was, only forty-two of the ministers yielded. They were promptly

[1] Quoted in R. Wodrow, *op. cit.*, Vol. I, p. 130.
[2] Ibid., p. 115.
[3] *Op. cit.*, Vol. II, p. 236.
[4] *Earnest Contendings*, p. 136.
[5] *An Informatory Vindication*, 1707, p. 8.

denounced as "dumb dogs that could not bark"—a description which finds a parallel in an English translation of George Buchanan's *Baptistes*, in which context it is not inappropriate to our present subject:

> . . . like dumb dogs that bark not, here you fret
> And fume about your sheepcotes, but the wolves,
> Which of you drive away?[1]

The compliant ministers were known also as the King's Curates, as distinct from the Bishop's Curates, and their ministrations were disdainfully refused by most of the people. Acceptance of the Indulgence meant virtually that the indulged constituted a little church within the church, under the government of the State. It was a subtle move of Lauderdale, expressed in innocent terms. Any outed minister, the decree ran, who has "lived peaceably and orderly," might re-enter his parish, if vacant, and occupy church and manse without necessarily acknowledging Episcopal authority. John Brown pointed out that this peaceable and orderly living included a negative compliance with tyranny, oppression of kirk and country, bloodshed, apostasy, and persecution of conscientious people.[2] For those to whom churches were not immediately available, an allowance at the rate of 400 merks per annum was promised until their settlement. The same offer extended to those not indulged, on promise of good behaviour. "Seeing by these orders we have taken away all pretences for conventicles," said the Act, "and provided for the wants of such as are, and will be peaceable; if any shall hereafter be found to preach without authority, or keep conventicles, our express pleasure is, that you proceed with all severity against the preachers and hearers as seditious persons, and contemners of our authority."[3] This showed how little both king and Government understood the basis of the Covenanters' resistance.

Yet even the historian Wodrow admits that "the Lord . . . had much good to bring out of it [i.e. the Indulgence], to the famishing souls of thousands . . . and they [the indulged ministers] could not but acknowledge they had as great and sensible assistance in the work of the gospel, as ever they had known. . . ."[4] Among those who accepted it was Robert Douglas, five times Moderator of the General Assembly, and preacher at Charles II's coronation in Scotland. Deprived of his charge at Greyfriars seven years earlier, Douglas now at seventy-five became "indulged minister"

---

[1] The translator is possibly John Milton, a known admirer of Buchanan. Cf. Isa. 56: 10.

[2] *History of the Indulgence*, 1783, p. 140.

[3] Wodrow, *op. cit.*, Vol. II, p. 131. Wodrow says that so far as he could discover, the allowance was never forthcoming to many of the ministers.

[4] Ibid., pp. 134f.

E

at Pencaitland, where he remained till his death in February 1674.

Whatever the motive that prompted it, this First Indulgence was a staggering *volte-face* and a concession which met the Covenanters more than half-way. Yet apart from incurring the inevitable opposition of the ejected, the regular Episcopalian clergy raised their voices against this action of the State. Their objections could scarcely have been on the grounds of Erastianism (however the term is interpreted), or they would surely have been forced to consider as anomalous their own position under a system which they had approved for several years. The devious-minded Sharp, whatever his true reasons, felt strongly enough about this new development to preach against it in Lauderdale's presence. His momentary boldness having deserted him, he afterwards expressed some sort of apology to the Commissioner. Sharp further showed his opposition indirectly, however, by refusing to admit any indulged minister to a charge in his diocese. Bishops in other parts of the country promptly took steps to fill vacant charges in order to exclude the indulged clergy.

Alexander Burnet, Archbishop of Glasgow, expressed a much stronger objection than the Primate. A meeting of his Synod of Glasgow in September 1669 agreed to a Remonstrance drawn up by James Ramsay, Dean of Glasgow, and Arthur Ross, later Archbishop of St. Andrews. Done with Burnet's approval, this document protested against the Indulgence as trespassing on their rights, and blamed the Government for turning a blind eye to nonconformity to the detriment of peace in the Church. It was not the Synod's intention to publicize the protest until some lobbying had been done among members of the Scottish Privy Council, but things went awry. Lauderdale somehow got a copy of it. He professed to smell treason, and took swift action to have it suppressed and its chief scribes cited before the Council. When the king himself read its contents he is quoted as exclaiming: "This damned paper shewes Bishops and Episcopall people are as bad in this chapter as the most arrant Presbyterian or remonstrator."[1] Burnet himself was confined in Glasgow while Parliament was in session, and the legislature took advantage of his enforced absence to pass a measure which he was expected to oppose—the Act of Supremacy.

This Act ordained that "His Majesty hath the supreme authority and supremacy over all persons and in all causes ecclesiastical within this kingdom; and . . . the external government and policy of the Church belongeth to him and his successors as an inherent right."[2] Not a single member opposed the Act in Parliament,

[1] *Lauderdale Papers*, Vol. II, pp. 139, 166.
[2] *Acts of the Parliaments of Scotland*, Vol. VII, p. 554.

except Leighton, and even he ended by accepting its terms—which decision he regretted for the rest of his life, feeling that it made the king their pope. Sharp, we learn, made "a long dark speech, and voted for it."[1]

"How comes that our kings are so great sticklers for prelacy, for this government of man's invention?" asked Fraser of Brea, a Covenanting leader who advocated non-resistance. "Why," he continued, "the cause is plain, it is that the king that hath the nomination of them, gives them their charters and rents, and when he has any thing ado in Parliament with the country, he is sure of 14 votes from his creatures, who will sacrifice honour, and conscience, and all to him."[2] "This abominable Act," says another Covenanter, "not only contains the grossest Erastianism and Popery, but makes that an inherent right of King Charles's Crown."[3]

Immediately the Act of Supremacy was passed, Charles declared the see of Glasgow vacant. This was virtually a deposition, which drastic exercise of the royal prerogative caused some alarm even among the English bishops to whom Erastianism hitherto had been no problem. Thus Burnet for a time "went off the stage, generally admir'd, even by the fanaticks themselves, for preferring his conscience to his gain, and for fearing nothing but to offend it," said Sir George Mackenzie, adding sententiously, "and by this example, we may see how advantageous it is, to adhere to the principles we have once own'd."[4] An examination of the respective careers of Archbishop Burnet and Sir George Mackenzie suggests that the high moral tone implied in the latter's words was typical of neither. To fill Burnet's place Robert Leighton was first appointed commendator or administrator, then a few months later was persuaded to accept the Archbishopric of Glasgow.

In view of the Indulgence and of this further setback to the Episcopalians, Presbyterian sympathizers taking a superficial glance at the situation might have been misled in having seen Lauderdale in conciliatory mood. Like Montrose twenty years earlier, he cared not for bishops, but he was first and foremost an avowed supporter of the royal absolutism. With a certain heavy joviality he could say to some who had been burdened with exorbitant fines for attending the banned gatherings: "Gentlemen, now ye know the rate of a conventicle, and shame falls them first fails."[5]

In September 1672 came the Second Indulgence, when the body

---

[1] Burnet, *op. cit.*, Vol. I, p. 398.
[2] *Prelacy an Idol . . . A Sermon.*
[3] W. Row, *The Life of Mr. Robert Blair*, 1848, p. 529.
[4] *Memoirs*, p. 159.
[5] R. Wodrow, *op. cit.*, Vol. II, p. 193.

of the faithful was really divided, and eighty ministers resumed parochial duties, albeit with grievous limitations. Most of them were settled in pairs in parishes; they could celebrate communion only on one day appointed for all the churches; and they were forbidden to leave their parish on any pretext whatever without permission from the bishop. Michael Shields, a contemporary writer, referred to "that woeful and church-renting Indulgence," a comment which sufficiently reflected the Covenanting attitude towards it, and deplored the fact that "so many Samsons, famous for contending and weathering out so many storms of hazard and dangers for their faithfulness, should have had their hair so easily cut by foundering upon these rocks of compliance."[1] John Brown of Wamphray declared that it was not merely inexpedient or unwise to take the bond offered by the Government; it was an offence against God. Brown added: "I cannot see how such a liberty can without sin be embraced or bargained for."[2]

Yet even these indulged ministers were occasionally driven to subterfuge to "please both a jealous people and ane usurping magistrate," on those occasions when ecclesiastical commissioners came around the country to enquire whether they made a practice of reading aloud two chapters of the Bible without comment. It is one of the minor mysteries of this period that this should have been considered a test of loyalty by the Episcopalian authorities, and of prelatic tendencies by the Presbyterians. The investigation was instituted after the bishops complained to the Council that some of the indulged ministers were expounding (not merely reading) a portion of Scripture before morning service—a pre-Restoration practice.

The Protesters at home and abroad condemned these Indulgences as barefaced Erastian breaches of the Covenant, and abjured the people in fiery language to have nothing to do with them, not to hear the intruded hirelings, disguised prelatists, or any without "a cleanly call." They told why. The king and Parliament had at first forbidden ministers to preach the Gospel and administer the Sacraments of the Church. Many had obeyed, some had disobeyed, the prohibition. Then the king, through Lauderdale, as we have seen, was graciously pleased to grant an Indulgence to some Presbyterian ministers—on certain conditions—to preach the Gospel and administer the Sacraments. Some had accepted, many had refused, that Indulgence. Therein lay the crux of the matter. Those who disregarded the king's prohibition did so on the ground that ministers of Christ's Church had not received their authority to preach His Gospel and administer His Sacra-

---

[1] *Faithful Contendings Displayed*, Preface, p. ix.
[2] "The Banders Disbanded," in *McWard's Tracts*, 1681, p. 20.

ments from king and Parliament; nor could they be deprived by the civil power of that authority. They would not receive, as an Indulgence granted out of the king's pleasure, a limited liberty to discharge their ministerial duties—while they claimed full liberty as a matter of right.

John Brown reasoned that acceptance of the Indulgence constituted a tacit recognition of power in the king to do whatever he pleased in ecclesiastical matters. Such a view was injurious to Christ as Head of the Church; contrary to Presbyterian principles; dependent on the 1669 Act of Supremacy; detrimental to the power of the people; served to promote Erastianism; was prejudicial to the good of the Church; tried to discredit the Covenanters' stand; strengthened the Episcopal hands; violated the Covenant; and condemned the authors of the Indulgence.[1] Logically Brown was right, as was John Blackadder who asserted that compliance was too much like admitting the existence of a right which was non-existent.[2] Similarly, when the Covenanters were asked the usual question, "Own ye the king's authority?" they saw very clearly that what was meant was not only his civil authority, but his claim to supreme headship over the Church.

The Irish Episcopalian Archbishop Ussher had obviously grasped the Covenanting dilemma when he posed the question, "Suppose the King shall command us to worship the devil. Would you . . . lay down your head upon the block and not . . . stand upon guard?"[3] To Robert McWard, acceptance of the Indulgence was a greater triumph for the king than had been achieved by the Highland Host and all his militia.[4] Nonconformists in England, however, looked upon the Scottish situation very differently, regarding the Government's Indulgences with amazement and envy. "What," exclaimed Edmund Calamy, one of their leaders, "what would our brethren in Scotland be at, and what would they have? Would to God we had these offers."[5]

In the days to come the situation was to be reversed, for Charles did offer similar Indulgences in England, and we find a Covenanting letter of 1687 contrasting the sad state of repression in Scotland with the "liberty and free toleration which is given in England."[6] What the letter did not reveal was that the Indulgences had in the southern kingdom similarly divided the Nonconforming party.

Another Act had been passed in Scotland in 1670, requiring

---

[1] *History of the Indulgence*, 1678. The above is a summary of Brown's conclusions.
[2] *Memoirs*, ed. A. Crichton, 1823, p. 264.
[3] *Power Communicated by God to the Princes*, 1688, p. 150.
[4] *Earnest Contendings*, p. 144; *infra.*, pp. 136f.
[5] Quoted by C. P. S. Clarke, *Short History of the Christian Church*, 1929, p. 378.
[6] M. Shields, *op. cit.*, p. 315.

anyone on oath to give information regarding conventicles. "Scarcely a year passes," remarks Wodrow, "but some new Declaration, Bond, or Oath was brought upon the subjects in Scotland; all of them dubious, many of them impossible to keep, and some of them evidently self-contradictory."[1] Thereafter Parliament further declared that punishment, even to exile, should be inflicted on those who had their children baptized by the non-conforming ministers, and also on those who for three successive Sundays absented themselves from the parish church. The object of all this legislation seems to have been to make Charles absolute monarch of the conscience of the Scottish people; dictator of their private as well as their public lives. In the words of a contemporary, "they would have their laws to reach thoughts as well as actions."[2]

In 1670 Archbishop Leighton sent a committee of the best Episcopalians on a travelling mission through the west, to try to persuade people to accept the concessions offered. (The settled clergy, scoffed Burnet, "could not argue much for anything."[3]) Its members were Laurence Charteris, James Nairn, Gilbert Burnet, Patrick Cook, Walter Paterson and James Aird. They might just as well have stayed at home. Burnet has left an interesting account of their dealings with the local communities:

> The people of the country came generally to hear us, though not in great crowds. We are indeed amazed to see a poor commonalty, so capable of arguing upon points of government, and on the bounds to be set to the power of princes, in matters of religion: upon all these topics they had texts of Scripture at hand; and were ready with their answers, to any thing that was said to them. This measure of knowledge was spread even among the meanest of them, their cottagers, and their servants. They were indeed vain of their knowledge, much conceited of themselves, and were full of a most entangled scrupulosity, so that they found or made difficulties in every thing that could be laid before them. . . . As soon as we were gone, a set of those hot preachers went round to all the places in which we had been, to defeat all the good we could hope to do. They told them, the devil was never so formidable as when he was transformed into an angel of light.[4]

After this and subsequent attempts had failed, Leighton despairingly resigned his see in December 1674. He affirmed that the irreconcilable Presbyterians had crowned him with insults, that the Kirk "abounded in furious zeal and endless debates about the empty name and shadow of a difference in government, in the

[1] *Op. cit.*, Vol. I, pp. 120f.
[2] A. Shields, *The Scots Inquisition*, 1745, p. 8.
[3] *Op. cit.*, Vol. I, p. 409.
[4] Ibid., p. 140.

meanwhile not having of solemn and orderly public worship as much as a shadow." He had been disappointed also that in 1671 his friends Gilbert Burnet, James Nairn and Laurence Charteris had declined bishoprics which had fallen vacant. For all his broadmindedness in other directions, Leighton never understood Covenanting principles; he dismissed them, indeed, as "trifling contentions" and referred to their resistance at one point as "a drunken scuffle in the dark."[1]

Robert Leighton, a man of ascetic habits, gave his entire income, apart from his own frugal expenses, to the poor. He has been called the "Fénelon of the Scottish Church,"[2] but his passive acquiescence in the Government's ecclesiastical policy has somewhat tarnished his reputation. The gentle divine who could condemn persecution as scaling heaven with ladders fetched out of hell, could also pronounce that "God hath given none power to resist and rise against the powers that are over us."[3] Yet "the holy wobbler" (Hay Fleming's term) did not harass the Nonconformists in his diocese, and was held by them in some esteem. Evidence suggests that it was he who induced the king to close the infamous Court of High Commission in 1665.

His ruling passion had been to achieve the unity of the Church in Scotland—an aim he shared with his king. As Bishop of Dunblane he had gone to London and laid before Charles a plan of comprehension, the main point of which was the proposal to sacrifice a considerable part of the Episcopal prerogatives in order to gain the Presbyterians. As a precedent he cited the concessions made by the African Church to the Donatists. It was a laudable scheme, but little came of it; other leading figures were less disinterested and less ingenuous than he. "Had he succeeded in moulding Presbyterian worship on the model of the English Liturgy," suggests Hay Fleming, "he would have forestalled the Church Service Society; and might have helped to hasten the advent of that movement which is threatening to turn churches into music-halls."[4]

Retiring to Sussex, Leighton engaged in works of charity until his death on 25th June, 1684, at the age of seventy-four. Leighton had always wanted to die at an inn, for it gave the impression of a pilgrim on his way home, to whom all the world was an inn, and who was weary with all the clamour of it. He got his wish, taking

[1] *Lauderdale Papers*, Vol. III, p. 76.
[2] A saintly man, Fénelon seems nevertheless to have approved Louis XIV's ruthless campaign against French Protestantism from 1684; cf. L. Sturzo, *Church and State*, 1939, p. 306.
[3] D. Butler, *Life and Letters of Robert Leighton*, 1903, p. 490.
[4] *Critical Reviews*, 1912.

his farewell of this earthly scene at the Bell Inn, Warwick Lane, London.

Lauderdale, who had been created duke in 1672, finding that his conciliatory policy had failed, and having lost the subduing influence of Leighton, reverted in 1677 to Rothes' policy of military spoliation. To this end he enlisted the aid of Graham of Claverhouse, known to Scottish history as "Bloody Clavers," as military leader. Lauderdale expressed the sentiment that it was "better that the west should bear nothing but windlestraws and sandy laverocks"—dog-grass and larks—"than rebels to the King."[1] He brought together a great army of militia, linked them with a band of marauding Highlanders (most of these Roman Catholics in so far as they professed any religion), and sent them, some 9,000 strong, among the industrious farmers and traders of the west.

The ostensible purpose of this was to crush a rebellion that did not actively exist. Burnet testifies that on one occasion Lauderdale said to him: "Would to God they *would* rebel, that so he might bring over an army of Irish Papists to cut all their throats."[2] In the event, the Highlanders proved no less effective. Their terms of reference were staggering. After authorizing the army to take free quarters while on the march and to seize such horses as were necessary for transporting ammunition and sick men, the Commission issued by the Privy Council continues:

> and for their encouragement, we hereby indemnify them against all pursuits civil and criminal, which may at any time hereafter be intented against them, or any thing they shall do in our service, by killing, wounding, apprehending, or imprisoning such as shall make opposition to our authority, or by seizing such as they have reason to suspect, the same being always done by order of our privy council their committee, or of the superior officer; and particularly we do hereby give them all such power and indemnity, as is usual and necessary for such forces as are raised by authority, or are at any time commanded to go upon such military expeditions. And lastly, we hereby command any such persons living within the bounds foresaid, as shall be pitched upon by the said military commander to arise and march with him under his command, and there to act and say as they shall be commanded by him, and that upon their highest peril. . . . [3]

The army commandeered horses beyond their immediate need to such an extent that none were left to pull the ploughs, and the land was left untilled. The invaders overturned loads on the public highway, killed cattle for no purpose, tortured people to make

[1] Sir W. Scott, *Tales of a Grandfather*, Vol. II, p. 30.
[2] *Op. cit.*, Vol. I, p. 476.
[3] R. Wodrow, *op. cit.*, Vol. II, p. 379.

them reveal where money and goods were hidden, robbed, raped, cut off fingers and hands. Many of the mutinous soldiers even threatened their officers if discipline were mentioned.

The invasion of the Highland Host, as it was called, did not lead immediately to the desired result confirmed by Patrick Walker when he agreed "that the very design of that Killing Time was to provoke the Lord's people" to take up arms, "that they might get the sham occasion to raise fire and sword in the west to make it a hunting-field," there being (here Walker quotes the Duke of York) " 'no other way of rooting out phanatism out of it.' "[1] James Kirkton draws substantially the same conclusion in regard to the governmental intention,[2] but the land remained quiet until the Highland Host had withdrawn, laden with booty which they had heaped up during their sojourn in the west. Comments Wodrow:

> One would have thought they had been at the sacking of some besieged town, by their baggage and luggage. They were loaded with spoil: they carried away a great many horses, and no small quantity of goods out of merchants' shops, whole webs of linen and woollen cloth, some silver plate bearing the names and arms of gentlemen. You would have seen them with loads of bed clothes, carpets, men and women's wearing clothes, pots, pans, gridirons, shoes, and other furniture, whereof they had pillaged the country....[3]

The same writer supplies a parish-by-parish account of the losses sustained by the people of Ayrshire alone. Carefully drawn up by some of the county gentlemen, it shows a total of £137,499 6s. 0d. Scots. Wodrow adds that taking into account the fact that all the details were not known at the time, the real losses of the people could be assessed at double that figure.[4] All this depredation was done within a maximum time of eight weeks.

Apart from the loss of money and goods, there existed a chronic state of indignation against the outrages of the dragoons. Victims were suspended from beams or branches by their thumbs; or a cord was pulled round the head and tightened by twisting a stick in it until the flesh was cut right through to the bone; or fuses were fastened between the fingers and kept burning till the flesh was consumed; or people were stripped naked miles from home and left to make their way back as best they could. One of Claverhouse's favourite ploys was to gather together the boys and girls of some country hamlet, assemble his dragoons in a line before the trembling children, then tell them to say their prayers before

[1] *Six Saints*, Vol. I, p. 7.
[2] *Op. cit.*, p. 390.
[3] *Op. cit.*, Vol. II, pp. 412f.
[4] Ibid., pp. 423–6.

he killed them all. Sometimes, as a further refinement, he would order his soldiers to fire a volley over the heads of the youngsters. Then this doughty warrior would tell them that he would spare their lives if they would reveal where their fathers and brothers and friends were in hiding.[1]

The persecution did not stop the conventicles. "We are met this day," said John Welsh, at a field communion at Maybole in 1678, "in the name of our Lord Jesus Christ, the King and Head of His Church. These meetings, ye know, are forbidden by authority, but there is One greater than they that commands the contrary of what they command, and His command must be obeyed."[2] At another such meeting John Kid bewailed the state of the country, adding: "There is no more religion seen at least amongst the most part, either upon the Lord's day, or on a week-day, than amongst those that live in the wilds of America."[3] J. H. Thomson quotes a letter dated 6th August, 1678, to someone in Carlisle, in which the writer reports that at a conventicle on the previous Sunday in Carrick there were more than 600 well-armed men, and continues: "I am informed that there is many a man in Galloway, if he hath but two cows, he will sell one cow for a pair of pistols."[4]

Archbishop Sharp had opposed the Indulgences and lent ready support to the congenial scheme of the Highland Host and other harsh measures against the Covenanters. This, however, was to mark the end of his unholy rule in the land. On 3rd May, 1679, he was assassinated by a group of nine zealots on Magus Moor, near St. Andrews. It was not altogether a premeditated crime. Though Sharp's death had long been resolved on, the original quarry sought on this occasion was the local Sheriff-Depute, William Carmichael, who had shortly before put to death some of their colleagues. Somehow they missed him, but took it as providential when news came that the Arch-Enemy *par excellence* was about to pass that way. Stopping the coach in which Sharp was travelling with his daughter, they gave him time to prepare for death, then fired at him. Thereafter, recounts one of the participants, "finding he was not yet dead, and remembering that it had been reported, that he had used Sorcery, in order to defend his Body, and that he was invulnerable; and withal to rid him of Life, with as little Torture as we might, we slew him with our Swords, and departed."[5]

Thus, says Alexander Shields, "that truculent traitor . . .

[1] R. Wodrow, *op. cit.*, Vol. 2, p. 512.
[2] *Sermons in Times of Persecution*, ed. J. Kerr, 1771, p. 643.
[3] Ibid., p. 13. Kid was executed in the following year.
[4] *The Martyr Graves of Scotland*, 1875, p. 43.
[5] *The Life of Mr. James Sharp* (anonymous), 1719, p. 172.

received the just demerit of his perfidie, perjury, apostasie, sour-ceries, villanies, and murders. . . ."[1] Patrick Walker dismisses the incident more tersely but equally strongly, referring to Magus Moor as the place where "that compend of wickedness, Bishop Sharp, got his just deservings."[2] Sharp was not, apparently, killed because he was an Episcopalian, but because he was a tyrant. It had been said of Archbishop Laud that nothing but the putting him to death in such an unjust manner as Charles I did could have raised his character; but not even death could do anything for James Sharp's reputation. "When Saul was breathing out cruelty," notes Wodrow, "he was converted; but this apostate went to his place."[3] Nevertheless, an absurdly fulsome inscription in Latin is still decipherable in Holy Trinity Church, St. Andrews. It refers to Sharp, incredibly, as a "most holy martyr," and thereafter, as "an example of piety, an angel of peace, an oracle of wisdom, and the personification of dignity." Holy Trinity, it may be added, is a Presbyterian church.

Sharp's murder, though it was swiftly repudiated by the Cove-nanting leaders, precipitated the second major rebellion of Charles's reign, both by the encouragement it gave to those who actually had approved the deed, and by the despair of those others who were justly apprehensive that the vengeance of the Government would be both general and terrible. John Buchan has truly said that the killing of Sharp was "the Rubicon which, once crossed, meant civil war à outrance."[4] To this incident we might apply the stanza attributed to Sir David Lindsay of the Mount, on the assassination of Cardinal Beaton in the previous century:

As for this cardinal, I grant
He was the man we weel could want,
    And we'll forget him soon;
And yet I think the sooth to say,
Although the loon is weel away,
    The deed was foully done.

[1] *A Hind Let Loose*, p. 123.
[2] *Op. cit.*, Vol. I, p. 217.
[3] *Op. cit.*, Vol. III, p. 41; cf. W. L. Mathieson, *op. cit.*, Vol. II, p. 273, for a some-what half-hearted attempt to cite Sharp's "private virtues."
[4] "The Making of Modern Scotland," in *Some Eighteenth Century Byways*, p. 132.

CHAPTER IX

THE SECOND REVOLT

THE INSURRECTION FLARED UP WHEN, ON 29TH MAY, 1679, A band of eighty Covenanters entered the town of Rutherglen, near Glasgow. They extinguished the bonfires blazing in honour of Restoration Day, and made a Declaration and Testimony at the Town Cross, after burning a copy of all the Acts of Parliament made in favour of Episcopacy since 1660. They mentioned specifically the Act of Rescissory and those Acts which re-established prelacy, renounced and condemned the Covenants, ejected the Presbyterian ministers, decreed 29th May as a holy day in remembrance of the king's birth and restoration, established the king's supremacy over civil and ecclesiastical causes, and offered sinful indulgences. The Covenanters publicly burned all the Acts directed against the Reformation, "as they have unjustly, perfidiously, and presumptuously burned our sacred Covenants."[1]

Thereafter things happened in quick succession—so much so, that within little more than a month of Sharp's murder a conventicle at Drumclog[2] had defeated a regiment of dragoons under Claverhouse himself (the latter's horse was shot from under him and he narrowly escaped with his life), the town of Glasgow was besieged by rebels, and the whole of the west was up in arms. A Declaration was issued at Hamilton, stating the reasons for continuing in arms. These were: first, the defence of the Protestant religion, the Covenants, and the kingly authority of Christ over His Church; second, the defence of the king's person and authority in the preservation and defence of the true religion and liberties of the kingdom; third, the attempt to obtain a free and unlimited Parliament and a free General Assembly.[3] An appeal to arms in resisting tyranny is referred to as "the last remedy." Regarding

---

[1] R. Wodrow, *op. cit.*, Vol. III, p. 67.
[2] J. H. Thomson tells of visiting this area and of finding a school erected on the site of the battle—a circumstance oddly symbolic of the Scottish tradition of education. Over the door was the inscription: "1839. On the battle field of Drumclog, this seminary of education was erected in memory of those Christian heroes, who on Sabbath, the 1st of June, 1679, nobly fought in defence of civil and religious liberty. Dieu et mon droit", *op. cit.*, p. 38.
[3] *A Cloud of Witnesses*, pp. 79f.

the second point here, there was some dissension among the rebels. It had been included in the National Covenant, but the more extreme elements now declared: "We had not the same cause to keep it as they the original compilers had to put it in."[1] However, after a struggle the more moderate spirits carried the day.

This rebellion proved to be more formidable than the march to the Pentlands thirteen years before, since it came at a time when the whole country was so incensed against Lauderdale that it was found impossible to subdue the revolted district without aid from England. Yet once again the ferocious and uncompromising attitude of the extremists, both in religion and politics, precluded the turning of the occasion into a national rising which might have secured a reasonable settlement from the Government. The former did not want a reasonable settlement. They would listen to no suggestion of compromise. They were fighting for a principle, and the Scottish capacity for that has persisted in ecclesiastical matters to this day. So typical is this kind of attitude of a section of the people, indeed, that more than eighty years after the Restoration we find the Secession Church issuing a statement that its members considered that they were "bound by our Covenants, National and Solemn League," and two years later, in 1744, these were made the terms of communion.[2]

The rebels were cruelly suppressed after this second uprising. It would be tedious to recount the complete story which traverses the well-worn track of 1651 with its feuds in the Covenanting camp and its characteristic "purging" of dissenters. The ministers, with that fanatical zeal which so often spelt the ruin of Covenanting enterprises, insisted that the object of the rising was the establishment of Presbyterianism as supreme over all other forms of church government. In this they prevailed over many of the country gentlemen and the more moderate clergy who thought that they should aim at something which might reasonably be attained—the exercise of their own form of worship unhindered by the State. In vain did these moderates point out that the first thing to be done was to defeat the Duke of Monmouth who had been sent to quell the rising. The zealots worked themselves into a frenzy, calling their more cautious brethren "the Erastian party," affirming that they were worse than the Malignants, and making all kinds of wild threats.[3]

They were crushed at Bothwell Bridge in June 1679 by a vastly superior governmental force.[4] The intercession of the Duke of

[1] A. Shields, *A Hind Let Loose*, p. 102.
[2] Cf. J. McKerrow, *History of the Secession Church*, 1839, p. 184.
[3] Cf. J. Fyfe, *Scottish Diaries and Memoirs*, 1550–1746, 1927, pp. 302f.
[4] See William Aiton, *A History of the Rencounter at Drumclog, and Battle at Bothwell*

Monmouth (an illegitimate son of the king) gave them a brief respite from their persecutors, but the arrival of the Duke of York a little later was the signal for renewed vengeance on the heads of the dissidents. The 1,200 prisoners taken at Bothwell were barbarously treated and confined in that same Greyfriars Churchyard where, forty years earlier, enthusiastic crowds had jostled in their eagerness to subscribe the Covenant. For three months the captives, without shelter, were exposed to all the vicissitudes of the Scottish climate. Thereafter, on the approach of winter, some wooden huts were erected which, comments Wodrow, "was mightily boasted as a great favour." The same author gives a harrowing account of the pathetic plight of the prisoners in Greyfriars.[1]

Two of their ministers, John King and John Kid, were hanged; five men were executed on Magus Moor to avenge the murder of Sharp, of which deed they were wholly innocent; some escaped; many got their liberty on the most humiliating terms; others died from exposure; the remaining 257 were sentenced to banishment to Barbadoes. These latter, on 15th November, were put aboard ship at Leith. For the first twelve days the ship lay at anchor. The prisoners were subjected to appalling cruelties. Robert Wodrow takes up the story:

> They were stowed under deck in so little room, that the most part of them behoved still to stand, to give room to such who were sickly, and seemingly a dying: they were pinned so close, they almost never got themselves moved, and were almost stifled for want of air. Two hundred and fifty seven of them being pent up in the room which could scarce have contained a hundred, many of them frequently fainted, being almost suffocated. The seamen's rudeness and inhumanity to them was singular. . . .

After giving further details of the confinement, in language which twentieth-century eyes would find offensive, Wodrow then quotes the words of James Corson, one of the victims "that all the trouble they met with since Bothwell, was not to be compared to one day in their present circumstances; that their uneasiness was beyond words: yet he owns, in very pathetical terms, that the consolations of God overbalanced all, and expresses his hopes that they are near their port, and heaven is open for them."[2]

It proved to be a prophetic word. The ship eventually set sail, but on 10th December it foundered off the Orcadian coast. The

---

Bridge, 1821. After Bothwell an English ballad called "Jockey's Downfall," by Milton's nephew, John Phillips, began: "How now, Jockie, what again? Does the Covenant ride thee still?" (*Roxburghe Ballads*, iv. 541.)

[1] *Op. cit.*, Vol. III, p. 125.
[2] *Ibid.*, pp. 130f.; cf. W. L. Mathieson, *op. cit.*, Vol. II, p. 282.

captain refused to uncover the hatches under which about 200 prisoners were locked, and only fifty others survived to be transported as slaves to the plantations. The ship's crew escaped, and were never even called to account for this dreadful deed. Law Mathieson, while admitting the captain's barbarous inhumanity, seems just as concerned to blame John Blackadder for having earlier persuaded the prisoners not to take the bond, which submission might have prevented their transportation.[1]

Since 1677 the work of prosecution had been largely in the hands of Sir George Mackenzie of Rosehaugh, the Lord Advocate, a man from whom the Covenanters could expect (and certainly received) less than impartial justice. "No Advocate," he boasted towards the close of his career, "has ever screwed the prerogative higher than I have. I deserve to have my statue placed riding behind Charles II in the Parliament Close."[2] Scott terms him "the Bluidy Advocate MacKenyie" (in "Wandering Willie's Tale") "who, for his worldly wit and wisdom, had been to the rest as a god."

The Duke of York visited Scotland in November 1679, and Robert McWard in a letter to either Cargill or Cameron (the recipient is not known for sure) lamented the favourable reception the Duke got. "What may the United Provinces think of us?" he asks, "when their Courants shall be filled with the stories of this solemn and sumptuous Reception, appointed for welcoming such a declared Enemy to Religion and Liberty?"[3] The state of Scotland after the uprising was worse than before. All over the southwest horses were seized, houses pillaged, people tortured and harassed. Even lending a plough to one alleged to have been at Bothwell was sufficient ground for savage reprisals. Life became so unbearable that many left Scotland for foreign countries at this time.[4]

Those who refused to take the oath of abjuration of the Covenant were shot down without trial. The last two years of Charles's reign began what was justifiably known as the Killing Times, when many a solitary grave was dug in haste, and many a rough tombstone recounted a plain unlettered tale of wrong and gave a strong assertion of faith. One such inscription, typical of those on the tombs of the martyrs, can still be seen near the churchyard of Irongray in Dumfriesshire. It reads:

Here lyes Edward Gordon and Alexander M'Cubine, Martyres,

[1] *Op. cit.*, Vol. II, p. 282.
[2] A. Smellie, *op. cit.*, p. 280. Mackenzie is chiefly now remembered for having been the founder of the Advocates' Library, Edinburgh, in 1680.
[3] Letter appended to *Faithful Contendings Displayed*, p. 334.
[4] R. Wodrow, *op. cit.*, Vol. III, p. 123.

hanged without law by Lagg and Cap. Bruce, for adhering to the
Word of God, Christ's kingly government in his house, and the
Covenanted work of Reformation against tyranny, perjury, and
prelacy.

Rev.xii.11. March 3, 1685

> As Lagg and bloodie Bruce command
> We were hung up by hellish hand;
> And thus their furious rage to stay
> We died near Kirk of Irongray.
> Here now in peace sweet rest we take
> Once murdered for religion's sake.

Thanks to Monmouth, an Act of Indemnity had been passed
for those who had fought at Bothwell, and in June 1679 a Third
Indulgence for ministers had been published. Conditions, however, were attached, and there were few who did not reject them.
An exception was Robert Law, writer of the famous *Memorialls*,
who was now restored to his former parish of New Kilpatrick.
Clemency was then thrown aside once more, and diligent search
made for those who had been out at Bothwell. Thumbkins and
lighted matches were freely used by the savage soldiers of the
Government in an attempt to force unwilling informers to reveal
their secrets. The Church went underground. "Where is the
Church in Scotland at this day?" exclaimed Alexander Peden. "It
is not amongst the Government clergy. I will tell you where the
Church is. It is wherever a praying young man or young woman
is at a dykeside in Scotland: that is where the Church is."[1]

One result of the 1679 rising was the elimination of the moderate Covenanters as a vital force in the country. Until then there
had been two sections of non-indulged clergy. The more extreme,
inspired by the exiles John Brown and Robert McWard, *in
absentia*, was openly rebellious and, moreover, began to advocate
"separation" from the indulged ministers. The more moderate
party, led by John Welsh and John Blackadder, was not clear on
the point of rebellion. Blackadder held that "the Lord called for a
testimony by suffering rather than by outward deliverance."[2] This
cleavage, which was in the rebels' camp before Bothwell Bridge,
greatly contributed to their defeat. Blackadder was imprisoned on
the Bass Rock, where he later died; Welsh escaped into England.

In his examination before the Council, Blackadder maintained
that he was under the strictest obligation to exercise his ministry,
whatever Acts of Parliament had been passed, for his commission
was from the Word of God. He had strongly deprecated the prac-

[1] K. Hewat, *Peden the Prophet*, 1911, pp. 82f.
[2] *Memoirs*, pp. 212ff.

tice of carrying arms to conventicles, and advised his colleagues continually to put little trust in weapons of war. With his departure a moderating influence was taken away from the Covenanters. Oppression once more had its natural consequences—wild men were made wilder, and control of the resistance movement passed completely into the hands of the extremists. James Atkine, Bishop of Galloway (1680–7), was given a special dispensation to live in Edinburgh, "because it was thought unreasonable to oblige a reverend prelate of his years to live among such a rebellious and turbulent people, as those of that diocese were. . . ."[1]

The Government continued to find its chief opponents in the Covenanters of the south-western counties. Two ministers, Richard Cameron and Donald Cargill, were the leaders, and their followers were known as "Society People," having organized themselves into local bands. By 1683, Gordon of Earlston records, there were eighty societies in Scotland, with 7,000 men in membership, many with wives and children as steadfast as they. Members were known also as Cameronians, Hillmen, Wanderers or Wild Whigs. (The latter term had been in use for about twenty years.) These people held that the Government had forfeited all right to the allegiance of the people, and that the king was worthy of death for his tyrannical rule.

No one could be a member of a Society Meeting who did any of the following things: ". . . took any of the bonds tendered by the Government, who paid cess, locality or militia money to the civil authorities or stipends to the curates or indulged clergy; made use of a government pass, voluntarily appeared before any court of law, supplied any commodities to the enemy, allowed another to do any of these things in their name, or who in any form recognized the ministry of the indulged or silent Presbyterians." While this is evidence of their exclusiveness, it shows also their determination to have nothing to do with those who for other than religious reasons might have had a grudge against the Government—a point further underlined by their attitude later to the political uprising under Argyle, which we shall discuss shortly.

At the beginning of June 1680, Henry Hall of Haughhead was surprised and seized at South Queensferry, near Edinburgh. He was found to be in possession of a Covenanting manifesto, known thereafter as the Queensferry Paper, which evidently was the joint product of Hall and Donald Cargill. It set forth at great length their theories of an ideal state: an ecclesiastical oligarchy with no obligations to any king. Though it was incomplete, the Queensferry Paper asserts a doctrine which must have been especially odious to Charles II and his colleagues—the absolute necessity

[1] *Athenae Oxonienses*, Vol. 4, p. 871.

of moral character in a ruler, no matter what office he holds. John Brown of Wamphray had made a similar point in declaring that the character of the authority determines the extent of the subject's obedience.

The Queensferry Paper was a stepping-stone to the more famous Sanquhar Declaration made on 22nd June, about which something fuller should be said. On that date, the anniversary of the battle of Bothwell Bridge, Richard Cameron and a band of twenty men with drawn swords rode up to the old Burgh Cross of Sanquhar. There they delivered themselves of an audacious Declaration. Unlike many of the Covenanting effusions, it is not long, and we propose to reproduce it now in full, both on account of its importance, and because it is a typical piece of Covenanting defiance:

It is not amongst the smallest of the Lord's mercies to this poor land, that there have been always some who have given their testimony against every course of defection (that many are yet guilty of) which is a token for good, that he doth not as yet intend to cast us off altogether, but that he will leave a remnant in whom he will be glorious if they, through his grace, keep themselves clean still, and walk in his way and method, as it has been walked in and owned by him in our predecessors of truly worthy memory in their carrying on of our noble work of reformation in the several steps thereof from popery, prelacy, and likewise Erastian supremacy so much usurped by him who (it is true so far as we know) is descended from the race of our kings, yet he hath so far deborded from what he ought to have been, by his perjury and usurpation in church matters, and tyranny in matters civil, as is known by the whole land, that we have just reason to account it one of the Lord's great controversies against us that we have not disowned him and the men of his practices (whether inferior magistrates or any other) as enemies to our Lord and his crown and the true Protestant and Presbyterian interest in these lands, our Lord's espoused bride and church.

Therefore, although we be for government and governors such as the Word of God and our covenant allows, yet we for ourselves and all that will adhere to us, as the representative of the true Presbyterian kirk and covenanted nation of Scotland, considering the great hazard of lying under such a sin any longer, do by these presents disown Charles Stuart, that has been reigning (or rather tyrannizing as we may say) on the throne of Britain these years bygone, as having any right, title or interest in the said crown of Scotland for government, as forfeited several years since by his perjury and breach of covenant both to God and his kirk, and usurpation of his crown and royal prerogatives therein, and many other breaches in matters ecclesiastic, and by his tyranny and breach of the very *leges regnandi* in matters civil. For which reason, we declare, that several years since he should have been denuded of being king, ruler or magistrate, or of having any power to act or to be obeyed as such. As also, we being under the standard of our Lord Jesus Christ, and his cause and covenants; and against all such as have strengthened him, sided with, or any wise acknowledge any other in the like usurpation and tyranny, far more against such as would betray or deliver up our free reformed mother-kirk into the bondage of Antichrist, the pope of Rome. And by this we homologate that testimony given at Ruther-glen the 29th of May 1679, and all the faithful testimonies of those who have suffered of late. And we do disclaim that Declaration published at Hamilton, June 1679, chiefly because it takes the king's interest, which we are several years since loosed from, because of the foresaid reasons, and others, which may after this (if the Lord will) be published.

As also we disown, and by this resent the reception of the Duke of York, that professed papist, as repugnant to our principles and vows to the most high God, and as that which is the great, though not alone, just reproach of our kirk and nation. We also by this protest against his succeeding to the crown; and whatever has been done, or any are essaying to do in this land (given to the Lord) in prejudice to our work of reformation. And to conclude, we hope after this none will blame us for or offend at our rewarding those that are against us, as the Lord gives opportunity. This is not to exclude any that have declined, if they be willing to give satisfaction according to the degree of their offence.

Given at Sanquhar, June 22d. 1680.

This Declaration, according to Hume Brown, was not a novelty in the history of the Christian Church. "Theologians Roman Catholic, Anglican, Episcopalian, and Presbyterian, all at one time or other have taught or enforced the right of subjects to cast off rulers accused of seeking to destroy the true religion."[1]

It is significant, first, that the Declaration directs its anathemas against Charles II as the chief author of the persecution; and that it does so, moreover, for his civil as well as for his ecclesiastical tyranny. We have met this latter point before in connection with the Covenanters. They were always quick to recognize that freedom of religion and civil liberty, as someone has put it, are like Hippocrates's twins—they weep or laugh, live or die together. Prelacy was associated as much with the absolutism of the throne in the State as in the Church.

Second, it is an ominous feature that the Cameronians should here repudiate the Hamilton Declaration as being too moderate. Next, the Sanquhar document does not fail to realize the import of the fact of the Roman Catholic Duke of York as heir-presumptive to the throne. It is in keeping with all this to find that these Covenanters made their abjuration a religious act. They prefaced

[1] *History of Scotland*, 1909, Vol. 2, p. 327.

and followed the oath of insurrection at Sanquhar by the worship of God, confident that they were disavowing King Charles in the interests of King Jesus; setting aside a despotism in order to establish a theocracy.

Finally, we should note that this was the first public statement of the Covenanters in which allegiance to Charles II was renounced, because of the supremacy he claimed over the Church. The sentence was futile, the gesture ostensibly fanatical, but it made Cameron a hero in the eyes of the persecuted. Nevertheless there is more clear-sightedness in the Sanquhar Declaration than is at first apparent. If it represented only a small minority in 1680, it is remarkable that nine years later it expressed the mind of Great Britain as a whole. Regarded as traitorous at its publication, it was true enough to become the basis for the Revolution Settlement. Richard Cameron constantly prophesied the extinction of the Stuart line "for their treachery, lechery, but especially their usurping the royal prerogatives of King Christ."[1]

The last night of Cameron's life was spent under a hospitable roof near the Water of Ayr. The next morning, 28th June 1680 (it is said), he looked at his hands after washing them, and laid them on his face with the words: "This is their last washing. I have need to make them clean for there is many to see them." The housewife's aged mother began to weep. "Weep not for me," said the minister, "but for yourself and yours, and for the sins of a sinful land; for ye have many melancholy, sorrowful, weary days before you."[2] That same day Cameron and his little band were surprised at Ayrsmoss by a troop of dragoons. When he saw there was no escape, Cameron said to his brother: "Michael, come let us fight it out to the last; for this is the day that I have longed for, and the death that I have prayed for, to die fighting against our Lord's avowed enemies; and this is the day that we will get the crown."[3] The rebels fought desperately, but they were heavily outnumbered and eventually overwhelmed.

In the course of the battle Cameron, the Lion of the Covenant, was killed and his head and hands cut off by Robert Murray and carried to Edinburgh, for the promised reward. The victor could not forbear from paying tribute to a fallen foe when he handed over the gruesome relics to the Council. "There," he said, "are the head and hands of a man who lived praying and preaching, and died praying and fighting." Cameron's father was at the time imprisoned in the Tolbooth for refusing to pay a fine imposed for holding conventicles in his house in Falkland. His son's head and hands were for some sadistic reason carried to him. He was asked if he knew them. He took them, kissed them, and said: "I know them, I know them, they are my son's, my dear son's. . . . It is the Lord, good is the will of the Lord, who cannot wrong me nor mine, but has made goodness and mercy to follow us all our days."[1]

Another Covenanter, David Hackston of Rathillet, was wounded and captured at Ayrsmoss. He was known to have been present at the assassination of Archbishop Sharp, though he denied that he had taken part in the deed. To the wounded man the Scottish Council meted out a dreadful penalty, incorporated thus in its minutes:

That his body be drawn backward on a hurdle to the Mercat Cross; that there be an high scaffold erected . . . where, in the first place, his right hand is to be struck off, and, after some time, his left hand. Then he is to be hanged up and cut down alive, his bowels to be taken out, and his heart shown to the people by the hangman; then his heart and his bowels to be burned in a fire prepared for that purpose . . . his head to be cut off, and his body divided into four quarters . . . that none presume to be in mourning for him, or any coffin brought. . . .[2]

It would be superfluous to comment upon a government which could devise such atrocities—even the ancient Romans allowed their crucified victims decent burial.

Just before his execution Hackston was brought before the Council and asked if he owned the king's authority. He answered that there could be no lawful authority but what was of God; that authority was in direct opposition to God by employing murderers in its service, using them to kill and oppress the Lord's people. Bishop Paterson asked him if ever Pilate and that judicature who were direct enemies to Christ were disowned by Him as judges. No answer appears to have been given. Taken before the Justiciary, Hackston declined the king's authority because he was a usurper of the prerogative of the Son of God, and declined the Court as having no power as competent judges because they had arrogated to themselves supreme power over the Church.

Two months later Donald Cargill, veteran preacher and former minister of the Barony, Glasgow, preached at Torwood from the significant text, "Thus saith the Lord God, Remove the diadem and take off the crown" (Ezekiel 21: 26). After the service of worship was over, Cargill, "sparing neither left-hand declensions nor right-hand extremes," excommunicated the king, the Duke of York, Monmouth, Rothes, Mackenzie, and Dalziel. This was the

[1] P. Walker, *op. cit.*, Vol. I, pp. 234f.
[2] R. Wodrow, *op. cit.*, Vol. II, p. 142.

Torwood Declaration, and similar pronouncements were made in other parts of the west. There is something very striking about the scene at Torwood which might lend itself to an effective painting.

A note of humour was curiously found in regard to Cargill's solemn pronouncement. Lauderdale was somehow forgotten at the morning service, but not for long, according to a letter which the Duke received from the Bishop of Edinburgh, saying: "Your Grace was forgotten by him in the forenoon; but uncanonicallie he brought you up in the afternoon, and after ane scurrilous apologie for his omission, he proceeded with his blunt thunder against you. . . ." But the Government did not regard the action lightly, and thereafter paid Cargill the compliment of raising the reward for his capture to 5,000 merks.

Two things should be noted about the Torwood Declaration: first, that the excommunication was the logical next step after the civil disowning of the king at Sanquhar; and second, that the sentence passed by Cargill was also implicitly founded upon the same grounds as were used afterwards in the British renunciation of the Stuarts. The principal reasons which the Cameronians gave, however, were these: the perjury of the king in breaking and burning the Solemn League and Covenant which he had twice sworn to uphold; his persecution of the cause which he had professed to be the cause of the Lord; and his disloyalty to God, as shown in his own flagrantly immoral conduct.

These were the points which Cargill stressed. He would probably have added, if challenged, that the civil liberties of citizens —simply as citizens—did not form the chief basis of his action. This would be as well, for rebellion against a lawful monarch must necessarily be legally weak, and be dependent rather upon its moral strength. The Covenanting appeal was to God and to conscience, which transcends legal considerations. The danger in such a position is that it may open the door to Antinomianism, but we shall see in the next chapter how the perspicacious Covenanters both realized and combated that danger.

On another occasion Cargill declared:

> But now you see what is the duty or office of a king . . . what has the king done and these rulers? Their exercise in these kingdoms has been to debauch folk from their obedience to God; in a word, it has been to exauterate that authority of God, and introduce and heighten men's authority; and has not that been that which all of them has been carrying on? Let the commands of men be great to you, and the commands of God be small; this they have employed themselves all into: but never a word of the commands of God, nor his authority.[1]

[1] J. Kirkton, op. cit., pp. 74f.(n.).

That the fight of the Covenanters was against Charles II the man, and not against kingship, was seen in August 1680, in a speech by John Malcolm from the scaffold in Edinburgh. This was, of course, a common Covenanting disclaimer. Malcolm denied the charge "that Presbyterians, and I amongst the rest, had cast off all fear of God and are against all good order and civil law," a point on which also there was unanimity among the Covenanters. Malcolm goes on: "I declare I adhere to kingly government, but not to perjury and tyranny, turning upside down Church and State, contrary to the Word of God, our Covenants. . . ."[1]

The Cameronians thus still held to the Protestant principle earlier expounded by George Gillespie, that infidelity or difference of religion does not of itself nullify the magistrate's legal authority. What they rejected was the false interpretation put upon it which made it an argument in defence of tyranny and arbitrary power. At that time, recounts Kirkton, "when Skene, Potter, and Stuart were hanged, Potter on the scaffold seemed to hesitate, and it was thought would have accepted of the pardon offered if he would say 'God save the King;' but his wife squeezing his arm, almost pushed him off the ladder, and said: 'Go die for the good old cause, my dear; see Mr. Skene (who was already executed) will sup this night with Christ Jesus?'"[2] James Renwick also reiterated the distinction between "magistracy or the office (in the abstract), and the persons invested with the office."[3]

Cargill was taken shortly afterwards, tried in Edinburgh, and asked the customary question: whether he acknowledged the king's authority. He answered that as the magistrate's authority was at present established by Act of Parliament, he denied the same. Regarding the excommunication carried out by him at Torwood, he declined to answer, since it was an ecclesiastical matter, and this a civil judicatory. He owned the lawfulness of defensive arms in case of necessity (a point made previously by John Brown of Wamphray), and denied that those who rose at Bothwell were rebels. Interrogated about the Sanquhar Declaration, he declined to give judgment till he had more time to peruse its contents. The Council enquired how he felt with regard to the killing of the Archbishop; Cargill would not commit himself here, but said that the Scriptures affirm that if the Lord gives a call to a private man to kill, then he might do so lawfully. He cited the instances of Phinehas and Jael.[4]

[1] *A Cloud of Witnesses*, p. 73.
[2] J. Kirkton, *op. cit.*, p. x (editorial footnote).
[3] *An Informatory Vindication*, p. 36.
[4] J. Howie, *op. cit.*, pp. 450–3.

Despite his advanced years, Cargill was condemned to death, the decision having been arrived at on the casting vote of the Earl of Argyle. "God knows," said the old man, as he climbed the scaffold steps on 28th July, 1681, "I go up this ladder with less fear and perturbation of mind than ever I entered a pulpit to preach."[1] His head was fixed on a spike on the Netherbow Port next that of Cameron. About the same time fifteen or sixteen others, including some women, suffered a like fate. Cargill's death deprived the Cameronians temporarily of a minister.

On the same day as Cargill, Walter Smith, a student of theology, was hanged. His case shows little of the sheer fanaticism which we found in Richard Cameron. Smith was a Covenanter, but not a Cameronian. The Council confronted him with the usual questions, and were in turn confronted with the usual answers expressed with moderation and firmness. He was asked if the king's falling away from the Covenant thereby loosed him (Smith) from his obedience, and loosed the king from his authority. Smith answered that the king was only to be obeyed in so far as he himself obeyed the Word of God and conformed to the Covenant. He was asked his opinion of the Torwood Excommunication, and declared that he thought "their reasons were just." When he was brought before the Council for the second time, Smith was asked if he owned the Sanquhar Declaration. It was read to him, and he admitted that all the articles were approved by him—except that he did not regard the declarers as the formal representatives of the Presbyterian Church, as they had called themselves. He must have been a remarkable young man: it must take a great amount of conviction and courage to disagree with a previous martyr—especially when one is about to be executed for substantially the same cause. Smith told the Council that what the king had done justified the people in revolting against him.

This left the Cameronians for a time without a clerical spokesman, but their resistance continued, heartened by their unflinching confidence that "God . . . still leaned from heaven to observe the doings of His moorland remnant."

---

[1] *A Cloud of Witnesses*, p. 10.

CHAPTER X

THE KILLING TIME

WILLIAM WORDSWORTH HAS CALLED THE DUKE OF YORK, brother of Charles II, "the vacillating bondman of the Pope." Patrick Walker, who knew the gentleman concerned but took no pleasure in the fact, ascribed to him an even more dubious affiliation—"the devil's lieutenant." This servant of the Covenanters' two greatest adversaries succeeded Lauderdale as Royal Commissioner in Scotland in 1681. The Duke was a Roman Catholic,[1] anxious to consolidate his position as heir-presumptive to the throne. He persuaded the Scottish Parliament to pass the Act of Succession, which declared that the kings of the realm derived their power from God, succeeding to it by lineal descent, and that no difference in religions could alter that circumstance. A bill for excluding him from the throne of England had been passed through the House of Commons in October 1680, but by the king's influence it was rejected by the Lords.

This was followed a few months later by the Test Act which required every holder of office to swear that he owned the Protestant religion, acknowledged the supremacy of the king in all causes, would not consult about any state matter without royal licence, and would never endeavour to alter anything in the government of the land—a most comprehensive statement! Never had the Scottish Parliament been so obliging in its abject subservience. It showed, remarks Dr. Cunningham, "that patriotism had long since left the house where they sat by passing this Act, and dooming the country to oriental despotism."[2] Significantly enough, a separate clause was appended which exempted the Duke of York himself from taking the oath. "The Test now became as great an instrument of persecution as the Covenant had once been," concedes Law Mathieson, who quotes from a letter written a few years later on the subject, thus: "I believe that both Covenant and Test were formed by Church Men to ruin each other by turns, and were tricks of kirk and church."[3]

[1] That same year, a Roman Catholic emissary who travelled extensively throughout the country reported to the Congregation of Propaganda in Rome that he had found 14,000 communicants in Scotland.
[2] *Church History of Scotland*, 1859, Vol. II, p. 228.
[3] *Op. cit.*, Vol. II, p. 307.

Even such a mild man as Sir James Dalrymple, President of the Court of Session, resigned his office rather than accept the Test; and eighty of the regular Episcopalian clergy, led by Laurence Charteris, refused to take it and resigned from their parishes. Twenty of them went to England, where Gilbert Burnet succeeded in getting them settled in parishes. So "self-contradictory" were the terms of the Test, according to Michael Shields,[1] that it was generally considered that he who took it implied that he was Presbyterian, Episcopalian, and Roman Catholic all at once. We quote this Act as an appendix (Appendix IV) for the purpose of showing how accurate is the criticism of it.

On 12th January, 1682, some fifty of the Covenanters published at Lanark a fresh declaration, and burned the Succession and Test Acts. Among their usual epithets they sensibly found room for the word "ridiculous" in their description of the latter Act. This declaration, substantially a repetition of previous Covenanting utterances, was the cue for an even more fierce war between the Society Men and the Government, in which Dalziel and Claverhouse earned for themselves infamous reputations. Their work was ably continued by the Bluidy Mackenzie (Sir George), the Lord Advocate, who was pitiless in his prosecutions. Victims were sent to slavery or fined, some shot, some hanged. Many were tortured. Part of an inscription on the gravestone of seven martyrs at Ayr reads: "Boots, thumbkins, gibbets, were in fashion then: Lord, let us never see such days again." It is small wonder that we find the Society People at a General Meeting in March 1682 resolving that each of its members should "provide for himself fit weapons, in case there should be any need requiring the same."[2]

Acceptance of the Test was extended to all people on pain of execution—which could be summary execution without trial. Many were thus put to death by the notorious Grierson of Lagg, the model of Scott's character of Redgauntlet:

Ye maun have heard of Sir Robert Redgauntlet of that Ilk, who lived in these parts before the dear years. The country will lang mind him; and our fathers used to draw breath thick if ever they heard him named . . . Redgauntlet was aye for the strong hand, and his name is kenned as wide as Claverhouse's or Tam Dalyell's. Glen, nor dargle, nor mountain, nor cave, could hide the puir Hill-Folk when Redgauntlet was out with bugle and bloodhound after them, as if they had been sae mony deer. And, troth, when they fand them, they didna mak' muckle ceremony. It was just, "Will ye tak' the Test,

---

[1] *Faithful Contendings*, p. 6.
[2] M. Shields, *op. cit.*, p. 19.

then?"—and if not, "Make ready; present; fire!"—and there lay the recusant.[1]

Robert Garnock and five others, brought before the Council in October 1681, delivered a paper to the judges containing a Protestation and warning, advising the latter to consider what they (the judges) were doing, and upon what grounds they passed sentence. They further declared that they were not rebels, for they disowned no authority that was according to the Word of God, and the Covenants by which the land was ruled. They charged the judges to consider how deep a sin covenant-breaking was. They were executed. The judicial ears had heard all this many times before.

The charge of rebellion against the State is one that has constantly been brought against Christians down through the ages for almost every persecution carried out against them. "If a Jezebel wants a Naboth's vineyard," one old writer points out in apt illustration, "and he stands up for his property, she will not want sons of Belial to bear witness that he 'blasphemed God and the king.' "[2] To the Romans the Christians were rebels because they would not swear by the life of Caesar or adore his image. Therefore, *Christianos ad Leones!*

Captured in November 1683 and charged with rebellion, John Nisbet was asked if he owned the king. He replied that while the king owned the way and work of God he thought himself bound both to own and fight for him; and when he quitted the way of God, he thought himself obliged to quit him. Just before his execution, Nisbet made a prophecy similar to that of Richard Cameron: "I am persuaded," he declared, "that Scotland's covenanted God will cut off the name of Stuart, because they have stated themselves against religion, reformation, and . . . Christ's kingdom and kingly government . . . and although men idolize them so much now, yet ere long there shall be none of them to tyrannize in covenanted Britain any more."[3] It is noteworthy that Nisbet, in common with many of his fellows, spoke thus of "Britain," thereby implying that England and Ireland were still bound by the Solemn League and Covenant.

Charles II ended his inglorious reign on 6th February 1685, in his fifty-sixth year, and received Roman Catholic absolution on his deathbed.[4] On looking back over his reign, we can perhaps trace two designs in his policy: first, to consolidate his own supremacy; second, to make the Church as comprehensive as

[1] "Wandering Willie's Tale" in *Redgauntlet*.
[2] *A Cloud of Witnesses*, Preface, p. xxix.
[3] J. Howie, *op. cit.*, p. 504; cf. M. Shields, *op. cit.*, p. 110.
[4] O. Airy, *Charles II*, 1904, pp. 411–14; J. Kirkton, *op. cit.*, p. 133.

possible, probably for the sake of the peace of the country. Hume Brown would add a third aim of Charles: that of filling his own purse.[1] Humanly speaking, the project was wise and even laudable to some degree. The Covenanting spirit upset his plans by running directly counter to him, particularly on the second issue.

For religion itself Charles cared not a button while he was well, and when left to himself he was inclined to decide spiritual matters on the basis of etiquette. Possibly that was what G. K. Chesterton had in mind when he suggested that Charles "could not keep the Ten Commandments, but he kept the ten thousand commandments." We remember, for example, that on one occasion he referred to Presbyterianism as being no religion for a gentleman,[2] but the king's religion of a gentleman, in Hallam's view, "was a religion of the boots and thumbscrew, which a good man must be very cold-blooded indeed if he did not hate and reject it from the hands that offered it."[3]

The king's cynicism led him to believe, in somewhat Hobbesian fashion, that no one did good except for the purpose of self-interest. He was unprincipled and mean, vindictive and remorseless. It is doubtful if he ever spared the lives of any whom motives of revenge or policy prompted him to destroy. Gilbert Burnet, who has a happy flair for the succinct summary, says of Charles: "A secularist, he shook off Presbyterianism as a viper, utilized Episcopacy as the readiest political tool, and finally put on Popery as a comfortable shroud to die in."[4] Referring to Charles's powers of dissimulation, James Kirkton adds dryly, "every man had at least fair words and big promises."[5] We can guess how such a personality was likely to be regarded in Scotland, especially by the Covenanters, whom the Scots people themselves characterized in their own expressive way as the "unco' guid."[6]

It is difficult to judge Charles fairly when we take into consideration his turbulent boyhood in the Civil War, his broken home, his wanderings on the Continent. His relations with Scotland, a land which he never once visited after 1651, were not creditable, but not all the wrong was done on one side. In any case, can we ever reasonably expect the Christian ethic where there is no Christian experience? It is tempting to judge him against an ideal—possibly one akin to Covenanting notions—and to cast Charles off as a

[1] Op. cit., Vol. II, p. 333.
[2] G. Burnet, op. cit., Vol. I, p. 195.
[3] Constitutional History, 1862, Vol. III, p. 334.
[4] Op. cit., Vol. II, pp. 464-74.
[5] Op. cit., p. 59.
[6] This is a peculiarly Scots expression which defies adequate translation into standard English parlance. It is used generally as a sly reference to those people who are thought to consider themselves more pious than others.

monster of iniquity. One can appreciate, however, that even a
Christian king would have been sore put to it to cope with the
Cameronians.[1]

Yet nothing illustrates Charles's rule so much as the contrast
between the jubilant enthusiasm shown on his Restoration twenty-
five years earlier, both in London and in Edinburgh, and the
niggardly, almost hurried funeral accorded him by his brother,
amid the gloomy foreboding of the majority of people in England
and Scotland. To Charles might well be applied with equal relevance the words spoken by John Knox of Mary of Guise more
than a century before: she "was unhappy to Scotland from the
first day she entered it unto the day she ended her unhappy life."[2]

Uninhibited by the nice scruple against saying anything dis-
paraging of the newly dead, the Cameronians took advantage of
the occasion to make a résumé of the deceased's dealings with
them. That they made out a sufficiently damning case can be seen
by the following excerpt:

> We do abhor the memory of his erection, and unhappy Restora-
> tion, after by many evidences he was known to be an enemy of God
> and the country; his nefarious wickedness in ejecting the ministers
> of Christ . . . and introducing abjured Prelacy; his atrocious arro-
> gance, in rescinding all Acts of Parliament for the works of Reforma-
> tion; his unparalleled perfidy and perjury, in making void and burn-
> ing the Covenants, his heaven-daring usurpation in arrogating to
> himself that blasphemous and Christ-dethroning supremacy; his . . .
> Indulgences to outed ministers, to divide and destroy the Church,
> his . . . tyranny over the consciences of poor people, pressing them
> to conformity with the time's abominations, contrary both to religion
> and reason, and imposing upon them conscience-debauching oaths;
> his absolute domination over the whole land in levying militia and
> other forces . . . for carrying on his wicked designs, his . . . arbitrary
> power, and bearing down the work of Reformation and enslaving
> the people; particularly in sending an host of savage and barbarous
> Highlanders several times upon a poor innocent people, to waste
> and destroy them; and imposing wicked taxations for the mainten-
> ance of these forces. . . . His cruelty over the bodies of Christians
> in chasing, catching and killing upon the fields many without sen-
> tence passed upon them or time previously to deliberate upon death;
> . . . drowning women, some of very young, and some of exceeding
> old age, imprisoning, laying in irons, exquisite tortures by boots,
> thummikins and fire-matches, cutting pieces out of the ears; banish-
> ing and selling as slaves old and young . . . bloodily butchering upon
> scaffolds . . . hanging, heading, mangling, dismembering alive, quar-
> tering dead bodies, oppressing many others in their estates; fore-

[1] For a totally different side of Charles's character, sketching his connection with
art and letters, see the *Scottish Historical Review*, Vol. III, 1906, pp. 41–52.
[2] *History*, Vol. II, p. 71.

faulting their possessions, robbing, pillaging their goods, casting . . .
out of their habitations, interdicting any to reset them, under the
pains of being treated after the same manner. . . .[1]

"Our Atlas fell indeed," sang the Roman Catholic poet Dryden,
"but Hercules was near." This Hercules, a man whom the Covenanters already knew only too well, succeeded his brother on the
throne. He had been expressively described on the gravestone of
James Harkness, one of the persecuted, as "that beist the Duke of
York." His was a cruel and revengeful disposition. He declined
to take the Coronation Oath for Scotland (which would have
bound him to uphold the Reformed religion), since it would
have hampered his designs for the re-establishment of Roman
Catholicism. The Scottish Estates, in abject submission, a state
which was becoming a habit with them, expressed their gratitude
for the blessings they owed to the sacred race of their most glorious king, and to "the solid, absolute authority with which they
were invested by the first and fundamental laws of the monarchy."

There was no slackening of the persecution. The giving or
taking of the National Covenant or of the Solemn League, or the
writing in defence thereof, or the owning of them as lawful, was
declared to be treason. This was followed by an Act which declared
that any person who preached at or attended a conventicle was to
be punished with death and confiscation of goods. Thus the
accession of James marked no change of policy towards the
Covenanters—so much the contrary, indeed, that the first twelve
months of the new reign were known as the "Black Year,"[2] when
people might have said with the Ettrick Shepherd:

> Our friends are waning fast away
> Baith frae the cliff and the wood;
> They are tearing them frae us ilka day;
> For there's naething will please but blood.

The name of Society People or Hill-Folk was now becoming
more and more common, and it was against them that the sharpest
edge of the persecution was directed. Their complete extermina-
tion seems to have been determined by the Government. The first
of their General Meetings had been held at Lesmahagow on
15th December, 1681, and it was decided to have four such meetings each year, at which representatives would be present from
every society. Nothing was to be done in matters concerning the
whole body without the knowledge and consent of the General
Meeting. This provision aimed at guarding against those "having

[1] J. Renwick, op. cit., pp. 41f.
[2] M. Shields, op. cit., pp. 165f. gives a summary of this year.

more zeal than knowledge."[1] Nevertheless they had already thrown off their allegiance to the king, and now resolved to make it known that they would not submit tamely to being butchered.

Their leader now was James Renwick, who in his twenty-second year had been ordained at Groningen in September 1683. The Dutch ministers who officiated on that occasion overlooked the fact that Renwick had declined to sign their formularies, and had protested against their church's corruptions. He had something of a history of nonconformity, for on graduation from Edinburgh University he had refused to take the customary oath of allegiance, and "publicly objected against the nauseous titles and compliments given to the then Duke of York, in the dedication of theses emitted by the class he was in."[2]

In November 1684 Renwick and his followers published an "Apologetical Declaration." This contained a warning to their persecutors that they counted them, and would punish them, as the enemies of God and His covenanted work, although they previously repudiated the principle of killing all those who differed from them. Even when driven almost to madness by persecution, the Cameronians declared "we utterly detest and abhor that hellish principle of killing all who differ in judgment and persuasion from us, as having no bottom on the Word of God, or right reason."[3] This makes nonsense of Agnes Mure Mackenzie's charge that those who refused to disown this Declaration were shot "for refusing to affirm that the murder of episcopalian ministers or of the King's servants was unlawful."[4]

The subscribers to the Declaration further stated that they would regard all who took part in the persecution—judges, soldiers, informers, false witnesses, as enemies to God and His cause. Their claim of the rights of people to rise up against a tyrannical ruler went no further than that of George Buchanan a century before. Yet we learn of only one curate, Peter Pearson of Carsphairn, who was killed by the Covenanters during all of the persecuting times. Pearson was shot by James McMichael, who, it is said, had thought that his friends were in danger. For this act McMichael was expelled from the fellowship of the Society People.[5]

The Apologetical Declaration was, however, more than negative. It set forth in the plainest terms the reasons for renouncing

[1] M. Shields, *op. cit.*, pp. 9ff.
[2] R. Wodrow, *op. cit.*, Vol. IV, p. 445.
[3] M. Shields, *op. cit.*, pp. 68f. There is some evidence to suggest that Renwick afterwards regretted the publication of this document.
[4] *The Passing of the Stuarts*, 1937, p. 259.
[5] *A Cloud of Witnesses*, p. 535.

allegiance to the king (they were referring to Charles II, who died three months afterwards): his perjury in breaking and burning the Solemn League and Covenant which he had twice sworn to observe; the rescinding of the Acts which he had vowed to uphold; his persecution of the cause which he had professed to be the cause of the Lord; and his disloyalty to God, seen in his personal immorality.

Renwick's manifesto was fixed to several market-crosses and posted up at church doors. The Government, which was never guilty of underestimating its adversaries, made this the pretext for greater severity. It at once required all people to take an Oath of Abjuration, renouncing the Declaration and provided thus for the sins of men to be visited upon wives and children: "You shall turn out all the wives and children of the forfeited estates from their habitations, if it shall appear they have conversed with their parents or husbands, or if they refuse to vindicate themselves by their oath." Every soldier was entrusted with the power of immediate execution with no pretence of trial. One victim of this was John Brown of Priesthill, in whose house, it was alleged, bullets and treasonable papers had been found. Brown refused to take the oath, and Claverhouse said: "Go to your prayers, for you shall immediately die." Three times during his prayers he was interrupted. The conclusion of the matter is told by Patrick Walker:

When ended, Claverhouse said, "Take goodnight of your wife and children." His wife standing by, with her child in her arms that she had brought forth to him, and another child of his first wife's, he came to her and said, "Now, Isabel, the day is come, that I told you would come, when I spake first to you of marrying me." She said, "Indeed, John, I can willingly part with you." Then he said, "That's all I desire, I have no more to do but die, I have been in case to meet with death for so many years." He kissed his wife and bairns, and wished purchased and promised blessings to be multiplied upon them, and his blessing. Claverhouse ordered six soldiers to shoot him; the most part of the bullets came upon his head, which scattered his brains upon the ground. Claverhouse said to his wife, "What thinkest thou of thy husband now, woman?" She said, "I thought ever much good of him, and as much now as ever." He said, "It were but justice to lay thee beside him." She said, "If ye were permitted, I doubt not but your cruelty would go that length; but how will ye make answer for this morning's work?" He said, "To man I can be answerable; and for God, I will take him in my own hand." Claverhouse mounted his horse, and marched, and left her with the corps of her dead husband lying there; she set the bairn upon the ground, and gathered his brains, and tied up his head, and straighted his body, and covered him with her plaid, and sat down and wept over him; it being a very desert place where never victual grew, and far from neighbours. . . .[1]

Andrew Hislop, a lad of seventeen, son of a widow in Annandale, was condemned to death for helping his mother care for a dying Covenanter and then bury him after he had died—a man whose name they did not even know. "I can look my death-bringers in the face without fear," said the boy stoutly, "and I have nothing to be ashamed of. . . ." After his execution the house of his mother, who had somehow eluded them, was stripped of all its possessions and then razed to the ground. "The broth was hell-hot in these days," recounted a contemporary, "they wanted long-shanked spoons that supped with the devil."[2] Michael Shields says that the Apologetical Declaration did much to deter "these intelligencers (concerning whom it was especially emitted) from that work which they were formerly employed in."[3] Shields adds that curates in some of the parishes were so terrified that they moved away in haste.

The Government had nothing to learn about terrorist tactics, however. Among many who discovered this was Sarah Kennedy of Penningham parish, whose husband William had been outlawed. Soldiers and sheriff-officers took the roof from her house and looted the contents. They made the woman, carrying an infant, walk with them six miles to Wigtown, leaving unattended in the roofless house three other children, the eldest of them only eight years old. Sarah Kennedy was kept in prison for eleven weeks. Says Wodrow: "This gentlewoman was no way obnoxious to the then laws, being a conformist with prelacy . . . only they would oblige her to swear she would never converse with her husband now put to the horn; but as soon as she knew where he was, she would discover him, and inform against him, that he might be apprehended. This she peremptorily refused."[4]

About this time Sir Robert Grierson of Lagg caused an old woman and a girl of eighteen to be drowned at Wigtown because they would not abjure the Declaration. The Abjuration read as follows: "I, A.B., do hereby abhor, renounce, and disown in the presence of Almighty God, the pretended declaration of war lately affixed at several parish Churches in so far as it declares a war against his sacred Majesty and asserts that it is lawful to kill such, and those that serve His Majesty in Church, State, army or

[1] *Op. cit.*, Vol. I, pp. 85f. Sir Walter Scott approves Walker's narratives as the best of all extant contemporary accounts of the persecuting times. So impressed was he by Walker's description of Brown's martyrdom that he said it reminded him of the Bible story of Ruth, and included it in two of his published works.
[2] Ibid., p. 329.
[3] *Op. cit.*, Vol. III, p. 155.
[4] *Op. cit.*, Vol. IV, p. 337.

F

country." With studied cruelty the girl was forced to watch her elderly companion die first, but even then she would not recant. She quoted from Romans chapter eight and sang a Psalm—"After Thy mercy think on me"—before the tide finally overwhelmed her.[1]

Many in Scotland suffered a like fate. *A Cloud of Witnesses* has the following typical terse statement: "The said Claverhouse authorized his troops to kill Matthew Mickelwrath without any examination, in the parish of Colmonnel in Carrick, anno 1685." The same work tells of seventy-eight similar cases, compressed into three of its pages.

One of those who eventually took the Oath of Abjuration was Alexander Shields. He did not do so without a struggle—and ever afterwards regretted his compliance as a great apostasy. The form of words he agreed to accept was: "I do abhor, renounce and disown in the presence of God that pretended Declaration in so far as it declares war against the King and asserts that it is lawful to kill all employed in Church, State, Army or Country." After he had done it, recounts Shields, "one that sat next said to me, I had done like a gentleman, which words gave my heart a knell, and I answered very confoundedly. . . ."

Meanwhile John Blackadder, one of the outed ministers, was languishing on the Bass Rock, where he had been imprisoned since April 1681. Bad food (for which the prisoners had to pay) and shocking living conditions had taken their toll of him so that his health began to fail. Though he was obviously dying, the old Covenanter refused to accept a certain measure of liberty (involving his transfer to the mainland) if any restraint were laid upon his ministry. He died in his dungeon at the age of seventy in December 1685. Appended to his *Memoirs* is a sermon from which shines out his steady confidence in the providence and purposes of God:

> The Lord takes such instruments and means and makes use of them for the deliverance of his church as may nonplus the wisest. . . . And therefore he will hide the instruments, manner and time of our deliverance so from our eyes, as the wisest of us shall not guess, when, or by what means or by whose hands he will turn back our captivity this day in Britain . . . I believe no man can tell what way or by whom our delivery shall come, but when it does come, it will be in such a manner as shall stop the mouth and boasting of all wise heads in the world that He alone can have the glory.

[1] This incident has prompted renewed discussion in recent years, and some have questioned its authenticity. See, however, the remarkable evidence adduced for the truth of these executions in Hector Macpherson's "The Wigtown Martyrs," in *Records of the Scottish Church History Society*, Vol. IX, 1947, pp. 166–84.

In 1685 there came a diversion from another quarter. The Earl of Argyle joined in a political conspiracy, the object of which was the overthrow of King James and the placing of the Duke of Monmouth on the British throne. The plot was premature, ill-planned and incompetently executed, and Monmouth was defeated and captured at the battle of Sedgemoor.

Argyle received no help from the Covenanters as a whole, which fact speaks well for their single-mindedness of purpose. (Alexander Peden, one of the Covenanting ministers, but not a Cameronian, was however in favour of any movement which had as its purpose the dethronement of James VII.) The contemporary Patrick Walker tells why they took no action, making four points: first, because the manifesto issued by the Argyle party was not in accordance with the Covenants; second, care had been taken not to place religion in the forefront, in case "the sectarian party should be irritate;" third, an old Covenanting standby, because it opened the door for an alliance with the Malignants; fourth, because several of the leaders of the insurrection had been responsible for condemning Covenanters to death.[1] This included Argyle himself who, previously a Covenanter, had at an earlier time forsaken the cause—and had even in the Privy Council given his casting vote for the condemnation of Donald Cargill in 1681. Argyle was beheaded in Edinburgh on 30th June, 1685.

The Covenanters gained no respite on account of their refusal to participate in this uprising, but rather suffered from it. The Government, before Argyle had been captured, was taking no chances of the Covenanters' being in league with him, and more than 200 of them who were prisoners at the time were removed to a small, airless vault in Dunottar Castle, where they had no space to lie or sit. Men and women alike were shut up in this dungeon where, through foul air and insufficient food, many of them died. The rest were eventually brought up, but not for release: they were sentenced to transportation. "Such was the judgment of the Government on the new sect from the dunghill," quotes A. M. Mackenzie, somewhat ghoulishly, "who kill by pretended inspiration, whose idol is the accursed Covenant."[2]

To the prisoners in Dunottar Castle, "above Eightscore, being Sixscore and two men, and Forty-six Women," according to Patrick Walker, Alexander Peden wrote a letter[3] in his own inimitable style, full of love and encouragement. In places Peden resembles Samuel Rutherford, as when he assures them that Christ is "the easiest merchant ever the people of God yoked with;

[1] *Op. cit.*, Vol. I, p. 102.
[2] *Op. cit.*, p. 264.
[3] The letter is quoted in full by Walker, *op. cit.*, Vol. I, pp. 110ff.

if ye be pleased with the wares, what of his graces makes best for you, he and ye will soon sort on the price; he'll sell good cheap, that ye may speir for his shop again, and he draws all the sale to himself." Then Peden goes on to speak more specifically of their present condition, writing to the prisoners:

> I counsel you to go no further than Christ; and now, when it is come to your door either to sin or suffer, I counsel you to lay your count with suffering, for an outgate coming out of any other airth will be prejudicial to your soul's interest. And for your encourage-ment, remember, he sends none a warfare on their own charges; and blest is the man that gives Christ all his money . . . and the less ye have, he has the more heart to frist you [i.e. give you credit], and so it is best for you to keep in with your old acquaintance. New acquaintance with strange lords is the ready way to make a wound in grace's side, which will not heal in haste; the sore may close before the wound dry up; for grace is a tender piece, and is very easily distempered with the backslidings of our present time; and if the wheels of it be once broke with sin, all the moyen in the world will not make it go about, until it be put in Christ's hand.

So the old saint who himself knew what it was to suffer for Christ's sake comforts his brethren. "I defy the world to steal a lamb out of Christ's flock unmist," he says, "what is a wanting at the last Day of Judgment Christ must make them all up." He concludes this section of his letter in the moving words: "Christ deals tenderly with his young plants, and waters them oft, lest they go back: be painful, and lose not life for the seeking. Grace, mercy and peace be with you." If these are the effusions of a fanatic, then they might be regarded as affording a clue as to what twentieth-century Christians need.

One of the criteria by which people in Scotland were now judged was their willingness to pray for the king. Robert McWard held that all subjects ought to pray for the conversion and salva-tion of their magistrates, even though the latter had become open tyrants and persecutors.[1] With reference to the king himself, some demurred over repeating the words "God save," because it might imply bidding him God-speed in his persecution. Possibly it was dictated to the Covenanters for that very purpose. Few scrupled to pray for the monarch in their own language. Captain Campbell offered to pray "that the Lord would give him a godly life here and a life of glory hereafter." He was answered that that was not enough, that he must pray for the king as supreme "over all per-sons and causes, ecclesiastic as well as civil." Campbell replied

---

[1] "The Banders Disbanded," in *McWard's Tracts*, 1681, pp. 48f.

that that would be praying for him as head of the Church—which prerogative was Christ's alone.[1]

This was one of the apparently unimportant points which gave the Covenanting theologians exercise for that dialectical skill so beloved of them. We cannot blame them: congenial discussion was at a premium in those days. Alexander Shields held forth at considerable length on the question of owning the ruler by saying "God save the King," and recorded his own form of prayer for the king in which he neither asks for his repentance nor for his salvation.[2] Others concerned themselves with such questions as, Is it lawful to hold communion with those who hold communion with the indulged?

That the Scottish Council sometimes became exasperated can be readily understood, especially when it was confronted with Mountain-Men such as John Nisbet. He would not acknowledge the Duke of York to be king because the Duke was a Roman Catholic. One of the members dryly commented that it seemed that he (Nisbet) would own no king but Mr. Renwick. Nisbet thus concludes his own account of the interrogation: "As to drinking of healths, never one of them spoke one word to me, east or west. As to praying for their king, one of them said he knew I was that much of a Christian that I would pray for all men. I told them I reckoned myself bound to pray for all; but prayer being institute by a holy God, who was the hearer of prayer, no Christian was obliged to prayer, when every profligate commanded them; and it was of no advantage to their cause, when they suffered such a thing."[3]

The next development in Scotland was a communication to the Privy Council from King James in the best tradition of the House of Stuart. Promulgated in February 1687, it stated that his prerogative enabled him to dispense with all laws, and formally charged the Council to rescind the penal laws against Roman Catholics, and to allow the celebration of the Mass in a chapel of Holyrood Palace. Not since the Reformation had the Church of Rome been accorded such liberty in the country. Feeling ran high at this, and the measure was opposed by Bishop Atkine of Galloway. But even the Council could not ignore the fact that Scotland dreaded a return to Rome, and James had to extend to moderate Presbyterians and to Quakers the toleration he desired for his coreligionists.[4] Included in this concession was James's proclamation that "by his sovereign authority, and prerogative royal, and

[1] R. Wodrow, *op. cit.*, Vol. IV, p. 49.
[2] *A Hind Let Loose*, pp. 454ff.
[3] J. Kirkton, *op. cit.*, p. 379(n).
[4] *Acts of the Parliament of Scotland*, Vol. VIII, pp. 576–653.

absolute power, he suspends, stops, and disables all penal and sanguinary laws, for nonconformity to the religion established by law." This did not extend to field-meetings however, which were still to be prosecuted with the utmost rigour.

The implications of this move were not lost on the Society People. "In the year 1687," says Michael Shields, their faithful secretary, "the cockatrice-egg was laid; which, if the Lord crush it not, threatens the production of the basilisk of popery itself; and that sleep-drink of this Antichristian intoxicating toleration was then brewed in hell, blinked in Rome, and propined to Scotland. . . ."[1] Alexander Shields agrees with his brother; in his opinion the king's design was "to advance his own absoluteness over all laws," and afterwards, "to undermine and overturn the Protestant religion and establish Poperie and idolatrie."[2]

James's rule in the country generally became so tyrannical, in secular as well as in ecclesiastical affairs, that even Sir George Mackenzie resigned his post in anger. He made it clear that he was not prepared to travel further with James "along the road of absolutism and Roman Catholicism." Regarding James's reign as a whole, the distinction between Divine Right and the autocratic claims of Rome is not one always clearly made in Covenanting literature, though Alexander Shields distinguished between papal endeavours to recover Scotland, and the fact that "the tyrants, *alias* kings of Europe . . . are advancing their prerogatives upon the ruins of the nations and churches privileges to such a pitch of absoluteness. . . ."[3] This was also, of course, the age of Louis XIV in France, who was ruthlessly waging a campaign to stamp out Protestantism in that country.

James, it would appear, was being pulled in different directions at once by the two influences most abhorrent to the Covenanters: his House's theory of Divine Right, and his penchant towards Rome. His three immediate predecessors had clung to the first; but the sporadic Calvinism of James VI, the pronounced Anglicanism of Charles I, and the chronic atheism of Charles II (at least in practice) had led them all away from Rome, albeit in different directions.

Nevertheless, most Presbyterians no longer had any scruples about complying and accepting the new concessions of James VII. Many of the original leaders of the outed ministers were dead; others, who had never actively fought against the Government, were weary of the strife of years, alienated by the action of the extremists, and content to end their days within the Church,

[1] *Op. cit.*, p. 308.
[2] *A Hind Let Loose*, p. 165.
[3] Ibid., p. 19.

though it may not have been to them their beloved Kirk of by-gone days. They were joined by some of their colleagues who had spent years of exile on the Continent, particularly in Holland, and who were glad of the opportunity to return to their native land.

There was perhaps a further reason behind their submission: the fear that a worse thing might befall the country, stemming from their knowledge of the king's avowed ecclesiastical purpose, and the need for some sort of unity against the threat from Rome. This was a fear which had haunted the land at other times since the Reformation, a perennial national bogey, but one which now assumed gigantic proportions to the eyes of the Covenanters—not without good reason. The priests, according to Sir John Lauder of Fountainhall, "were beginning openly to keep their meetings."[1] Robert Wodrow quotes a letter from a Jesuit at Liège in which James is represented as having told a priest "that he would either convert England or die a martyr, and he had rather die the next day and convert it, than reign 20 years piously and happily, and not effect it."[2] James must have been a big disappointment to the Jesuits.

[1] *Historical Observes of Memorable Occurrents*, Bannatyne Club, 1840, p. 243.
[2] *Op. cit.*, Vol. IV, p. 403; cf. A. Shields, *A Hind Let Loose*, p. 174.

CHAPTER XI

THE REVOLUTION SETTLEMENT

THE SOCIETY PEOPLE WERE EXCLUDED FROM THE NEW ACTS
of Indulgence, as they had thrown off allegiance to the king.
They would not, in any case, have accepted them. The
massacre of the Waldensians about this time was looked upon by
the Cameronians as the result of "the sin and danger of com-
pounding with or trusting enemies, whose offers are snares, and
who know not to keep oath or promise either to God or to man."

We would not wish, however, by quoting the above remark in
isolation from Michael Shields's *Faithful Contendings*, to give a
wrong impression of the Society People's attitude towards fellow-
sufferers in other lands. They never lost sight of the vision of the
Church Universal, despite all their intolerance. Among the causes
of fasting specified by them is "the little extent of . . . our sympathy with the sufferings of other churches, as France, Hungary
and Piedmont."[1] Impoverished and harassed as they were, we find
the Society People at their General Meeting on 1st August, 1688,
making plans and raising money to be sent to Barbadoes to pur-
chase the freedom of fourteen of their fellow-countrymen in
bondage. "If there be more of the money than purchases your
relief," said their letter to the exiles, "apply it to the supply of your
necessity in your home-coming. But" (Scots thrift will out), "you
are desired to keep account of the way how you dispose of it."[2]

Regarding the fate of the Waldensians as an awful warning,
they poured scorn on the new Indulgence. Field conventicles
were still banned, their adherents still outlawed. All this time, it is
significant to observe, Government agents were travelling
throughout the country "offering all their liberty to go either to
Mass, or to the Quakers, or to the prelatic curates, or to the
tolerated meetings of Presbyterians."[3] The shadow of the Reformation was declining; Rome was gaining converts in high

---

[1] M. Shields, *op. cit.*, p. 342; cf. W. H. Goold, "Historical Retrospect of the
Reformed Presbyterian Church," in *Commemoration of the Bicentenary of the Westminster Assembly*, 1843, p. 178.

[2] M. Shields, *op. cit.*, pp. 344f.

[3] Ibid., p. 355.

places.[1] Much more now could the Cameronians apply to themselves the words of James Guthrie: "Do not all these things, put together, much heighten the danger of the Protestant religion in Scotland?"[2]

They continued in opposition, continued with their secret meetings, and averred that the king's intention was merely to facilitate the extension of popery in the land—as indeed it was.[3] They sought solace, as ever, in Old Testament analogies, and James Renwick expressed their rather curious logic thus: "We shall never ken better that God is our covenanted God than by this, that we are brought into captivity."[4] "O happy shall they be," exclaimed Michael Shields, "who shall be found marked among the mourners of Zion, for they shall be spared."[5] The dangers of this vein of thought need no comment.

Renwick is found to be a more level-headed reporter when he said of the Government agents: "I think we never heard of a generation of persecutors where spirits were more set on edge by hell fire than these; they persecute without compassion . . . so that they have given up not only with all things like Christianity, but with very human reason itself."[6] The authors of *Naphtali* had twenty years earlier characterized the tyranny as worse than the Spanish Inquisition.[7] Alexander Shields maintained that the conduct of the Government would have made "Turks and pagans ashamed."[8] Renwick advised his followers to "disobey all tyrannical power, cost what it will,"[9] and on another occasion stated that "the land defiled with blood cannot be cleansed but by the blood of him who shed it."[10]

The danger that this might have led on to anarchy was seen and counteracted by Alexander Shields in a section of his work *A Hind Let Loose*, published anonymously in 1687 in Utrecht. A few months later copies of this book began to filter into Scotland. "As tyranny is a destructive plague to all the interests of men and Christians," declared Shields, "so anarchy, the usual product of it, is no less pernicious, bringing a community in a paroxysm as

---

[1] For the origins of this revival see D. Maclean, "Roman Catholicism in Scotland in the Reign of Charles II," in *Records of the Scottish Church History Society*, Vol. III, pp. 43–54.

[2] "Some Considerations," in M. Shields, *op. cit.*, p. 521.

[3] Confirmed by the moderate Royalist, W. L. Mathieson, *op. cit.*, Vol. II, pp. 328–36.

[4] *Prophetic Sermons*, p. 27.

[5] *Op. cit.*, pp. 341f.

[6] *Prophetic Sermons*, p. 212.

[7] *A Hind Let Loose*, p. 165.

[8] Ibid., p. 114.

[9] *Prophetic Sermons*, p. 104.

[10] "A Letter Concerning the Oath of Abjuration," in M. Shields, *op. cit.*, p. 507.

deadly and dangerous."[1] James Renwick himself makes a similar point after the Society People had been accused not only of casting off all magistrates, but of setting up their own rulers in the magistrates' place, and of "cutting off all as open enemies who did not acknowledge our imaginary government."[2]

As with Gillespie and Rutherford forty years before, so it was with these later Covenanting writers: anarchy and antinomianism had no place in their religious and political outlook. The laws of the land were to be obeyed so far as conscience would allow, and active opposition to the magistrate was not to be lightly undertaken. Summoned before the Scottish bishops in 1685, Alexander Shields agreed with them that all powers were ordained of God, but added that "every power assumed by man is not so by His approbative and perceptive will." The Covenanters would have whole-heartedly endorsed the view of a modern writer who says: "The right of the individual to liberty . . . does not imply his right to do anything he pleases."[3] This was Robert McWard's position when he said: "We never laid any ground for excess on the right hand, while we pleaded against evils on the left."[4] Branded as outlaws, the Covenanters have not always been given credit for this sort of thoughtful reasoning.

Thus the Cameronians were unanimous in censuring disorderliness of all kinds. That was their reaction, for example, to the wild extravagances of the Gibbites or "Sweet Singers of Borrowstounness." This group had originated under the auspices of "Meikle" John Gibb, a sailor. He gathered round him a band of about thirty, mostly women, and retired with them to the wilds, with some notion of becoming perfect through keeping themselves unspotted from the world and renouncing every characteristic of fallen man. With admirable impartiality they condemned equally Covenanters and Covenanting declarations, alcohol, tobacco, all semblance of comfort, Bibles with human addenda, the king and his agents, the educated clergy, and the calendar. Just before he became king, James "was so well pleased with Gibb's blasphemies, that he favoured him extraordinarily,"[5] and approved of his burning the Bible.[6] The latter end of this group was worse than the first. The Scottish Council ultimately banished some of them to America, where Gibb's exhibitions of wizardry brought him some small fame among the Indians.[7]

[1] P. 211.
[2] *An Informatory Vindication*, p. 22.
[3] J. N. Figgis, *op. cit.*, p. 102.
[4] Letter appended to *Earnest Contendings*, p. 373.
[5] A. Shields, *A Hind Let Loose*, p. 155.
[6] *Ibid.*, p. 168.
[7] J. K. Hewison, *op. cit.*, Vol. II, p. 343.

Another point which the Cameronians stressed was that difference of religious opinion (or the fact of a heathen magistrate) did not in itself constitute a valid reason for disobedience,[1] though it might incapacitate a person from exercising authority. The law of the land, for example, prohibited a Roman Catholic king. James was a Roman Catholic. The syllogistic conclusion roused the Covenanters to arms against him. It would have been different, Alexander Shields points out with penetrating logic, "if this James VII-II had been King before he was a Roman Catholic; if we had no more to object, we should not have quarrelled his succession." Shields warns his readers in the Preface to *A Hind Let Loose* that what he has to say goes against prevailing views in an age

wherein fancy hath greater force than faith, and nothing is pleasing but what is parasitical, or attempered to the palate of the greatest, not of the best; and naked truth, without the fairdings of flattery, or paintings of that pakiness which is commonly applauded as prudence now-a-days, is either boggled at, or exposed to scorn and contempt; and reason, if roundly written, except it meet with an honest heart, is commonly read with a stammering mouth, which puts a T before it, and then it is stumbled at as Treason.

There is strictly little originality about this work of Shields's; all it says had been said previously by Major, Buchanan, Rutherford, Stewart and John Brown. *A Hind Let Loose* is important chiefly because it draws together the various strands of democratic thought expressed by its predecessors.

Meanwhile in England, Sir Edward Hales was persecuted because he, a Roman Catholic, had held a government post contrary to English law. It was, however, a contrived action, and the judges by a large majority gave James the verdict he desired: the king is sovereign, the laws are his laws which he may dispense with in case of necessity, and his kingly power did not originate in the people and cannot be taken away from him.[2]

It says much for the loyalty of his adherents that James Renwick, a man with a price on his head, was able to travel and preach up and down the length of the country for more than four years without being arrested, although he was continually hunted by the royal forces. Against him was issued an edict of the Privy Council in September 1684, declaring:

We command and charge all and sundry our lieges and subjects, that they nor none of them presume, nor take in hand to reset, supply, or intercommune with the said Mr. James Renwick, rebel

[1] A. Shields, *A Hind Let Loose*, p. 311.
[2] R. Wodrow, *op. cit.*, Vol. IV, p. 388.

aforesaid; nor furnish him with meat, drink, house, harbour, victual, nor no other thing useful or comfortable to him; or to have any intelligence with him by word, writ, or message, or any other manner of way whatsoever, under the pain of being esteemed art and part with him in the crimes aforesaid, and pursued therefor with all rigour to the terror of others. And we do hereby require all our sheriffs and other officers to apprehend and commit to prison the person of the said Mr. James Renwick wherever they can find him.

It may not be an impeccable piece of literature, but the admirable care obviously taken over the wording of the edict indicates the Council's fear of the influence of the "rebel aforesaid." There was no chance that the Government would listen to some such advice as that of Alexander Shields (latterly Renwick's chief colleague) to "contain themselves within Gamaliel's bounds—that if this work be of men it will come to nought, but if it be of God it cannot be overthrown."[1]

In 1686 Renwick published *An Informatory Vindication of a Poor, Wasted, Misrepresented Remnant of the Suffering, Anti-Popish, Anti-Prelatic, Anti-Erastian, Anti-Sectarian, True Presbyterian Church of Christ in Scotland*. It seems a surprising title for a work designed to answer accusations of schism brought against the Society People! A General Meeting on 7th December, 1687, had resolved that this work should be sold "at eight-pence per book, and at seven-pence unstitched."[2] Despite the implication of the above title, there is evidence that Renwick did his best to curb the extremism of some of his followers, particularly after Alexander Shields had joined him. He was not unsuccessful in this, for by the time he was captured he had made the people, even those who opposed him, distinctly uneasy about the king's designs. He reminded them of how John Knox had declared one Mass more fearful to him than 10,000 armed Papists; of how Andrew Melville had denounced James VI for not exterminating Catholic rebels; of how the Covenanted Assembly had denied toleration even to the Protestant sects. To the majority, however, it was all so much wasted breath. The authority of such precedents in Scottish history was now recognized in practice by the Hill-Folk alone.

After Renwick had been captured and brought to Edinburgh, the Chancellor, Lord Perth, at his trial asked how he differed so much from other Presbyterians, who owned the authority of the king. Renwick answered that he adhered to the old Presbyterian principle which the Covenant had obliged all to maintain. From this, he added meaningfully, some had apostatized for a little liberty, they knew not how short, as they (his judges) had done

---

[1] Life of Renwick in *Biographia Presbyteriana*, Vol. II, p. 49.
[2] M. Shields, *op. cit.*, p. 319.

for a little honour.[1] These words were to find an echo less than a century later in Benjamin Franklin's statement: "They that can give up essential liberty to obtain a little temporary safety deserve neither liberty nor safety."[2]

Renwick was condemned on three charges: disowning the king's government—or, as he himself expressed it, the usurped authority and tyranny of the Duke of York; preaching that it was not lawful to pay the cess levied by the king; and teaching that it was lawful for people to carry arms in self-defence while attending Gospel ordinances. On the second charge a Covenanting manifesto[3] had declared that to pay the cess is to assist the Government in the execution of their "hell-hatched and heaven-daring decrees, orders, and laws," and that the argument that it is payable by law is a "pitiful plea" which will not acquit before God the men who acquiesce in payment. The court pronounced the inevitable sentence.

That Renwick was not the impossible fanatic some take him to be is seen further in a visit paid to him in the condemned cell by a curate. In the course of conversation the curate asked his opinion of the latest religious toleration. Renwick answered he "was against the thing as not conform to the rule, but as for the men who embraced it, he judged them godly men."[4] On the scaffold he said to the great crowd of spectators: "Ye that are the people of God, do not weary in maintaining the testimony of the day, in your stations and places; and whatever you do, make sure an interest in Christ, for there is a storm coming, which will try your foundations."[5] Renwick thanked the Lord who had honoured him with the crown of martyrdom—an honour denied even to the angels—and died, two days after his twenty-sixth birthday, the last preacher-martyr for the Covenants, on 17th February, 1688. Before the year was out the Stuarts were in exile, the persecution past.

Thomas Carlyle, it is interesting to discover, has words of high praise for the Cameronians, and these are perhaps the more weighty because of such a comparatively unlikely source. He declared:

Since Protestantism went silent, no Luther's voice, no Zisca's drum proclaiming that God's truth was not the Devil's lie; and the last of the Cameronians (Renwick was the name of him, honour to the name of the brave!) sank, shot, on the Castle Hill of Edinburgh,

[1] J. K. Hewison, *op. cit.*, Vol. II, pp. 507ff.
[2] *Historical Review*, 1759.
[3] "The Banders Disbanded," in *McWard's Tracts*, 1681, pp. 221, 238.
[4] R. Wodrow, *op. cit.*, Vol. IV, p. 451.
[5] Ibid., p. 454.

there was no partial impulse of faith among nations. Herein we say in that astounding faith of theirs lies the miracle. It is a faith undoubtedly of the more prodigious sort, even among faiths; and will embody itself in prodigies.[1]

We may add here the verdict of the historian Henry Hallam on the Covenanting era generally:

> It was very possible that Episcopacy might be of Apostolical institution; but for this institution houses had been burned and fields laid waste, and the Gospel had been preached in wildernesses and its ministers had been shot in their prayers, and husbands had been murdered before their wives, and virgins had been defiled, and many had died by the executioner, and by massacre, and in imprisonment, and in exile and slavery, and women had been tied to stakes on the sea-shore till the tide rose to overflow them, and some had been tortured and mutilated; it was a religion of the boots and the thumbscrew, which a good man must be very cold-blooded, indeed, if he did not hate and reject from the hands that offered it. For after all, it is much more certain that the Supreme Being abhors cruelty and persecution than that he has set up bishops to have a superiority over presbyterys.[2]

When Charles II died, his ancestral House was secure on the throne of Britain. Yet there was one point at which it was vulnerable—its use in the interests of the Church of Rome. After the Earl of Perth, Scotland's Chancellor, and his brother, Lord Melfort, a Secretary of State, had announced their conversion to Rome and set up a private chapel for the saying of Mass, there was a riot by the citizens of Edinburgh against the open exercise of Roman worship in the capital. The Earl barely escaped with his life. That was in January 1686. Since then, the non-Covenanting Presbyterians who had accepted James's offer of toleration, and who had been reinforced by exiles returning from Holland, were rapidly building up an organization which offered an alternative to Episcopacy. The Episcopalian clergy, for their part, were almost equally hostile to toleration both to Presbyterians and to Romans. As for the peers and politicians, they were becoming increasingly alarmed by the freedom given to Roman Catholics.[3]

The Cameronians claimed that they saw portents in the skies, and now indeed events were moving rapidly towards the downfall of James VII. For some time past certain of the Scottish Presbyterian leaders who were still in exile in Holland had been putting their grievances before William, Prince of Orange, who had

---

[1] *French Revolution*, 1837, Vol. III, p. 102.

[2] Quoted by R. H. Story, "The Revolution Settlement" in *St. Giles' Lectures*, First *Series*, 1881, p. 231.

[3] On this point see W. C. Dickinson and G. Donaldson, *A Source Book of Scottish History*, 1954, Vol. 3, pp. 190, 194f.

married Mary, eldest daughter of James and heir-presumptive to the British crown. As the despotism and the Roman tendencies of the king became more and more pronounced, both in Scotland and in England, pressing invitations were sent to William, seeking his aid in maintaining the civil and religious liberties of both kingdoms. (The English had their own particular grievances against James which we need not discuss here.)

On 3rd November, however, the Scottish prelates, with the exception of two absentees, met together and sent a letter to the king, containing the most extravagant eulogies. After saluting him as "the darling of heaven," they vowed their steadfast allegiance to him, "as an essential part of their religion." They went on to profess their amazement at learning of the possibility of a Dutch invasion which, they averred, "excites our prayers for a universal repentance to all orders of men," and concluded by wishing the king "the hearts of your subjects, and the necks of your enemies."[1] It is difficult to imagine anything more sickeningly servile, and at the same time more despotic and persecuting in tone and intention. The significance, moreover, is perhaps underlined in that this is the last officially recorded act of Scottish Episcopalianism as the "national" Church. The notoriety which it acquired during the Covenanting era served as a death blow to Episcopacy as a major factor in Scottish ecclesiastical life. At the present time (1963) communicants of the Episcopal Church in Scotland comprise just under 1 per cent of the total population.

So inextricably linked were the Episcopalians with a tyrannical form of government that even some modern adherents seem compelled to go to surprising lengths to defend the latter Stuarts and Archbishop Sharp, or at least to denigrate the Covenanters. One such scholar, purporting to write a history of Scotland, civil and ecclesiastical, in recent years contrived to produce a book which dismissed and depreciated the Covenanters in nine frigid lines.

In the closing months before the Revolution, the crisis had been accelerated by the birth of a son to James on 30th June, 1688—an heir who would have displaced Mary, and who would presumably have ensured the Roman Catholic succession. In order to combat this danger, and because also he considered the time was ripe, William of Orange landed at Torbay on 5th November 1688. Crowds flocked to his standard, the kingdom expressed its approval, and James found it politic to slip quietly out of England and spend Christmas on the Continent.

In Scotland a Convention of Estates, seeing how the wind was blowing, declared James to have forfeited his throne. They bolstered up this Declaration by a valid legal argument which they

[1] R. Wodrow, *op. cit.*, Vol. IV, p. 468(n).

brought out at a convenient season, but which they had previously chosen to ignore. This concerned James's refusal to take the Coronation Oath for Scotland on his accession in 1685.[1] The Crown was then settled on William and Mary as joint monarchs. The date was 11th April, 1689. The restored Stuart dynasty had lasted less than thirty years.

James's cause was lost, although a wild horde of Irish and Highlanders under Claverhouse carried on a campaign on his behalf for some months before the latter general, a faithful soldier for his king to the end, whatever their respective faults, was killed at the battle of Killiecrankie on 27th July, 1689. His followers were soon thereafter suppressed. A Cameronian regiment played a notable part in this struggle against the Jacobite troops. One authority on the period, indeed, taking a serious view of the strength of the army under Claverhouse, goes so far as to suggest that in Scotland the victory for Protestantism "could never have been achieved unless these 'bonny fighters' had been unified in an invincible legion by the spirit of the Covenant."[2]

Nothing vindicates the position of the Covenanters through the persecuting years so much as the fact that their consistent arguments for renouncing the Stuart kings, which had led to the sacrifice of several thousand Presbyterian lives, became now the reasons offered to the world for the righteousness of the invasion of Britain by a foreign liberator.[3] It was a startling *volte-face*, for it drew at last an admission by official circles in England and Scotland that the abuse of power destroys the right to exercise it, and that a people may depose their rulers. That there was some clear-headed thinking as well as fanaticism among the Society People (another point we have all along tried to bring out) can be seen in their decision, when they had heard of William's landing, "that it would be a reproach, when now the quarrel would be stated for religion and liberty, if they who have borne arms hitherto for the defence thereof, should now lay them by as indifferent."[4]

Further to this point, Daniel Defoe has an interesting comment originating from the Pentland Rising of 1666:

We leave all those who afterwards thought it lawful to join in the Revolution, and in taking arms against the oppressions and arbitrary government of King James, to judge whether these good men had not the same individual reasons and more for this Pentland expedition. And it is answer enough . . . that those men died for that lawful

[1] P. Hume Brown, *History of Scotland*, Vol. II, p. 349.
[2] J. K. Hewison, *op. cit.*, Vol. II, p. 532. This view is supported by J. Skelton, *Essays in History and Biography*, 1883, p. 139.
[3] On this point see M. Shields, *Faithful Contendings*, p. 392.
[4] Ibid., p. 365.

resisting of arbitrary power which has been justified as legal, and acknowledged to be justifiable by the practice and declarations of the respective Parliaments of both kingdoms.[1]

Parliament abolished Episcopacy in Scotland at a session from which the bishops discreetly absented themselves. "The bishops, I know not where they are," wrote one nobleman sardonically, "they are the Kirk Invisible."[2] Wherever they were, they certainly had not taken to the hills in defence of principle. Parliament further ratified the Confession of Faith, settled the Presbyterian Church government, and rescinded all fines and forfeitures.

The Society People, meanwhile, resolutely testified against both Jacobites and Dutch, styling the latter "a promiscuous conjunction of reformed Lutherans, Malignants, and Sectaries." Although these Covenanters fought on William's behalf, it was for them merely a continuation of their fight against James. Moreover, although they helped to purge the churches of Scotland of their "intruded hirelings," they regarded William's motives for invasion as being too lame and defective, because they ignored the "covenanted work of Reformation." William's Government did not rescind the Act Rescissory, by which the Drunken Parliament had in 1661 erased much that was worthiest in the Church's record of achievement; and this omission was a sore point with the Cameronians. "Is there," demanded Michael Shields, "any positive act to be found amongst the archives of the nation, by which that heaven-daring Act Recissory is repealed? If there is not, the whole legal establishment of the true Protestant Presbyterian form of Church government must stand yet publicly condemned."[3]

The tactical blunder committed by the extreme Cameronians, accordingly, was that although that Act had not been repealed, and although the Covenants had not been reimposed, they had gained the substance of what they had contended for, but had at the same time forgotten that the Covenants were but a means to an end, called forth not only by the spirit of the time, but by the special circumstances of the day.[4] Unhappily, the Covenants had now become a kind of fetish which was to perpetuate schism in the Scottish Church.

In stark contrast to irresponsible mobs in other parts of the country, the true Covenanters behaved decently towards the curates, "those plants which our heavenly Father never planted."[5]

[1] Quoted by J. Howie, *op. cit.*, p. 356.
[2] M. Napier, *Memorials of Montrose*, 1862, p. 601.
[3] *Op. cit.*, Preface, p. viii. For a comprehensive account of the Society People's objections to the Settlement, see John Howie's Appendix to this volume by Michael Shields.
[4] P. Hume Brown, *op. cit.*, Vol. II, p. 454.
[5] *Naphtali*, p. 200.

"How would they tremble and sweat," said Patrick Walker, "if they were in the Grassmarket, going up the ladder, and the rope before them, and the lad with the pyoted coat at their tail." We mention this point because of the outrageous legend which, still current and assiduously cultivated in neo-Jacobite circles, with lurid illustration charges the Covenanters with taking dire revenge on the curates.

The vacancies caused in certain parts of Scotland were not only a source of acute difficulty for some time, but were also keenly resented. In 1690, for example, there was only one Presbyterian minister in the Synod of Aberdeen and Banff, containing 100 parishes. In 1694 there were eight, in 1697 fifteen. The Lord's Supper was not administered in Aberdeen till 1704 by Presbyterian clergy.[1] On the other side of northern Scotland, the minister of Lochcarron was for a time obliged to carry firearms to protect himself from his parishioners,[2] and not until 1716 did a Presbyterian preach in peace in Dingwall.[3] Even in Aberfoyle, not far from Glasgow, a curate installed himself and remained in possession until his death in 1732.[4]

As Dr. King Hewison has suggested, the Revolution Settlement was to the Cameronians what the second temple must have been to the old men who remembered and hankered after the magnificence of the former one in Solomon's day. The great majority of the Cameronians would not join in the worship of the restored Church of Scotland at the Revolution—which Settlement, incidentally, dealt a mortal blow not only to Episcopacy, but to the theory of the Divine Right of Presbytery. The lineal descendants of the Cameronians (diminished by sundry unions down the years) survive as a Church to this day, and still bear the old name, though their official designation in Scotland is "The Reformed Presbyterian Church." With congregations in North America and Ireland as well in Scotland, the Church is a remnant standing as a witness of the bitter struggle fought by its founders against the tyranny of the House of Stuart.

[1] Spalding, *Miscellanies*, Vol. II, p. 72.
[2] Scott's *Fasti*, Vol. V, p. 98.
[3] Ibid., Vol. V, p. 283.
[4] Minutes of Dunblane Presbytery.

CHAPTER XII

COVENANTERS OVERSEAS

PERHAPS IT WOULD BE HELPFUL TO ADD AT THIS POINT A short section on the career and cause of some of those forced to leave Scotland during the persecuting times. In the Covenanting era Holland provided an asylum for refugees from other lands, and to Scotsmen the atmosphere of that country was particularly congenial. The people of the Netherlands had had a long and bitter struggle to achieve their freedom. It was commonly reported that about 100,000 of them had been burned, strangled, beheaded, and buried alive during the reign of Charles V, which barbarous policy was maintained by his son, Philip II, husband of Mary Tudor.

A century had elapsed since the Dutch had thrown off the yoke of Spain and of Roman Catholicism, and for the intervening period the United Provinces had been a distinctively Protestant state. The Dutch Church was Calvinist and Presbyterian—though orthodox Scots of the Covenanting era tended to regard the Dutch Church as somewhat latitudinarian in matters of belief. Moreover, the latter was not altogether free of an Erastian tinge which was especially odious to the Covenanters. Nevertheless, the Covenanters found in Holland a welcome haven, as did Jews and Jansenists.

The Scots had maintained a settled ministry in Rotterdam since the arrival of the Rev. Alexander Petrie in August 1643. There was in that Dutch port a large number of Presbyterians who had cashed in on the commercially lucrative prospects then offered there. These took the opportunity of relieving those of their fellow-countrymen who had left home for conscience' sake. Among those who aided our exiled Scots were the magistrates of Rotterdam. Large sums were given out of the town chest, of which the Scottish Consistory were almoners. The church treasurer's book bears ample evidence, moreover, of the extreme delicacy with which they administered the money placed at their disposal by the benevolence of magistrates and private individuals. The money was always voted and paid out in the presence of the session, upon whose members the strictest secrecy was enjoined.

It was to Holland that Livingstone, Brown and McWard, three of the stalwarts among the outed ministers, took their flight; and it was from that country that the two latter poured forth their fiery tracts and treatises in defence of the thoroughgoing Covenanting position. McWard became second minister in Rotterdam, his services highly valued by the whole congregation, and by those trading to the port. He had both piety and presence, and his anxiety to promote personal and family religion endeared him to his flock. From ship to ship, as well as from house to house, he systematically went, speaking of the things pertaining to the kingdom. His friend, John Brown, of whom we have spoken earlier, may with some justice be called the father of Cameronianism.

The literary activities of Brown and McWard so gravely alarmed the Scottish administration that, spurred on by Archbishop Sharp, Charles II in 1676, through his envoy-extraordinary in the United Provinces, demanded that these two ministers and Colonel James Wallace be expelled from Dutch territory. With this demand was coupled the threat that if the States-General demurred, there might be a rupture of diplomatic relations. Eventually the Dutch authorities reluctantly yielded, and the three were obliged to leave the country. Their absence, however, was only temporary. Brown returned to Holland, residing first of all near Utrecht, where the two others had gone, and latterly at Rotterdam, where he died in 1679. One of John Brown's last acts was to participate in the ordination of Richard Cameron.

The latter was ordained by Brown, McWard and a Dutch minister called Koelmann. Cameron seems to have been the first of a number of young Scotsmen to repair to Holland for the purpose of securing a congenial teaching in theology. Alexander Shields was another such. In 1680, five years after graduating in Arts at Edinburgh University, Shields was enrolled as a student of theology in the University of Utrecht, and probably spent two or three years in Holland at this time. In London several ministers took him by surprise and persuaded him to be licensed by them (one of them was Nichol Blackie or Blaikie, minister of Roberton, who had been ejected in 1662). Shields remained only a licentiate until his appointment in 1691 as chaplain to the Cameronian regiment.

Robert McWard collected and arranged the papers of Samuel Rutherford, and gave to the world the first edition of the famous *Letters*, published in Rotterdam in 1664. He died in Holland in 1682. Robert Wodrow gives a brief account of later Covenanting nonconformists who retired to Holland.[1] Even there, however, they were not out of danger, but were sometimes attacked and

[1] *Op. cit.*, Vol. IV, p. 414.

violently assaulted by the agents of James VII. Some were even kidnapped, and taken forcibly to be executed in England. "And sometimes," narrates Wodrow, "there was a search procured by king James from the States, but they kindly gave some advertisement, that Scots people might be on their guard, as particularly one for Sir James Stewart. . . ."[1]

Shortly after he became monarch of the united kingdom in 1603, James I seized the estates of the rebellious Ulster chiefs, and promised religious freedom to Presbyterians and Puritans who would settle there. Between 1608 and 1616, more than 40,000 Presbyterians and many Puritans, lured by this promise, moved to Ulster. Hence the term "Scotch-Irish" which is well known in the New World. James forgot his promise, persecutions followed after his death, and immigration to the New World became the hope of the Presbyterians. To Maryland and Pennsylvania especially, then, many Presbyterians repaired, and in the next century more than half a million Celtic Presbyterians came to America.

Of the 4,000 Presbyterians who are said to have emigrated to New England between 1620 and 1640, the majority were of English and Dutch origin. The situation changed during the latter half of the century. After the battle of Dunbar in 1651, Oliver Cromwell despatched Scottish prisoners in shiploads to the plantations of North America, to be sold as bondmen.[2] During the thirty-eight years thereafter till the Revolution, thousands of Scottish Covenanters were either transported to America as a penalty for alleged crimes, or sought there a refuge from protracted persecution at home.[3] Many of those accused of being concerned in the 1666 Pentland Rising, for example, were condemned to transportation and servitude. The same sentence was pronounced upon 250 Covenanters in 1679 after the battle of Bothwell Bridge, and also upon 100 of the Dunottar captives in 1685 after the Monmouth rebellion. In the former case, however, shipwreck substituted death for bondage, while in the latter many died of fever on the voyage, and the remainder, on their arrival in New Jersey, were declared by the colonial magistrates to be free men.[4] This ship, which had sailed from Leith on 5th September, 1685, arrived at Perth Amboy about the middle of December, and there set ashore nearly 100 men, women and children, Covenanters taken from Scottish prisons and banished to America. No less than twenty-nine of their companions, including two ministers

[1] *Op. cit.*, p. 513.
[2] R. Webster, *History of the Presbyterian Church in America*, p. 66. A list of the prisoners in one of the ships sent out at this time is preserved in the collections of the Massachusetts Historical Society.
[3] J. H. Burton, *The History of Scotland*, Vol. VII, 1876, pp. 176, 234, 277.
[4] R. Wodrow, *op. cit.*, Vol. IV, p. 333.

and their leader, George Scot of Pitlochie, had died during the fifteen-week voyage, from fever, rotten food and maltreatment. The survivors included two Covenanting pastors—Archibald Riddel[1] and John Frazer. They settled in New Jersey on the site which afterwards became Woodbridge. Some of their fellow-countrymen were about the same time banished to the Carolinas, and again we learn of many deaths on the voyage due to ill-usage.[2] Others were transported to Jamaica.

In the library of Edinburgh University there survives a curious old document signed by twenty-eight of those thus exiled, including six women, giving their testimony. They would have men know (after they had expressed the customary abhorrence of Popery, Prelacy and Erastianism, and their support of the Covenants), that they approved the fight carried on at Pentland, Drumclog, Bothwell Bridge and Lanark; that they endorsed the Queensferry Paper and the Torwood Excommunication. They testify against the king, Parliament, Privy Councillors, local sheriffs and provosts for the persecution; and against the regular and indulged clergy for their acquiescence in it. "Thus we leave you, dear friends, wives, children, and families," it concludes, somewhat pathetically, "on the hand of him who is a husband to the widou, a stay to the orphant, and a hiding place to His people, and the shadou of a great rock in a wearie land; to whom be glory for ever. Amen."[3]

A further sixteen men and five women were banished to America in April 1687, because they would not acknowledge the present authority to be according to the Word of God, would not disown the Sanquhar Declaration, and would give no undertaking to desist from hearing James Renwick. The voyage which they and others took at this time was always hazardous. As late as 1715, the brig *Eagle Wing* was taking seven to ten weeks for the crossing, and sometimes longer. Once it was three months on the way, and forty-two of the passengers and crew died and were buried at sea. Only passage could be purchased, a space between decks would then be assigned, and the passengers made that their home until America was reached. They supplied their own bed and bedding and supplies, for nothing could be purchased aboard ship.

Not all of those who came to the New World at this epoch came unwillingly. Among the 290 colonists from Leith and Montrose

[1] Riddel had been minister of Kippen prior to his imprisonment from 1677 to 1685. On the voyage home after the Revolution he fell into French hands, and with his son suffered nearly two years' incarceration before finally being resettled in his old parish.
[2] J. G. Fyfe, *op. cit.*, p. 339, gives a brief graphic picture from a contemporary diary.
[3] *Laing MSS.*, Vol. 344, No. 110.

COVENANTERS OVERSEAS 183

in 1684 were "gentlemen and merchants of very good repute."
The deputy Governor of New Jersey, in a letter of the same year,
testifies that "the Scots coming now, and settling, advance the
province more than it hath advanced these ten years."[1] George
Bancroft, the nineteenth-century American statesman and historian, writing in 1837, gives a similar testimony thus: "Scottish
Presbyterians of virtue, education, and courage, blending a love
of popular liberty with religious enthusiasm," emigrated "in such
numbers as to give to the rising commonwealth a character which
a century and half have not effaced."[2]

So the Covenanters came to America, most of them unwillingly
through banishment, some of their own accord in order to escape
the persecution.

Their foes doubtless expected that such rude transplanting
would quench the fire of Cameronian stubbornness, but the exiles
took their faith with them, and it is interesting to discover that
there are now more Covenanters in North America than in Scotland and Ireland combined.[3] A century later, when the War of
Independence was being fought, a contemporary said in a letter
of the uprising: "Call this war, my dearest friend, by whatsoever
name you may, only call it not an American Rebellion, it is nothing
less than an Irish-Scottish Presbyterian Rebellion."[4] As their ancestors had in the past resisted European rulers' claims to decide
what religion should be allowed in their domains, so the descendants found that not only "new truths would break forth from the
Word of God" (John Robinson's phrase), but even a new form
of community in the foundation of new states.

So conspicuous and fruitful a source of emigration was Scotland
at this epoch, that landowners of New Jersey, anxious to direct
the stream into their own channel, anticipated the advertising
agencies of later times, and circulated among the Scottish people
an attractive description of the territory for sale in their province,
with assurances of complete religious liberty.[5]

[1] Smith's *History of New York*, p. 177.
[2] *History of the United States*, 1834–76, Vol. II, p. 412.
[3] The Reformed Presbyterian Church in North America (General Synod) still
holds restricted communion and "the principles of dissent from all immoral civil
institutions." With the Reformed Presbyterian Church of North America (Old
School), the total number of members in American Churches claiming direct
descent from the Scottish Covenanters is just under 8,000, according to the *American
Churches Handbook*. In Scotland, numbers have fallen to less than 600, with about
five times as many in Northern Ireland.
[4] Extract from a letter of Captain Johann Heinrichs of the Hessian Jager Corps,
written from Philadelphia, 18th January, 1778; see *Pennsylvania Magazine of History
and Biography*, XXII, p. 137.
[5] See the "Brief Advertisement concerning East New Jersey in America,"
appended to George Scot of Pitlochie's *Model of the Government of the Province of
East New Jersey, and Encouragements for such as Design to be Concerned there*, 1685.

It was during the persecuting times in Scotland that Ninian Beale, a God-fearing colonel and an elder of the Kirk, founded a Scottish colony in the district of Maryland where afterwards arose the city of Washington. He attracted to the new settlement 200 Presbyterian fellow-countrymen, constituted them into a congregation provided with a pastor, and afterwards assigned to them land for a church.

About 1674 a group of Scotch-Irish Presbyterians from Donegal came with their preacher and settled along the east shore of the Elizabeth River, near Norfolk, Virginia. The neighbouring territories of Maryland and Pennsylvania attracted the Celts because of their guarantee of religious liberty. The Covenanting defeat at Drumclog (1679) brought America a further supply of captive Covenanters. After 1680 emigration became more systematic, partly to relieve the sufferers from religious persecution, partly as an outlet of commercial enterprise. The proprietors of East New Jersey, who got their title to the land in 1682, included five Scots, and they persuaded many hundreds of their fellow-countrymen to move in. Letters home by settlers brought out many friends or kinsfolk. This part of the Atlantic seaboard consequently acquired, and for long retained, a strong Scottish and Presbyterian character. The new provincial capital, Perth Amboy, was named in honour of the Earl (later Duke) of Perth (who afterwards became a Roman Catholic under James II), one of the proprietors. The descendants of these Presbyterians had much to do with the foundation and prosperity of the "College of New Jersey" (1746), which grew to be Princeton University.

Far to the south, meanwhile, Stuart's Town (South Carolina) was settled by Lord Cardross and William Dunlop (later Principal of Glasgow University), many of whose Covenanting colleagues were men of high social standing.[1] For two years (1684-6) it was the southern outpost of British settlement in those parts, until overwhelmed by a Spanish force from Florida. After Argyle's rebellion, a further supply of Scots prisoners went to the American colonies.

Those who during the persecution left Scotland to seek asylum in the western world formed themselves into praying societies, as they were wont to do in their own land, upon the basis of Reformation principles. They kept themselves distinct from other religious

This Edinburgh-published book contains a collection of letters from colonists to their friends at home.

[1] Ramsay, *History of South Carolina*, Vol. II, p. 23, states that "to the Scotch South Carolina is indebted for much of its early literature. A great proportion of its physicians, clergymen, lawyers, and schoolmasters were from North Britain." The city of Savannah in Georgia still has a large congregation which curiously calls itself an "Independent Presbyterian Church."

bodies in North America, regarding them as in no way disposed to enter into the full spirit of the Covenanted Reformation.[1] It is significant that the Covenanting remnant in Scotland after the Revolution Settlement never claimed that the obligation of the Covenants extended to the American colonies.[2] Acceptance of the Covenants could not therefore be imposed as a condition of Communion.

Another difference between Covenanters in America and in Scotland lay in the fact that the Scottish Covenanters disowned the authority of the civil government; they did not, like those who assumed that name in America, claim its protection; they did not apply to courts or magistrates for the recovery of debts, damages, etc., or the protection of constables to their presbytery, as those assuming that name did in America. Doing so was at home esteemed highly censurable; they did not act so inconsistently as to claim protection where they refused allegiance.

The Covenanters were thinly scattered from Nova Scotia to South Carolina and far into the interior. They built their first churches of logs among the dense forests. Sometimes the ordinances were administered in private dwellings, or in barns, sometimes in the open air. The ministers were few—they laboured industriously and sacrificially, riding long distances on horseback, often over unfrequented roads, pursuing mountain paths, riding through unforded streams, shelterless often at night, in constant danger from wild beasts and wilder Indians. The Covenanters took no active part in civil affairs in America while the colonies were subject to Britain. They would not sustain the British Government in this land.[3]

A section of the Covenanters, led by the Rev. Alexander Craighead[4] in the first half of the eighteenth century, renewed their Covenants, declaring not only their religious convictions, but also their right to civil independence; indeed the followers of Craighead made a public demand for national independence from Great Britain. They circulated the daring doctrine; it breathed the spirit of the early Scottish Covenanting manifestoes. From this bold statement of rights and principles the writer of America's Declaration of Independence admits that he received aid, and drew inspiration.[5] "But how pitiful their disappointment, when the Federal Constitution was adopted, without reference to Divine Providence, or the mention of God's name in it! What

[1] See *Reformation Principles Exhibited by the Reformed Presbyterian Church in the U.S.A.*, 1807.
[2] W. Findlay, *Observations on "The Two Sons of Oil,"* 1812, pp. viif.
[3] J. C. M'Feeters, *The Covenanters in America*, 1892, pp. 58f.
[4] Craighead later withdrew from the Covenant at Octorara, Pennsylvania, in 1743.
[5] J. C. M'Feeters, *op. cit.*, pp. 59f.

cause of shame was there when they saw human slavery established by law! They promptly dissented from the Government and have continued to do so, considering it defective in morality and religion because it made no acknowledgment of God as the source of all power and authority, and did not administer law according to the requirements of His Word."[1]

Before the outbreak of the American Revolution the numerical strength of the Presbyterians increased so rapidly as a result of the Scotch-Irish immigration that this religious group became increasingly important in the affairs of the province of Pennsylvania. In 1774 Benjamin Franklin, computing the total population of Pennsylvania at 350,000, estimated that Scotch-Irish accounted for one-third of that number. Allowing for the fact that not all Scotch-Irish were Presbyterians, one would consequently place the number of Presbyterians in Philadelphia at the close of the colonial era in the neighbourhood of 100,000.[2]

In 1782 a number of ministers abandoned the Covenant, but the Church rode the storm. In 1798 a presbytery was reorganized which developed into a synod, to be again disturbed by division in 1833 when about half the ministers and members departed; yet she survived and quietly multiplied in congregations and missions. Again in 1891 she suffered further loss of pastors and people, when her principles, especially her dissent, were subjected to public criticism.[3]

There was a certain unhealthy exclusivism found here and there. As late as May 1868 George H. Stuart of Philadelphia was suspended from his office as ruling elder in the anti-Union Reformed Presbyterian Church, and from worship in the church. His offence: he was charged with "hymn-singing and communing with Christians of other denominations." (That he was unquestionably guilty was seen later in his whole-hearted support of the Moody and Sankey campaign in Philadelphia.)

The Reformed Presbyterians in the United States still stand upon the principle of political dissent. They give four reasons for this: (1) The compact by which the political society is bound fails to acknowledge the relation of the nation to God; there is no proper and adequate acknowledgment of this in the United States constitution. (2) Official trusts are committed to godless men. (3) It is the only way of action in the face of a morally defective constitution and its legitimate consequences. (4) It is the most effective way for the reformation of the nation. Political dissent is not regarded as a denial of the legitimacy of the government,

[1] J. C. M'Feeters, op. cit., p. 61.
[2] Writings of Benjamin Franklin, ed. by A. H. Smyth, Vol. IV, p. 337(n).
[3] J. C. M'Feeters, op. cit., p. 63.

but rather as a refusal to incorporate with the political society of the nation.

In the 1960 Report of the Committee on Political Dissent of the Synod of the Reformed Presbyterian Church, convened at Sterling, Kansas, the last paragraph says: "If the oath to support and defend the Constitution means our approval of the secular character of the Constitution, then we cannot take that oath and maintain a consistent testimony to the Lordship of Jesus Christ, and we cannot vote for others to take the oath as our representatives." Comments one of their ministers: "The debate centered on the 'if'. The committee was not willing, or rather, felt it was not able to say that to take the oath DOES mean this, and it was made rather clear on the floor that the Supreme Court is the only body with authority to say one way or the other, and they have not to this date; therefore, it is evident that we as a church are maintaining as a term of communion a position based on an ASSUMPTION . . . which has not yet been proved to be true, namely, that to take the oath does mean that we are approving the secular nature of the Constitution."[1]

---

[1] Personal letter to the author.

CHAPTER XIII

CONCLUSION

"THERE CAME OUT, AFTER THIRTY YEARS' STRUGGLING," wrote Thomas Carlyle, "what we call the *Glorious Revolution*, a Habeas Corpus Act, free parliaments, and much else. Alas! is it not too true that many men in the van do always, like the Russian soldiers, march into the ditch of Schwiednitz, and fill it up with their dead bodies, that the rear may pass over them dry shod, and gain the honour? How many . . . poor peasant Covenanters, wrestling, battling for very life in rough, noisy places, have to struggle and suffer and fall, greatly censured, bemired, before a beautiful Revolution of eighty-eight can step over them in official pumps, with universal three times three."[1]

The Cameronians objected strongly to the fact that in connection with the Revolution Settlement made in 1689 the Covenants were not renewed, and they hesitated to accept an agreement of any sort devised by an uncovenanted king. It was bigoted, but it was logical. We can understand their attitude only by recalling that for them the Covenants were Covenants with God Himself after the Scriptural manner. This explains the continued resistance which they showed to the rule of Charles II and James VII, and the odd tenacity with which they stuck to their guns even after the last of the Stuarts had been exiled. That the Covenants were binding perpetually had been declared by James Guthrie in his dying speech, thus: "These sacred and solemn public oaths of God, I believe can be loosed or dispensed with by no person or party, or power, upon earth, but are still binding upon these kingdoms and will be for ever hereafter."[2] James Renwick, basing his belief on the Old Testament, stated plainly that the Covenants were binding on posterity,[3] and Alexander Shields declared them "unrepealably and indispensably binding."[4] Another Covenanting writer, Patrick Walker, spoke of the allegiance to the Covenants as "an oath which no power on earth could loose,"[5] and John

---

[1] *Heroes*, Lecture IV.
[2] *Naphtali*, p. 229.
[3] *The Test of Some Persecuted Ministers*, 1688, p. 33.
[4] *A Hind Let Loose*, p. 214.
[5] *Op. cit.*, Vol. I, p. 11.

Brown of Wamphray devotes fifteen pages in illustration of the heinous sin of covenant-breaking.[1]

Nor were the Covenanters alone in such a high conception of the term. Philip Nye, an English Independent, and a distinguished member of the Westminster Assembly, had said about the Solemn League and Covenant and its violation: "A truce-breaker is reckoned up amongst the vilest of Christians, so a covenant-breaker is listed amongst the worst of heathens."[2]

This was a vital point with the Covenanters when they were pressed to give up their adherence to their Covenants. The Test Act of 1681 attacked their stand on this question, and demanded an assertion that people felt themselves under no obligation from the Covenants to work for changes in Church or State.[3] This was, of course, a further attack along the general front of religious freedom. On the other hand, as with other religious men—St. Columba or their own John Knox, for example—the Covenanters had on occasion little pity or sympathy for such as they considered to be wilful enemies of the truth. If religion were the absolute thing they believed it to be, then doubtless their attitude was the highest piety. To show relentings towards the enemies of God was to trifle with the eternal salvation of their fellow-men (in this they were not far from the Church of Rome). The idea that others might have perceived some different aspect of truth was beyond their comprehension. They alone had the whole truth—and if defence of that truth left little room for toleration or liberty of conscience in others, then so it ought to be. We find traces of the same dogmatism in Luther, who applied it to political as well as to religious discussions; and in Calvin, who founded his religious principle on the ground of truth (as he saw it) rather than on liberty of conscience. Perhaps a healthy dose of dogmatism is an integral part of a Reformer's equipment. If we are to condemn him for it, then we must choose carefully on what ground we base our condemnation, lest our own flank be exposed, our own "liberalism" traced to spiritual lethargy.

We of this age have the advantage of being able to see all sides of the problem. The Covenanters, for the most part, had no opportunity of coolly assessing a nicely-graded less or more. They either had to obey God or obey the king. For them it was as simple as that. Men are less often than they think faced with an absolute choice of good or evil, black or white. Life tends to be more complex—and greys are difficult to deal with. In a time when prudence advocated compromise, the Covenanters renounced the wisdom

[1] *Apologetical Relation*, pp. 167ff.
[2] "Exhortation at Westminster," in *The Covenants and the Covenanters*, p. 146.
[3] R. Wodrow, *op. cit.*, Vol. II, p. 194.

of this world and flung their whole weight on the side of God and of what they regarded as the eternal verities. Their very whole-heartedness is counted against them: the intervening centuries have taught us that it is both immature and unfashionable to display strong religious feeling.

Thus a favourite point at which the Covenanters are considered vulnerable by their critics is found in their view of toleration, lucidly expressed in Covenanting terms by their own James Durham: "Toleration," he says, "doth either account little of errour, as being no hurtful thing, and so there can be no esteem of truth; or it doth account little of the destruction of souls; both which must be abominable."[1] As with Tertullian, they would have no truck with heresy or compromise or "black error". It is easy to dismiss their attitude as impossible, with the facile contempt of the more enlightened who people our twentieth century, and to forget that tolerance is a relative term. There are some who need seriously to question whether they themselves are consistently tolerant in the truest sense: whether they do not apply their touchstone only in the case of those who are more "liberal" than they. It ought also to operate in their judgment on the most rabid Fundamentalist; it ought to be tempered by the warning that the frontier between their vaunted "broad-mindedness" and religious indifference may be soon involuntarily crossed.

In view of the tendency to judge the Covenanters by modern standards, with little regard for the spiritual and physical torture which men endured in that age, we should ask why they were what they were; what motivated them; what sustained them through weary years. And we shall find, for example, that the answer lies chiefly in their confidence of being the chosen of God. Failure and disaster with them was regarded as being for "the punishment of former sins, and for future trial." Success or good fortune was the God-given assurance of the protection of the Everlasting Arms. When a thick mist on one occasion suddenly descended and concealed Alexander Peden from his pursuers, "the Lord had let doon a flap of His cloak to screen puir Auld Sandie."[2] And who shall say that He didn't!

But the Covenanters' supreme conviction that their cause was right was illogically carried over to mean also that the course which they advocated was likewise right and justifiable. In this they made a tragic mistake. Thus there was the possibility (despite much controversy it remains little more than that) of the slaughter of prisoners by the Covenanters after their triumph at Philiphaugh in 1645. The editor of Kirkton's *History* quotes the

---

[1] *A Dying Man's Testimony to the Church of Scotland,* 1659, p. 153.
[2] K. Hewat, *Peden the Prophet,* 1911, p. 61.

story of how the Covenanters shot 100 Irish prisoners, on which a minister (Bishop Henry Guthry identifies him with David Dickson) is said to have observed: "This wark gaes bonnilie on."[1] Patrick Walker, on the other hand, denying that prisoners were slain at the later battle of Drumclog (1679), adds that "by withholding our sword from shedding of their blood" they brought themselves "under that curse of doing the work of the Lord deceitfully."[2] If something like a massacre did occur at Philiphaugh, it would have been quite in character for the Covenanters to have explained it away by quoting the example of Samuel and Agag, and that of the resourceful Jael—a lady for whom we have never had much admiration. Alexander Shields's *A Hind Let Loose* finds in certain verses of Esther justification for retaliating against those who would destroy the faithful.

The Covenanters tended to renounce all things for which they could find no Scriptural warrant. Every man was to have "liberty to utter and declare his mind with knowledge to the comfort and edification of the Church," as Knox had put it a century earlier.[3] But that was heady wine which tended to raise up a class of "saints of God" who alone could interpret His will—a will which indeed they often portrayed as strait and narrowing, devoid of that mercy which should ever be linked with the concept of a holy God's dealings with sinful men. The slavish Covenanting adherence to the letter of Scripture which led them into dubious courses of action makes us appreciate what the translators of the King James version of the Bible meant when, doubtless with one eye on the Scots of that time, they spoke in the Dedication of the possibility of being "maligned by self-conceited brethren, who run their own ways; and give liking unto nothing but what is framed by themselves, and hammered on their anvil." Three and a half centuries later we know what they mean.

Under Covenanting rule, scrupulous care was given to "preaching to the times." When he was still Presbyterian minister at Newbattle, Robert Leighton was reprimanded for not preaching up the times. He asked who did, and was told that all the brethren did. "Well," came his mild rejoinder, "if all of you preach up the times, you may surely allow one poor brother to preach up Christ Jesus and eternity."[4] It was unusual for the zealots to be thus worsted in a verbal duel.

Often in the attitude of the rebels there was apparent an odd lack of seemliness, particularly towards pious men of other

---

[1] *Op. cit.*, pp. 48f.(n.), quoting from the *Memoirs of the Somerville Family.*
[2] *Op. cit.*, Vol. II, p. 77; see also M. Shields, *op. cit.*, p. 201, on this question.
[3] *History*, Vol. II, p. 243.
[4] J. N. Pearson, *Life of Leighton*, 1835, p. xvi.

parties. Saintly attributes were put down as the weak and timid vacillations and hesitations of a character incapable of strenuous convictions, for this was essentially an age of action. Here again Robert Leighton was a target for their abuse, because he was both a good man and an Episcopalian—a combination which they found incredible. For them there was no dividing line, no differentiation, between toleration on one hand, submission or apathy on the other. Those who were not for them were against them. This was a faith bordering on the esoteric: ". . . a dark lanthorn of the spirit, where none can see but those who bear it."

Even if the curates had been saints they would have been rejected, such was the mood of carping criticism which the men of the Covenant for the most part displayed towards everything in any way linked with the Government. Yet even in this it seems clear that it was not the curate or bishop they objected to, but the man's office. In dealing with opponents, the Covenanters never put themselves in the latter's place. All who disagreed with them were promoters of "Popery, Prelacy, Erastianism, schism, error, tyranny or defection." This type of attitude is expressed in the words of Walter Chalmers Smith:

> And there's none of them but would as soon
> Criticize the Almighty as not,
> And see that the angels kept tune
> And watch that the sun and the moon
> Didn't squander the light that they'd got.

Admittedly it is not easy for some to appreciate fully the Covenanting position. "The Covenant," said W. Landels, "though right in spirit, and originally a protection to liberty, became hostile to liberty when subsequently they sought to enforce it to the letter."[1] Andrew Lang, that staunch advocate of everything with a royalist flavour, might be right in his suggestion that the Arminians were the sole remnant who knew what liberty meant. Even if we do not stop to define our terms, and concede that point, Lang never appreciated the alternative: take away the Covenanting protest, and regal despotism of an even more extreme type would have been speedily established in Scotland.

In another sense, however, the Covenanters' stand was neither unreasoning nor unreasonable. The National Covenant was, as we have seen, a legitimate legal document by which the Covenanters had tried to obtain their legal rights. It had been declared unlawful to support it, by "the blasphemous encroachment of the tyrant upon the prerogative of God, in making and rescinding oaths at

[1] "The Scottish Covenanters," in *Exeter Hall Lectures*, 1861, p. 38.

his pleasure.''[1] But how could they depart from it just because
persecution was increased, and when religious liberty, far from
being given, was restricted to an intolerable degree? These were
proud men who, when their enemies asked if they thought the
king's power was limited, rightly pointed out that they knew of
no power but the Almighty's to be unlimited.

The one plea that can be made for Charles II, chief author of
the persecution (for James merely continued his brother's policy,
in essentials, towards the Covenanters), is that what the extremists
demanded, and went on demanding, was the acceptance of the
Solemn League and Covenant, and the suppression of Episcopacy
in England. Now these were measures which, after the Restoration,
Charles simply was not able to take, even had he wished. False and
unprincipled he certainly was, but we cannot say how far the
determination to force both Covenants upon him was the cause
of the suffering inflicted upon Scotland during his reign and with
his consent and approval. He was soon made to feel how impossible it was to set right a time so out of joint.

In that sense we may have a certain sympathy towards Charles,
a man whose nature was far as the poles apart from these rugged
men who assumed in such facile fashion the characters of the Old
Testament heroes whose words were ever on their lips, and whose
deeds were at once their delight and their example.[2] Their standards of ethics, both personal and social, were strictly Biblical, and
the Ten Commandments were regarded as the sum of human duty
in a rather Calvinistic manner. So Emily Brontë, in *Wuthering
Heights* makes Mrs. Dean say of such: "He was, and is yet, most
likely, the wearisomest, self-righteous Pharisee that ever ransacked
a Bible to rake the promises to himself, and fling the curses on his
neighbours.''

The horrible scruples felt by one section of the Covenanters
against granting any quarter in the hour of victory may be traced
to the mental habit of dividing mankind into servants of God and
servants of the devil—a division not unknown in our own times.
In support of it may be adduced the fact that it is of the very
essence of the Gospel that there is a great gulf fixed in this world
and the next between saved and unsaved. It was this conviction
which was the motive-force behind many of the Covenanters'
actions. And no one is more dangerous than the man who is
fighting for his religion.

Moreover, for the Covenanters, religion and politics were

[1] M. Shields, *op. cit.*, p. 30.
[2] D. M. G. Stalker points out that Rutherford's *Lex Rex* appeals to the Old
Testament four times as much as to the New. For an interesting article on this
Covenanting predilection for the Old Testament see Mr. Stalker's essay in *Records
of the Scottish Church History Society*, Vol. X, 1950, pp. 186–95.

G

necessarily bound up together: if it had not been so our picture would have been clearer. They objected as emphatically to despotism in affairs of State as to Erastianism in the Church. "Persecution for conscience' sake, and oppression in civil liberty, flow from the same spring, are carried on by the same measures, and lead to the very same miserable end"—so wrote Robert Wodrow in the Dedication of his *History*. "Take away the liberty of Assemblies," Knox had exclaimed, "and you take away the liberty of the evangel." Yet with equal zeal Knox was the foremost to stand up on behalf of his nation's freedom in defiance of autocratic rulers. It was the same with his successors in Scotland's fight for spiritual liberty. Their banner, while it was inscribed "For Christ's crown and covenant," was equally an expression of their hatred of civil misrule.

The Assertory Act of 1669 had declared that the ordering of all things relating to the external government of the Church and all ecclesiastical matters and persons was inherent in the person of the sovereign. That was enough for the Protesters: Episcopacy was identified in their minds with the crudest variety of Erastianism—and they would have none of it. Prelacy and the royal supremacy were mixed up together. Each supported the other. "The monstrous dragon of Erastian Prelacy," said Thomas Forrester in 1684, "hath charmed the nation into ane amazing stupidity."[1]

Nevertheless, it was one thing for the Covenanters to stand out boldly in defence of their principles—and quite another for them to take some of the steps they did to remedy the disease. It does not involve our agreement with every facet of their policy to say that their persistence against the efforts of the State to extinguish their freedom of conscience was entirely justified. When we consider the background against which they lived out their lives, we can readily understand how it necessarily brought a perilous margin between genuine suffering for conscience' sake and a sheer bigotry which was far from the spirit of the Gospel which they professed to uphold. We can see how opinions can differ so radically about the Covenanters, and how in surprisingly few historians of this period there is a completely impartial-sounding voice (if history allows such a thing at all). If this was the age of partisanship, some of it has infected later writers. Their colouring is always intensified: lights are heightened, shades darkened, according to the sympathies of the reporter.

---

[1] *Review and Examination of . . . the Controverted Points of the Covenants*. Formerly curate of Alva, Forrester had resigned and sided with the Covenanters. After the Revolution he became the colleague of Alexander Shields at St. Andrews, and was later Principal of the University there.

We must regard the reigns of Charles II and James VII as a whole—as a chapter in Scotland's fight for spiritual independence —or we shall be lured into wrong decisions and misplaced emphases. Man always falls far short of the ideal for which he strives (Browning finds divine encouragement here), but that he does so is criticism probably of himself, certainly not of the ideal. The faults of the Covenanters were the faults natural to their own temperament and to the intense atmosphere in which they lived. They were goaded beyond all endurance by the Government— and are condemned beyond all reason by those few writers who since then have somewhat ineffectually tried to explain away the atrocities of that Government. Such condemnation is undeserved, both by its very nature, and even more by the fact that it is a tacit criticism of that deposition of the Stuart dynasty which was the will of the vast majority of the Scottish and English peoples. Only the Covenanters, preaching "living truths for dying times," maintained a consistent opposition during those last years of tyranny. To them might apply Josiah Quincy's words: "Blandishments will not fascinate us, nor will threats of a 'halter' intimidate. For, under God, we are determined that wheresoever, whosoever, or howsoever we shall be called to make our exit, we will die free men."[1] The democratic principles of the English-speaking world today reflect that teaching in regard to civil rights which was the Reformed tradition in Scotland.

For us today it is mean work to be hyper-critical of those who fought and died in contributing towards the happy Church-State relationship and the religious freedom which we enjoy in our time.[2] Theodore Roosevelt, in his book *The Winning of the West*, expresses thus the debt his countrymen owe to the seventeenth- and eighteenth-century Scots: "It is doubtful if we have realized in the leadership of our country the part played by that stern and virile people, the Scotch-Irish, whose predecessors taught the creed of Knox and Calvin. They . . . became the vanguard of our civilization. . . . These were the men who first declared for American Independence. . . . They were the kinsfolk of the Covenanters; they deemed it a religious duty to interpret their own Bible. . . . For generations their whole ecclesiastical and scholastic systems had been found fundamentally democratic."[3]

In 1638, some 60,000 people were said to have thronged the

---

[1] *Observations on the Boston Port Bill*, 1744.
[2] We say this despite the view held by a correspondent expressed in the *Glasgow Herald* of 14th March, 1962, thus: "It is surely enough that Scotland is still to-day partially sunk in Covenanting gloom without having to be grateful to the Covenanters for it."
[3] Vol. I, p. 195; see also "The Scottish Ancestors of President Roosevelt," *Scottish Historical Review*, Vol. I, 1904, pp. 416–20.

streets of Edinburgh when the National Covenant was signed; 300,000 were estimated to have subscribed throughout the country, and some of the greatest nobles were then its supporters. Fifty years later the fight was won—and the Covenant at the time was represented only by eighty pastorless societies[1] and a membership of 7,000 souls. None of them were nobles or people of influence; some had "mean Education and little other Learning, then what they learned in the Gospel of Him, who is meek and lowly";[2] all of them had the unsearchable riches of Christ in their hearts.

An English historian provides a fitting summary. J. A. Froude, Anglican deacon, after years of careful research among all available records, spoke of the Covenanters as benefactors of mankind, in these terms:

> And now suppose the Kirk had been the broad, liberal, philosophical, intellectual thing which some people think it ought to have been, how would it have fared in that crusade; how altogether would it have encountered those surplices of Archbishop Laud or those dragoons of Claverhouse? It is hard to lose one's life for a "perhaps", and nothing more. For more than half the seventeenth century, the battle had to be fought out in Scotland, which in reality was the battle between liberty and despotism; and where except in an intense, burning conviction that they were maintaining God's cause against the devil, could the poor Scotch people have found the strength for the unequal struggle which was forced upon them? Toleration is a good thing in its place; but you cannot tolerate what will not tolerate you, and is trying to cut your throat. Enlightenment you cannot have enough of, but it must be the true enlightenment, which sees a thing in all its bearings. The Covenanters fought the fight and won the victory; and then, and not till then, came the David Humes with their political economies, and steam-engines, and railroads, and political institutions, and all the blessed or unblessed fruits of liberty.[3]

But let theirs be the last word, spoken by one of the first Protesters, with little thought of any personal application. The word is Samuel Rutherford's, in a letter to the Earl of Cassillis, dated 9th September, 1637. He writes: "Your honourable ancestors, with the hazard of their lives, brought Christ to our hands, and it shall be cruelty to posterity if ye lose Him to them." There is no doubting the relevance of that message for the world today.

---

[1] Alexander Shields, who succeeded Renwick as leader of the Cameronians, had only the status of probationer, and was not ordained minister until after the Revolution.
[2] *Naphtali*, 1693, p. 19.
[3] *The Influence of the Reformation on the Scottish Character*, 1895, Vol. I, p. 180.

THE KING'S CONFESSION, 1580 [1581]

WE ALL AND EVERY ONE OF US UNDERWRITTEN, PROTEST, THAT, after long and due examination of our own consciences in matters of true and false religion we are now thoroughly resolved in the truth by the Word and Spirit of God; and, therefore, we believe with our hearts, confess with our mouths, subscribe with our hands, and constantly affirm, before God and the whole world, that this only is the true Christian faith and religion, pleasing God, and bringing salvation to man, which is now by the mercy of God, revealed to the world by the preaching of the blessed evangel; and is received, believed, and defended by many and sundry notable kirks and realms, but chiefly by the Kirk of Scotland, the King's majesty, and three estates of this realm, as God's eternal truth, and only ground of our salvation; as more particularly is expressed in the Confession of our Faith, established and publicly confirmed by sundry acts of Parliament, and now of a long time hath been openly professed by the King's majesty, and whole body of this realm both in burgh and land. To the which Confession and Form of religion we willingly agree in our consciences in all points as unto God's undoubted truth and verity, grounded only upon His written Word. And therefore we abhor and detest all contrary religion and doctrine; but chiefly all kinds of Papistry in general and particular heads, even as they are now condemned and confuted by the Word of God and Kirk of Scotland. But, in special we detest and refuse the usurped authority of that Roman Antichrist upon the Scriptures of God, upon the kirk, the civil magistrate, and consciences of men; all his tyrannous laws made upon indifferent things against our Christian liberty; his erroneous doctrine against the sufficiency of the written Word, the perfection of the law, the offices of Christ, and this blessed evangel; his corrupted doctrine concerning original sin, our natural inability and rebellion to God's law, our justification by faith only, our imperfect sanctification and obedience to the law; the nature, number and use of the holy sacraments; his five bastard sacraments, with all his rites, ceremonies and false doctrine, added to the ministration of the true sacraments without the Word of God; his cruel judgment against infants departing without the sacraments; his absolute necessity of baptism; his blasphemous opinion of transubstantiation or real presence of Christ's body in the elements and receiving the same by the wicked, or bodies of men; his dispensations with oaths, perjuries, and degrees of marriage forbidden in the Word; his cruelty against the innocent divorced; his devilish mass; his blasphemous priesthood; his profane sacrifices for the sins of the dead and the quick; his canonization of men; calling upon angels and saints departed; worshipping of imagery, relics, and crosses; dedicating of kirks, altars, days; vows to creatures; his purgatory, prayers for the dead; praying or speaking in a strange language; his processions, and blasphemous litany, and multitude of advocates or mediators; his manifold orders, auricular confession; his desperate and uncertain repentance; his general and doubtsome faith; his satisfactions of men for their sins; his justification by works; his opus operatum, works of supererogation, merits, pardons, peregrinations, and stations; his holy water, baptising of bells, conjuring of spirits, crossing, sayning, anointing, conjuring, hallowing of God's good creatures, with the superstitious opinion joined therewith; his worldly monarchy, and wicked hierarchy; his three solemn vows, with all his shavelings of sundry sorts; his erroneous and bloody decrees made at Trent, with all the subscribers and approvers of that bloody bond, conjured against the kirk of God. And finally, we detest all his vain allegories, rites, signs, and traditions brought into the kirk without or against the Word of God, and doctrine of this true reformed kirk; to the which we join ourselves willingly in doctrine, faith, religion, discipline, and use of the holy sacraments, as lively members of the same in Christ our Head: promising and swearing, by the great name of the Lord our God, that we shall continue in the obedience of the doctrine and discipline of this kirk, and shall defend the same, according to our vocation and power, all the days of our lives; under the pains contained in the law, and danger both of body and soul in the day of God's fearful judgment.

And seeing that many are stirred up by Satan, and that Roman Antichrist, to promise, swear, subscribe, and for a time use the holy sacraments in the kirk deceitfully, against their own conscience, minding hereby, first, under the external cloak of religion, to corrupt and subvert secretly God's true religion within the kirk, and afterward, when time may serve, to become open enemies and persecutors of the same, under vain hope of the Pope's dispensation, devised against the Word of God, to his greater confusion, and their double condemnation in the day of the Lord Jesus: We, therefore, willing to take away all suspicion of hypocrisy, and of such double-dealing with God and His kirk, protest, and call the Searcher of all hearts for witness, that our minds and hearts do fully agree with this our Confession, promise, oath, and subscription; so that we are not moved for any worldly respect, but are persuaded only in our conscience through the knowledge and love of God's true religion imprinted in our hearts by the Holy Spirit, as we shall answer to Him in the day when the secrets of all hearts shall be disclosed.

And because we perceive, that the quietness and stability of our religion and kirk doth depend upon the safety and good behaviour of the Kings Majesty, as upon a comfortable instrument of God's mercy, granted to this country, for the maintaining of His kirk, and ministra-

THE KING'S CONFESSION, 1580 [1581]

tion of justice among us, we protest and promise solemnly with our hearts, under the same oath handwrit, and pains, that we shall defend his person and authority with our geare, bodies, and lives, in the defence of Christ, His evangel, liberty of our country, ministration of justice, and punishment of iniquity, against all enemies within this realm or without, as we desire our God to be a strong and merciful Defender to us in the day of our death, and coming of our Lord Jesus Christ; to whom, with the Father, and the Holy Spirit, be all honour and glory eternally. Amen.

APPENDIX II

THE NATIONAL COVENANT, 1638

THE CONFESSION OF FAITH, SUBSCRIBED AT FIRST BY THE KING'S Majesty and his household in the yeere of God 1580; thereafter by persons of all rankes, in the year 1581, by ordinance of the Lords of the Secret Councell, and Acts of the Generall Assembly; subscribed againe by all sorts of persons in the yeere 1590 by a new ordinance of Councell, at the desire of the General Assembly, with a generall band for maintenance of the true religion and the King's person; and now subscribed in the yeere 1638 by us noblemen, barons, gentlemen, burgesses, ministers, and commons, under subscribing, together with our resolution and promises, for the causes after specified, to maintaine the said true religion, and the King's Majestie, according to the Confession foresaid and Acts of Parliament. [Here is repeated the King's Confession, see Appendix I.]

Likeas many Acts of Parliament, not only in general do abrogate, annul and rescind all laws, statutes, acts, constitutions, canons, civil or municipal, with all other ordinances, and practique penalties whatsoever, made in prejudice of the true religion, and professors thereof; or of the true kirk, discipline, jurisdiction, and freedom thereof; or in favours of idolatry and superstition, or of the Papistical kirk: As Act 3. Act 31. Parl. 1. Act 23. Parl. 11, Act 114. Parl. 12. of King James VI. That Papistry and superstition may be utterly suppressed according to the intention of the Acts of Parliament, repeated in the 5th Act, Parl. 20. King James VI. And to that end they ordain all Papists and Priests to be punished with manifold civil and ecclesiastical pains, as adversaries to God's true religion, preached, and by law established, within this realm, Act 24. Parl. 11. King James VI.; as common enemies to all Christian government, Act 18. Parl. 16. King James VI.; as rebellers and gainstanders of our sovereign Lord's authority, Act 47. Parl. 3. King James VI.; and as idolaters, Act 104. Parl. 7. King James VI. But also in particular, by and attour the Confession of Faith, do abolish and condemn the Pope's authority and jurisdiction out of this land, and ordains the maintainers thereof to be punished, Act 2. Parl. 1. Act 51. Parl. 3. Act 106. Parl. 7. Act 114. Parl. 12. King James VI. do condemn the Pope's erroneous doctrine, or any other erroneous doctrine repugnant to any of the articles of the true and Christian religion, publicly preached, and by law established in this realm; and ordains the spreaders and makers of books or libels, or letters or writs of that nature to be punished, Act 46. Parl. 3. Act 106. Parl. 7. Act 24, Parl.

11. King James VI. do condemn all baptism conform to the Pope's kirk, and the idolatry of the mass; and ordains all sayers, wilful hearers, and concealers of the mass, the maintainers and resetters of the priests, Jesuits, trafficking Papists, to be punished without any exception or restriction, Act 5. Parl. 1. Act 120. Parl. 12. Act 164. Parl. 13. Act 193. Parl. 14. Act 1. Parl. 19. Act 5. Parl. 20. King James VI. do condemn all erroneous books and writs containing erroneous doctrine against the religion presently professed, or containing superstitious rites and ceremonies Papistical, whereby the people are greatly abused, and ordains the home-bringers of them to be punished, Act 15. Parl. 11. King James VI. do condemn the monuments and dregs of bygone idolatry, as going to crosses, observing the festival days of saints, and such other superstitious and Papistical rites, to the dishonour of God, contempt of true religion, and fostering of great error among the people; and ordains the users of them to be punished for the second fault, as idolaters, Act 104. Parl. 7. King James VI.

Likeas many Acts of Parliament are conceived for maintenance of God's true and Christian religion, and the purity thereof, in doctrine and sacraments of the true Church of God, the liberty and freedom thereof, and her national, synodal assemblies, presbyteries, sessions, policy, discipline, and jurisdiction thereof; as that purity of religion, and liberty of the Church was used, professed, exercised, preached, and confessed, according to the reformation of religion in this realm; As for instance, the 99th Act, Parl. 7. Act 25. Parl. 11. Act 114. Parl. 12. Act 160. Parl. 13. of King James VI. ratified by the 4th Act of King Charles. So that the 6th Act, Parl. 1. and 68th Act, Parl. 6. of King James VI. in the year of God 1579, declare the ministers of the blessed evangel, whom God of his mercy had raised up, or hereafter should raise, aggreeing with them that then lived, in doctrine and administration of the sacraments; and the people that professed Christ, as he was then offered in the evangel, and doth communicate with the holy sacraments (as in the reformed Kirks of this realm they were presently administrate) according to the Confession of Faith, to be the true and holy Kirk of Christ Jesus within this realm. And decerns and declares all and sundry, who either gainsay the word of the evangel received and approved as the heads of the Confession of Faith, professed in Parliament in the year of God 1560, specified also in the first Parliament of King James VI. and ratified in this present Parliament, more particularly do express; or that refuse the administration of the holy sacraments, as they were then minisrated, to be no members of the said Kirk within this realm, and true religion presently professed, so long as they keep themselves so divided from the society of Christ's body. And the subsequent Act 69. Parl. 6. of King James VI. declares, that there is no other face of Kirk, nor other face of religion, than was presently at that time, by the favour of God, established within this realm: "Which therefore is ever styled God's true religion, Christ's true religion, the true and Christian religion, and a perfect religion;" which by manifold Acts of Parliament, all within this realm are bound to profess, to subscribe the articles thereof, the Confession of Faith, to recant all doctrine and errors repugnant to any of the said articles, Act 4. and 9. Parl. 1. Acts 45, 46, 47. Parl. 3. Act 71. Parl. 6. Act 106. Parl. 7. Act 24. Parl. 11. Act 123. Parl. 12. Act 194 and 197. Parl. 14. of King James VI. And all magistrates, sheriffs, etc., on the one part, are ordained to search, apprehend, and punish all contraveners: For instance, Act 5. Parl. 1. Act 104. Parl. 7. Act 25. Parl. 11. King James VI.; and that notwithstanding of the King's Majesty's licences on the contrary, which are discharged, and declared to be of no force, in so far as they tend in any wise to the prejudice and hinder of the execution of the Acts of Parliament against Papists and adversaries of true religion, Act 106. Parl. 7. King James VI. On the other part, in the 47th Act, Parl. 3. King James VI. it is declared and ordained, Seeing the cause of God's true religion and his Highness's authority are so joined, as the hurt of the one is common to both; that none shall be reputed as loyal and faithful subjects to our sovereign Lord, or his authority, but be punishable as rebellers and gainstanders of the same, who shall not give their confession, and make their profession of the said true religion: and that they who, after defection, shall give the confession of their faith of new, they shall promise to continue therein in time coming, to maintain our sovereign Lord's authority, and at the uttermost of their power to fortify, assist, and maintain the true preachers and professors of Christ's religion, against whatsoever enemies and gainstanders of the same; and namely, against all such, of whatsoever nation, estate, or degree they be of, that have joined and bound themselves, or have assisted, or assist, to set forward and execute the cruel decrees of the council of Trent, contrary to the true preachers and professors of the Word of God; which is repeated, word by word, in the articles of pacification at Perth, the 23d of February, 1572, approved by Parliament the last of April 1573, ratified in Parliament 1587, and related Act 123. Parl. 12. of King James VI.; with this addition, "That they are bound to resist all treasonable uproars and hostilities raised against the true religion, the King's Majesty, and the true professors."

Likeas all lieges are bound to maintain the King's Majesty's royal person and authority, the authority of Parliaments, without the which neither any laws or lawful judicatories can be established, Act 130 and 131. Parl. 8. King James VI. and the subjects' liberties, who ought only to live and be governed by the King's laws, the common laws of this realm allenarly, Act 48. Parl. 3. King James I. Act 79. Parl. 6. King James IV.; repeated in the Act 131. Parl. 8. King James VI.; which if they be innovated and prejudged, "the commission anent the union of the two kingdoms of Scotland and England, which is the sole act of the 17th Parl. of King James VI. declares," such confusion would ensue as this realm could be no more a free monarchy; because, by the fundamental laws, ancient privileges, offices, and liberties of this kingdom, not only the princely authority of his Majesty's royal descent hath been these many ages maintained, but also the people's security of their lands, livings, rights, offices, liberties, and dignities preserved. And therefore, for the preservation of the said true religion, laws, and liberties of this kingdom, it is statute by the 8th Act, Parl. 1. repeated in the 99th Act, Parl. 7. ratified in the 23d Act, Parl. 11. and 114th Act, Parl. 12. of King James VI. and 4th Act, Parl. 1. of King Charles I. "That all Kings and Princes at their coronation, and reception of their princely authority, shall make their faithful promise by their solemn oath, in the presence of the eternal God, that, enduring the whole time of their lives, they shall serve the same eternal God, to the uttermost of their power, according as He hath required in His most holy word, contained in the Old and New Testament: and according to the same word, shall maintain the true religion of Christ Jesus, the preaching of His holy word, the due and right ministration of the sacraments now received and preached within this realm, (according to the Confession of Faith immediately preceding,) and shall abolish and gainstand all false religion, contrary to the same; and shall rule the people committed to their charge, according to the will and command of God revealed in His foresaid word, and according to the laudable laws and constitutions received in this realm, nowise repugnant to the said will of the eternal God; and shall procure to the uttermost of their power, to the Kirk of God, and whole Christian people, true and perfect peace in all time coming: and that they shall be careful to root out of their empire all hereticks and enemies to the true worship of God, who shall be convicted by the true Kirk of God of the foresaid crimes." Which was also observed by his Majesty, at his coronation in Edinburgh 1633, as may be seen in the order of the coronation.

In obedience to the commandment of God, conform to the practice of the godly in former times, and according to the laudable example of our worthy and religious progenitors, and of many yet living amongst us, which was warranted also by act of Council, commanding a general band to be made and subscribed by his Majesty's subjects of all ranks; for two causes: one was, For defending the true religion, as it was then reformed, and is expressed in the Confession of Faith above written, and a former large Confession established by sundry acts of lawful General Assemblies and of Parliaments, unto which it hath relation, set down in publick Catechisms; and which hath been for many years, with a blessing from Heaven, preached and professed in this Kirk and kingdom, as God's undoubted truth, grounded only upon His written word. The other cause was, For maintaining the King's Majesty, his person and estate; the true worship of God and the King's authority being so straitly joined, as that they had the same friends and common enemies, and did stand and fall together. And finally, being convinced in our minds, and confessing with our mouths, that the present and succeeding generations in this land are bound to keep the foresaid national oath and subscriptions inviolable.

We Noblemen, Barons, Gentlemen, Burgesses, Ministers, and Commons under-subscribing, considering divers times before, and especially at this time, the danger of the true reformed religion, of the King's honour, and of the publick peace of the kingdom, by the manifold innovations and evils generally contained, and particularly mentioned in our late supplications, complaints, and protestations; do hereby profess, and before God, His angels, and the world, solemnly declare,

That with our whole heart we agree, and resolve all the days of our life constantly to adhere unto and to defend the foresaid true religion, and (forbearing the practice of all novations already introduced in the matters of the worship of God, or approbation of the corruptions of the publick government of the Kirk, or civil places and power of kirkmen, till they be tried and allowed in free Assemblies and in Parliaments) to labour, by all means lawful, to recover the purity and liberty of the Gospel, as it was established and professed before the foresaid novations. And because, after due examination, we plainly perceive, and undoubtedly believe, that the innovations and evils contained in our supplications, complaints, and protestations, have no warrant of the word of God, are contrary to the articles of the foresaid Confession, to the intention and meaning of the blessed reformers of religion in this land, to the above-written Acts of Parliament; and do sensibly tend to the re-establishing of the Popish religion and tyranny, and to the subversion and ruin of the true reformed religion, and of our liberties, laws, and estates; we also declare, That the foresaid Confessions are to be interpreted, and ought to be understood of the foresaid novations and evils, no less than if every one of them had been expressed in the foresaid Confessions; and that we are obliged to detest and abhor them, amongst other particular heads of Papistry abjured therein. And therefore, from the knowledge and conscience of our duty to God, to our King and country, without any worldly respect or inducement, so far as human infirmity will suffer, wishing a further measure of the grace of God for this effect: we promise and swear, by the GREAT NAME OF THE LORD OUR GOD, to continue in the profession and obedience of the foresaid religion; and that we shall defend the same, and resist all these contrary errors and corruptions, according to our vocation, and to the uttermost of that power that God hath put in our hands, all the days of our life.

And in like manner, with the same heart, we declare before God and men, That we have no intention nor desire to attempt any thing that may turn to the dishonour of God, or to the diminution of the King's greatness and authority; but, on the contrary, we promise and swear, That we shall to the uttermost of our power, with our means and lives, stand to the defence of our dread Sovereign the King's Majesty, his person and authority, in the defence and preservation of the foresaid true religion, liberties, and laws of the kingdom; as also to the mutual defence and assistance every one of us of another, in the same cause of maintaining the true religion, and his Majesty's authority, with our best counsel, our bodies, means, and whole power, against all sorts of persons whatsoever; so that whatsoever shall be done to the least of us for that cause, shall be taken as done to us all in general, and to every one of us in particular. And that we shall neither directly nor indirectly suffer ourselves to be divided or withdrawn, by whatsoever suggestion, combination, allurement, or terror, from this blessed and loyal conjunction; nor shall cast in any let or impediment that may stay or hinder any such resolution as by common consent shall be found to conduce for so good ends; but, on the contrary, shall by all lawful means labour to further and promote the same: and if any such dangerous and divisive motion be made to us by word or writ, we and every one of us shall either suppress it, or, if need be, shall incontinent make the same known that it may be timeously obviated. Neither do we fear the foul aspersions of rebellion, combination, or what else our adversaries, from their craft and malice, would put upon us; seeing what we do is so well warranted, and ariseth from an unfeigned desire to maintain the true worship of God, the majesty of our King, and the peace of the kingdom, for the common happiness of ourselves and our posterity.

And because we cannot look for a blessing from God upon our proceedings, except with our profession and subscription, we join such a life and conversation as beseemeth Christians who have renewed their covenant with God; we therefore faithfully promise for ourselves, our followers, and all others under us, both in publick, and in our particular families, and personal carriage, to endeavour to keep ourselves within the bounds of Christian liberty, and to be good examples to others of all godliness, soberness, and righteousness, and of every duty we owe to God and man.

And, that this our union and conjunction may be observed without violation, we call the LIVING GOD, THE SEARCHER OF OUR HEARTS, to witness, who knoweth this to be our sincere desire and unfeigned resolution, as we shall answer to JESUS CHRIST in the great day, and under the pain of God's everlasting wrath, and of infamy and loss of all honour and respect in this world: most humbly beseeching the LORD to strengthen us by His HOLY SPIRIT for this end, and to bless our desires and proceedings with a happy success; that religion and righteousness may flourish in the land, to the glory of GOD, the honour of our King, and peace and comfort of us all. In witness whereof, we have subscribed with our hands all the premises.

THE article of this Covenant, which was at the first subscription referred to the determination of the General Assembly, being now determined; and thereby the five articles of Perth, the government of the Kirk by bishops, and the civil places and power of kirkmen, upon the reasons and grounds contained in the Acts of the General Assembly, declared to be unlawful within this Kirk, we subscribe according to the determination aforesaid.

THE SOLEMN LEAGUE AND COVENANT, 1643

WE NOBLEMEN, BARONS, KNIGHTS, GENTLEMEN, CITIZENS, BUR-
gesses, Ministers of the Gospel, and Commons of all sorts,
in the kingdoms of Scotland, England, and Ireland, by the
providence of GOD, living under one King, and being of one reformed
religion, having before our eyes the glory of God and the advancement
of the kingdom of our Lord and Saviour JESUS CHRIST, the honour
and happiness of the King's Majesty and his posterity, and the true
publick liberty, safety, and peace of the kingdoms, wherein every one's
private condition is included: And calling to mind the treacherous and
bloody plots, conspiracies, attempts, and practices of the enemies of
GOD against the true religion and professors thereof in all places,
especially in these three kingdoms, ever since the reformation of religion; and how much their rage, power, and presumption are of late,
and at this time, increased and exercised, whereof the deplorable state
of the church and kingdom of Ireland, the distressed estate of the
church and kingdom of England, and the dangerous estate of the
church and kingdom of Scotland, are present and publick testimonies;
we have now at last (after other means of supplication, remonstrance,
protestation, and suffering), for the preservation of ourselves and our
religion from utter ruin and destruction, according to the commend-
able practice of these kingdoms in former times, and the example of
GOD's people in other nations, after mature deliberation, resolved and
determined to enter into a mutual and Solemn League and Covenant,
wherein we all subscribe, and each one of us for himself, with our
hands lifted up to the most High GOD, do swear,—

I. That we shall sincerely, really, and constantly, through the grace
of GOD, endeavour, in our several places and callings, the preservation of the reformed religion in the Church of Scotland, in doctrine,
worship, discipline, and government, against our common enemies;
the reformation of religion in the kingdoms of England and Ireland,
in doctrine, worship, discipline, and government, according to the
Word of GOD, and the example of the best reformed Churches; and
shall endeavour to bring the Churches of GOD in the three kingdoms
to the nearest conjunction and uniformity in religion, confession of
faith, form of church government, directory for worship and cate-
chising; that we, and our posterity after us, may, as brethren, live in
faith and love, and the Lord may delight to dwell in the midst of us.

II. That we shall in like manner, without respect of persons, endeavour the extirpation of Popery, Prelacy, (that is, church government by Archbishops, Bishops, their Chancellors, and Commissaries, Deans, Deans and Chapters, Archdeacons, and all other ecclesiastical officers depending on that hierarchy,) superstition, heresy, schism, profaneness, and whatsoever shall be found to be contrary to sound doctrine and the power of godliness; lest we partake in other men's sins, and thereby be in danger to receive of their plagues; and that the Lord may be one, and His name one, in the three kingdoms.

III. We shall, with the same sincerity, reality, and constancy, in our several vocations, endeavour, with our estates and lives, mutually to preserve the rights and privileges of the Parliaments, and the liberties of the kingdoms; and to preserve and defend the King's Majesty's person and authority, in the preservation and defence of the true religion and liberties of the kingdoms; that the world may bear witness with our consciences of our loyalty, and that we have no thoughts or intentions to diminish his Majesty's just power and greatness.

IV. We shall also, with all faithfulness, endeavour the discovery of all such as have been or shall be incendiaries, malignants, or evil instruments, by hindering the reformation of religion, dividing the King from his people, or one of the kingdoms from another, or making any faction or parties amongst the people, contrary to this League and Covenant; that they may be brought to publick trial, and receive condign punishment, as the degree of their offences shall require or deserve, or the supreme judicatories of both kingdoms respectively, or others having power from them for that effect, shall judge convenient.

V. And whereas the happiness of a blessed peace between these kingdoms, denied in former times to our progenitors, is, by the good providence of GOD, granted unto us, and hath been lately concluded and settled by both Parliaments; we shall each one of us, according to our place and interest, endeavour that they may remain conjoined in a firm peace and union to all posterity; and that justice may be done upon the wilful opposers thereof, in manner expressed in the precedent article.

VI. We shall also, according to our places and callings, in this common cause of religion, liberty, and peace of the kingdoms, assist and defend all those that enter into this League and Covenant, in the maintaining and pursuing thereof; and shall not suffer ourselves, directly or indirectly, by whatsoever combination, persuasion, or terror, to be divided or withdrawn from this blessed union and conjunction, whether to make defection to the contrary part, or to give ourselves to a detestable indifferency or neutrality in this cause which so much concerneth the glory of GOD, the good of the kingdom, and honour of the King; but shall, all the days of our lives, zealously and constantly continue therein against all opposition, and promote the same, according to our power, against all lets and impediments whatsoever; and, what we are not able ourselves to suppress or overcome, we shall reveal and make known, that it may be timely prevented or removed: All which we shall do as in the sight of God.

And, because these kingdoms are guilty of many sins and provocations against GOD, and His Son JESUS CHRIST, as is too manifest by our present distresses and dangers, the fruits thereof; we profess and declare before GOD and the world, our unfeigned desire to be humbled for our own sins, and for the sins of these kingdoms: especially, that we have not as we ought valued the inestimable benefit of the gospel; that we have not laboured for the purity and power thereof; and that we have not endeavoured to receive CHRIST in our hearts, nor to walk worthy of Him in our lives; which are the causes of other sins and transgressions so much abounding amongst us; and our true and un-feigned purpose, desire, and endeavour for ourselves, and all others under our power and charge, both in publick and in private, in all duties we owe to GOD and man, to amend our lives, and each one to go before another in the example of a real reformation; that the Lord may turn away His wrath and heavy indignation, and establish these churches and kingdoms in truth and peace. And this Covenant we make in the presence of ALMIGHTY GOD, the Searcher of all hearts, with a true intention to perform the same, as we shall answer at that great day when the secrets of all hearts shall be disclosed; most humbly beseeching the LORD to strengthen us by His HOLY SPIRIT for this end, and to bless our desires and proceedings with such success, as may be deliverance and safety to His people, and encouragement to other Christian churches groaning under, or in danger of, the yoke of anti-christian tyranny, to join in the same or like association and Covenant, to the glory of GOD, the enlargement of the kingdom of JESUS CHRIST, and the peace and tranquillity of Christian kingdoms and common-wealths.

OATH REQUIRED BY THE TEST ACT, 1681

I, A.B., SOLEMNLY SWEAR, IN PRESENCE OF THE ETERNAL GOD, WHOM I invocate as judge and witness of my sincere intention in this my oath, that I own and sincerely profess the true protestant religion, contained in the Confession of Faith, recorded in the first parliament of king James VI. and that I believe the same to be founded on and agreeable to the written word of God: and I promise and swear, that I shall adhere thereunto during all the days of my life-time, and shall endeavour to educate my children therein, and shall never consent to any change or alteration contrary thereunto; and that I disown and renounce all such principles, doctrines, or practices, whether popish or fanatical, which are contrary unto, and inconsistent with the said protestant religion, and Confession of Faith: and, for testification of my obedience to my most gracious sovereign Charles II. I do affirm and swear, by this my solemn oath, that the king's majesty is the only supreme governor of this realm, over all persons, and in all causes, as well ecclesiastical as civil; and that no foreign prince, person, pope, prelate, state or potentate, hath or ought to have any jurisdiction, power, superiority, pre-eminency, or authority ecclesiastical or civil, within this realm, and therefore, I do utterly renounce and forsake all foreign jurisdictions, powers, superiorities, and authorities; and do promise, that from henceforth I shall bear faith and true allegiance to the king's majesty, his heirs and lawful successors; and, to my power, shall assist and defend all rights, jurisdictions, prerogatives, privileges, pre-eminencies, and authorities belonging to the king's majesty, his heirs and lawful successors: and I further affirm and swear by this my solemn oath, that I judge it unlawful for subjects, upon pretence of reformation or any pretence whatsomever, to enter into covenants or leagues, or to convocate, convene or assemble in any councils, conventions or assemblies, to treat, consult, or determine in any matter of state, civil, or ecclesiastic, without his majesty's special command, or express license had thereunto, or to take up arms against the king, or those commissionate by him; and that I shall never so rise in arms, or enter into such covenants or assemblies, and that there lies no obligation upon me from the national covenant, or the solemn league and covenant (so commonly called) or any other manner of way whatsomever, to endeavour any change or alteration in the government, either in church or state, as it is now established by the laws of this kingdom: and I promise and swear, that I shall, with my utmost power, defend, assist, and maintain his majesty's jurisdiction foresaid, against all deadly; and I shall never decline his majesty's power and jurisdiction, as I shall answer to God. And finally, I affirm and swear, that this my solemn oath is given in the plain genuine sense and meaning of the words, without any equivocation, mental reservation, or any manner of evasion whatsomever; and that I shall not accept or use any dispensation from any creature whatsomever. So help me God."

BIBLIOGRAPHY

Volumes marked * are particularly useful for any study of the Covenanting period.

Airy, O., *Charles II*, 1904.
Airy, O. (ed.), *Lauderdale Papers*, 3 vols., 1884–5.
*Baillie, R., *Letters and Journals*, 3 vols., 1841–2.
Balfour, J., *Historical Works*, Vol. IV, 1825.
Blackadder, J., *Memoirs*, ed. A. Crichton, 1823.
*Brown, John (of Wamphray), *An Apologeticall Relation . . .*, 1665.
Brown, John (of Wamphray), *The History of the Indulgence*, 1678.
Brown, P. H., *History of Scotland*, Vol. II, 1911.
Brown, P. H., *Surveys of Scottish History*, 1919.
Brown, T., *Church and State in Scotland*, 1891.
Buchan, J., *Montrose*, 1928.
*Buchanan, G., *De Jure Regni apud Scotos* (in *The Presbyterian's Armoury*, Vol. III), 1846.
Burleigh, J. H. S., *A Church History of Scotland*, 1960.
*Burnet, G., *History of His Own Time*, Vols. I, II, 1724–.
Butler, D., *Life and Letters of Robert Leighton*, 1903.

Campbell, W. M., *The Triumph of Presbyterianism*, 1958.

Dickinson, W. C. and Donaldson, G., *A Source Book of Scottish History*, Vol. III, 1954.
Durham, J., *A Dying Man's Testament to the Church of Scotland*, 1659.
Firth, C. H. (ed.), *Scotland and the Commonwealth*, 1651–3, 1895.
Firth, C. H. (ed.), *Scotland and the Protectorate*, 1654–9, 1899.
Fyfe, J. G., *Scottish Diaries and Memoirs*, 1550–1746, 1927.

*Gillespie, G., *Aaron's Rod Blossoming*, and other works in *The Presbyterian's Armoury*, Vols. I–II, 1846.
Grub, G., *An Ecclesiastical History of Scotland*, Vol. III, 1861.
Guthrie, J., *Causes of God's Wrath against Scotland*, 1653.
Guthry, H., *Memoirs*, 1748.

Hanna, C. A., *The Scotch-Irish*, 2 vols., 1902.
Henderson, G. D., *Religious Life in 17th Century Scotland*, 1937.
*Hewison, J. K., *The Covenanters*, 2 vols., 1908.
Howie, J., *Scots Worthies*, 1902.

Jaffray, A., *Diary and Memoirs*, ed. J. Barclay, 1883.
Johnston, J. C., *Treasury of the Scottish Covenant*, 1887.
*Kirkton, J., *The Secret and True History of the Church of Scotland*, ed. C. K. Sharpe, 1817.
Knox, J., *History of the Reformation*, ed. W. C. Dickinson, 2 vols., 1949.

Lauder, Sir J. (of Fountainhall), *Historical Observes of Memorable Occurrents*, 1840.

Law, R., *Memorialls*, ed. C. K. Sharpe, 1818.

McCrie, C. G., *The Confessions of the Church of Scotland*, 1907.

McCrie, T. (the Younger), *Sketches of Scottish Church History*, 2 vols., 1846–9.

Mackenzie, A. M., *The Passing of the Stuarts*, 1937.

Mackenzie, Sir G., *Memoirs of the Affairs of Scotland*, ed. T. Thomson, 1818.

Mackenzie, Sir G., *Vindication of the Government of Charles II*, 1691.

Mackenzie, W. C., *Life and Times of John Maitland, Duke of Lauderdale, 1616–1682*, 1923.

Macpherson, H., *The Cameronian Philosopher: Alexander Shields*, 1932.

*Macpherson, H., *The Covenanters under Persecution*, 1923.

Macpherson, J., *The Doctrine of the Church in Scottish Theology*, 1903.

McWard, R., *Earnest Contendings for the Faith*, 1723.

McWard, R., *The Poor Man's Cup of Cold Water*, 1678.

Maidment, J. (ed.), *The Spottiswoode Miscellany*, 2 vols., 1844–5.

*Mathieson, W. L., *Politics and Religion in Scotland . . . from the Reformation to the Revolution*, 2 vols., 1902.

Millar, J. H., *Scottish Prose of the Seventeenth and Eighteenth Centuries*, 1912.

Morton, A. S., *Galloway and the Covenanters*, 1914.

Napier, M., *Memorials of Montrose and His Times*, 2 vols., 1848–50.

Orr, R. L., *Alexander Henderson*, 1919.

Pearson, J. N., *Life of Leighton*, 1829.

*Renwick, J., *An Informatory Vindication*, 1707.

Renwick, J., *Prefaces, Lectures and Sermons*, 1776.

Rutherford, S., *A Free Disputation against Pretended Liberty of Conscience*, 1649.

Rutherford, S., *A Peaceable and Temperate Plea*, 1642.

Rutherford, S., *Divine Right of Church Government and Excommunication*, 1646.

Rutherford, S., *The Due Right of Presbyteries*, 1644.

*Rutherford, S., *Lex Rex* (in *The Presbyterian's Armoury*), 1846.

*Shields, A., *A Hind Let Loose*, 1797.

Shields, A., *The Scots Inquisition*, 1683.

*Shields, M., *Faithful Contendings Displayed*, 1780.

Smellie, A., *Men of the Covenant*, 1908.

Steven, W., *The History of the Scottish Church, Rotterdam*, 1832.

Stewart, Sir J. (of Goodtrees), *Jus Populi Vindicatum*, 1669.

*Stewart, Sir J. (of Goodtrees) and Stirling, J., *Naphtali*, 1667.

Thomson, J. H. (ed.), *A Cloud of Witnesses*, 1871.

Thomson, J. H., *The Martyr Graves of Scotland*, 2 vols., 1875, 1877.

Thomson, T. (ed.), *The Booke of the Universall Kirk of Scotland*, 3 vols., 1839–45.

Ussher, J., *Power Conceded by God to the Princes*, 1688.

Walker, J., *Theology and Theologians of Scotland*, 1872.
*Walker, P., *Six Saints of the Covenant*, 2 vols., 1901.
Watt, H., *Recalling the Scottish Covenants*, 1946.
*Wodrow, R., *The History of the Sufferings of the Church of Scotland from the Restoration to the Revolution*, 2 vols., 1721–2.

Acts of the General Assembly from 1638, ed. A. Peterkin, 1838.
Acts of the Parliament of Scotland, 1593–1707, 1858 etc.

INDEX